HISTORY MAKERS

HISTORY MAKERS

INTERVIEWS

Fred Schultz

NAVAL INSTITUTE PRESS
Annapolis, Maryland

Naval Institute Press
291 Wood Road
Annapolis, MD 21402

Library of Congress Cataloging-in-Publication Data
Schultz, Fred, 1956–
History makers : interviews / Fred Schultz.
p. cm.
ISBN 1-55750-899-2 (alk. paper)
1. United States—History, Naval—20th century.
2. Navigation—United States—History—20th century.
3. Naval history, Modern—20th century. 4. Navigation—History—20th century. 5. Interviews—United States. I. Title.

E746 .S38 2000
359'.0092'273—dc21

00-042726

Printed in the United States of America on acid-free paper ♾
07 06 05 04 03 02 01 00 9 8 7 6 5 4 3 2
First printing

To J. Fred and Shelby Schultz, my parents and strongest supporters,
and to Susan Hottle-Schultz, my love

Contents

Acknowledgments

First thanks go to Fred Rainbow, the U.S. Naval Institute's Director of Periodicals and Seminars and editor-in-chief of its monthly professional journal, *Proceedings.* Fred never wavered in his endorsement of my schemes; not once did he question my judgment regarding an interview and often offered helpful suggestions. Besides that, I'm grateful that he also has been my biggest supporter in the publisher's office and pushed this project relentlessly.

The real person in control of the Periodicals and Seminars Division is Jaci Day, and I thank her for her friendly efficiency and for keeping us all in line. Thanks also to Liese Carrington and all the other administrative people who have assisted with tape transcripts, mail, expense accounts, and telephone calls over the years. Particularly helpful to me were Nicole Rummel and Linda McCabe.

I also thank Paul Stillwell, the Director of the Naval Institute's History Division and my predecessor at *Naval History* for allowing me to call on his encyclopedic mind so frequently.

Then come the editorial, production, and public relations people who produce and promote *Proceedings* and *Naval History.* Their professionalism is outweighed only by their good humor. Many thanks go to Dee Matney and Adrienne Richardson, the workhorses of the staff, who always manage to get the magazines out on time, with something on every page; to Julie Olver, who good-naturedly keeps us in M&Ms and editorially above water while we work on projects like this; to Dave Hofeling, for his photographic expertise and his light touch—on and off the course (and in the ring); to LeAnn Bauer, for turning the random pictures we assemble into art; to Kevin Clarke, for his expertise in getting us into the papers; to Colin Babb, for his "action" shots of Tom Brokaw; and to John Miller, who has on several occasions kept me from "falling on my sword" while talking to top military brass. I especially thank old pro Mac Greeley for warning me not to go "too Hollywood" and for introducing me to my first martini after an interview—"what real journalists do," he told me.

I also acknowledge here past Naval Institute staffers who participated in some of these discussions: Follin Armfield (who alternated questions with me in our interview of Caspar Weinberger); Linda O'Doughda (a fine editor and intellect who landed the Fairbanks interview for us); Bruce Gibson (whose experience as an editor in naval aviation topics proved invaluable in our discussion with Jim Lovell); Ray Whitney (for his perspectives as a diver during our interview with Jean-Michel Cousteau); and Scott Belliveau (my old office mate and sorely missed source of unproductive fun and laughter, for his knowledge of a vast array of trivia and arcana).

Critical to the publication of interviews, obviously, are the people with the thankless job of transcribing often unintelligible audiotapes. For their yeoman's work over the years, I thank the many skilled transcribers who have helped us in this regard.

Finally, I thank former Senior Acquisitions Editor Mark Gatlin and current Manufacturing Supervisor Eddie Vance for being the first at the Naval Institute Press to express a glimmer of interest in this project; thanks also to Press Director Ron Chambers for his approval and to Acquisitions Editor Eric Mills for seeing the project through.

And most important, I'm forever grateful to my wife Susan for having listened patiently to all my stories—several times.

Introduction

All reporters must learn the art of the interview, the most basic of all journalistic endeavors. Direct quotes seem somehow more pure than any information that passes through the filters of a reporter's interpretation and analysis. I always keep in mind something one of my interview subjects told me years ago: "The historians can write whatever they want to," scolded Doc Watson, a blind Grammy Award–winning musician from the hills of North Carolina, "because most of them don't get it right anyway." For that reason alone, interviews are the best, if still imperfect, means of arriving at the truth.

Our collection of history makers spans a decade of the 127-year-old U.S. Naval Institute, and it includes sea service officers, explorers, journalists, movie stars, historians, and filmmakers, all with a connection—some more obvious than others—to naval and maritime affairs and naval history. That each of these personalities granted us interviews in the first place is a strong affirmation of this venerable organization's reputation. We haven't been turned down often. And once we penetrated the buffers surrounding some of the biggest names presented here, none hesitated to talk with us. Each offers a unique perspective, and all have been memorable for one reason or another.

Take the julep-voiced Shelby Foote: historian, author, playwright, and the colorful star commentator on Ken Burns's popular PBS miniseries, *The Civil War.* We've tried for years to get Mr. Foote to review books for both the Naval Institute *Proceedings* and *Naval History* magazines, but his drawling answer is always, "I find book reviews a great waste of time." So we were gratified that he didn't feel the same way about interviews. I'll never forget his answer to one of my questions. Puffing on his pipe, he surged forward in his chair when I asked him what he would tell any critics who might denigrate his historical work—since he uses no source citations—as not being scholarly enough. The edited version of his answer appears here, and I'll leave the real tenor of his remarks to the reader's imagination.

My colleague Scott Belliveau and I had arranged to drive David McCullough—the white-haired, silver-tongued host of the PBS series *The American Experience*—from Washington for a lecture he was to deliver at the U.S. Naval Academy. We were early, so we each lit a cigar and stood outside the hotel before deciding to "loiter" in the elegant lobby until the prescribed time we were to meet. When we approached the front desk, announcing that we were there to pick up the Pulitzer Prize–winning historian, the concierge calmly picked up the telephone and said, "Cancel security."

We turned out not to be the hooligans we apparently appeared to be—considering we both were sporting beards at the time, as I recall—and the interview we conducted turned out to be a highlight of both our careers. Mr. McCullough, a fellow Pennsylvanian, has in fact been a friend and frequent correspondent ever since.

To my great pleasure, we have met on several occasions. Indeed, I'll be forever grateful to Mr. McCullough for once introducing me to former Congressman James Symington as the editor of "one of the best magazines in the country." Our most unforgettable meeting, however, was the celebration of Herman Wouk's eightieth birthday at the Library of Congress and Mr. Wouk's donation of manuscripts to the library from several of his best-known works, most notably, *The Winds of War* and *War and Remembrance.* While we did not conduct an interview with Mr. Wouk, he did agree to make a rare appearance at one of our events. Similar occurrences happen frequently, as our periodicals and seminar programs often work hand-in-hand. The powerful words from a speech Mr. Wouk delivered at the Naval Institute's annual Annapolis Seminar are featured here, as are remarks from columnist Art Buchwald, *Baltimore Sun* bureau chief Robert Timberg, and *Washington Post* Pentagon correspondent Tom Ricks.

When Ernest Borgnine—"the Real McHale"—arrived at the U.S. Navy Memorial on Pennsylvania Avenue in Washington, World War II destroyer veterans were taking photos of each other beside the famous Lone Sailor statue that stands in the center of the memorial's courtyard. Being an old four-stacker destroyer sailor himself, Borgnine joined the group, had his picture taken with the other veterans, and signed autographs. Then he strolled to the memorial entrance, where I introduced myself: "Good morning, Mr. Borgnine," I said, "my name is Fred Schultz." Without missing a beat, the Oscar-winning actor replied, "Well, I can't help that!"

Alas, what I thought was the stage-setter for a totally light-hearted interview certainly was not. My first question involved his reasons for joining the U.S. Navy. He told of his growing up during the Great Depression; to him the Navy seemed his only salvation. He began to sob. Then, he actually broke down and cried as he recalled his first Mother's Day on board a Navy destroyer, far from home. I was afraid this might end up being the longest short interview I'd ever conducted, but once we began talking about his antics in the old *McHale's Navy* television series, a twinkle returned to Borgnine's eye, and he talked candidly about his service in the Navy and how it affected his acting career.

I also talked about military service and its importance with Gene Hackman. I can't count how many people have told me he is their favorite actor, then asked why in the world I was interviewing him. What most don't know is that he lied about his age and joined the Marine Corps before his seventeenth birthday. Hackman credits his military service with instilling discipline that he otherwise lacked. I talked to him while he was on a book tour touting his swashbuckling novel, *Wake of the Perdido Star*, cowritten with underwater archaeologist and long-time friend of the Naval Institute, Dan Lenihan. What struck me the most about our interview was that the two of them seemed so at ease as we talked. They were so comfortable with photo editor and photographer Dave Hofeling and me that they agreed to have a drink with us after the interview. Dave and I pondered later how many people in the bar recognized Mr. Hackman and wondered exactly who we were.

Another Hollywood legend we had the opportunity to meet was the late Douglas Fairbanks Jr., the cinema's original Sinbad the Sailor. On the heels of the release of his book, *A Hell of a War*, I accompanied the Naval Institute's History Division Director Paul Stillwell and Associate Editor Linda O'Doughda to Mr. Fairbanks' Madison Avenue office in New York City. We assembled in a museum-like room, with photos and memorabilia of Hollywood's Golden Age covering nearly every inch of wall space. Mr. Fairbanks greeted us, his trademark red carnation attached to his lapel. (We were told that he walked to the office every day and never went anywhere without the carnation.) He obliged us by agreeing to attend the Naval Institute's Annual Meeting and sign books there. My task was to pick up him and his wife in Alexandria, Virginia, following the taping of Larry King's radio program, which I did dutifully. On the way to a reception at the Naval Institute's headquarters, I stopped at home to pick up my wife for the event.

So we're probably the only people in town who can say that Douglas Fairbanks once dropped by our house.

After lunch with my old friend and colleague Lisa Furgatch, who had agreed to photograph my interview with Walter Cronkite, we entered the New York headquarters of CBS—the aptly named "Black Rock" building on West 52nd Street—and went to the floor where the retired anchor of that network's evening news program still maintained an office. Camera crews from the Discovery Channel's *The Cronkite Report* were leaving when we arrived, so we waited a few minutes in his reception room. Mr. Cronkite—once described as "the most trusted man in America"—then came to the door and invited us inside.

His office was not as imposing as I would have imagined, but it did feature several Emmy Awards, a model of the space shuttle, and a large selection of books. We began by talking about his role in reporting on the World War II invasion of Normandy, but I especially relished his recalling a segment of his popular series, *The 20th Century*, based on an article from the Naval Institute's *Proceedings.* I am also pleased to report that when he later called the office to amend a misrecollection, our administrative assistant, Marcia Owens, resisted her skepticism when he said, in his characteristically low rumble, "This is Walter Cronkite."

Ben Bradlee was sitting behind his desk on the executive floor of *The Washington Post* when I arrived. I had heard him just two days earlier on the radio, talking about his World War II service in the Navy as described in his autobiography, *A Good Life.* I phoned his office immediately and inquired about an interview. About a half-hour later, I got a call from Mr. Bradlee's long-time assistant, Carol Leggett, who asked, "How does Friday sound?" Then I quickly bought Mr. Bradlee's book and set out to talk to the man portrayed by Jason Robards in *All the President's Men.* The movie (based on Bob Woodward and Carl Bernstein's book by the same name) details how the *Post* broke the story of the Watergate break-in and all the fallout from it. Even though Mr. Bradlee played a major role in the downfall of a president of the United States, he made it clear in our interview that he took great offense at anyone's questioning his patriotism. Like him or not, agree with his politics or not, you still have to admire Ben Bradlee.

I once had a Watergate experience myself, but in a completely different vein. Retired Coast Guard Rear Adm. Sid Wallace had agreed to provide a venue for my interview with U.S. Navy veteran, explorer, and best-selling author Robert Ballard. We parked ourselves at a long conference table in Admiral Wallace's Watergate law office, overlooking the placid Potomac

River. Dr. Ballard, credited with having located the wrecks of the *Bismarck*, the *Lusitania*, and the *Titanic*, among many others, lambasted the efforts of deep-sea salvors, who were threatening at that time to raise a section of the *Titanic*.

Another undersea explorer I met is Jean-Michel Cousteau, the son and last surviving family member of the legendary Jacques Cousteau. What struck me most about my discussion with Jean-Michel was the poignancy with which he recalled his reconciliation with his father before he died. Perhaps more striking was the stark contrast of that passage with his vitriolic remarks about the current state of the Cousteau Society and the manner in which his stepmother is operating it.

In a few cases, our interviews have even made some news. One involved a trip to the little Yankee town of Walpole, New Hampshire, where Florentine Films, presided over by documentary filmmaker Ken Burns, appears to be the town's principal industry. I had to wait a few minutes for Mr. Burns in his office, which is in a renovated barn next to his house. In it are memorabilia from many of his PBS programs: a basketful of autographed baseballs here, a portrait of Abraham Lincoln there, and videotapes—lots of videotapes. On the floor was a set of page proofs from a new book I had never heard of, Tom Brokaw's *The Greatest Generation*, with a note from Tom asking Ken what he thought of it. Mr. Burns and I sat at his kitchen table, talking about various things, including his opinion on the quality of cable television documentaries. It became obvious that he doesn't think much of them. His words were so strong in the interview, in fact, that reaction to it from other documentary producers appeared later in the "Style" section of *The Washington Post*.

I returned to my office with that image of Tom Brokaw's book in my mind, only to find a package of promotional material relating to *The Greatest Generation* on my desk. Would Mr. Brokaw, I wondered, be available to talk when he was scheduled to be in Washington the following week? I called the publicist for his book publisher, who told me his schedule was full; an interview was out of the question. Then I called his office at NBC News and spoke to his assistant, who suggested that I fax a request to NBC. A last-ditch call to the publicist received the same answer. The night before Mr. Brokaw was supposed to be in town, however, just as I was bemoaning the whole process of lining up these interviews to my wife, I got a call at home. Mr. Brokaw would be happy to speak with me, his publicist said, the next day. My call directly to his office had paid off.

Photographer Colin Babb and I arrived early and ordered something to drink at the hotel restaurant where we to meet Mr. Brokaw. As our drinks arrived, I spotted him, obviously just arriving from a New York shuttle flight. Overhearing his disappointment that his room was not yet ready, I introduced myself. "Why don't we do the interview right now?" he suggested. So we talked for about an hour, and he seemed grateful when he left us for some extra time to get settled into his room before he was to interview Secretary of State Madeleine Albright for that night's news. When Colin and I went to pay our restaurant check, the hostess told us that Mr. Brokaw had paid it already. We shouldn't have been surprised by this gesture from someone who, I later learned, made NBC satellite facilities in the Persian Gulf available for U.S. Marines to phone home.

The words of some of the personalities who appear here were nearly overshadowed by the aura that seemed to surround them. Retired Navy captain Bill Horn called us one day to ask whether we would be interested in interviewing a Japanese kamikaze pilot. Without much thought, I immediately said yes. But then I began to assess what that meant. How could a kamikaze pilot be alive to tell his tale? I soon learned that Kaoru Hasegawa, the chief executive of the largest packaging manufacturer in Japan, had come to the United States to gather details about the most important day of his life. In spring 1945, sailors from the U.S. destroyer *Callaghan* shot down his Frances bomber before it could crash into their ship and then rescued the severely injured pilot. Mr. Hasegawa eventually learned many of the details from the very men who rescued him from the waters off Okinawa. In fact, he is now an honorary member of the USS *Callaghan* Survivors Association and has met with the group annually at various locations across the country since 1995.

I was excited when Vice Adm. John Bulkeley agreed to an interview. Made famous as Lieutenant Brickley in the movie *They Were Expendable*, he received the Medal of Honor for evacuating Gen. Douglas MacArthur from the Philippines early in World War II, and he made news for refusing to cooperate with Fidel Castro when he commanded the naval base at Guantanamo Bay, Cuba. Before we got down to brass tacks, however, Admiral Bulkeley wanted to show me something. There, in the boardroom of the Naval Institute's old headquarters in Preble Hall at the Naval Academy, he dropped his trousers and pointed to the wound he had incurred during the war. This was the beginning of what would turn out to be an amiable and frequent exchange of phone calls and correspondence. The admiral always spelled out his name when he called, and answered the phone, "On board!" I enjoyed my interplay with the gruff old guy and was especially gratified when, only weeks before his death, he told me he thought I was "one of the good guys." So was he.

When photographer Dave Hofeling and I arrived at James Webb's office overlooking the Iwo Jima Memorial in Arlington, Virginia, the Marine Corps Vietnam War veteran, former secretary of the Navy, and best-selling author was riding high on the impending release of Paramount Pictures' *Rules of Engagement*. He had written the story on which the movie—starring Tommy Lee Jones and Samuel L. Jackson—was based and talked about his on-off-on relationship with the project, saying some fairly provocative things concerning the machinations of making a movie in Hollywood.

I did not know then that Mr. Webb had declined interview requests from other media on the subject and had referred them instead to me. In due time a *Wall Street Journal* reporter called for permission to quote our interview—congratulating me on my "scoop." The day that *WSJ* hit the street I heard from William Friedkin, the movie's director, phoning to take exception to Mr. Webb's remarks. The result of that conversation was that Mr. Friedkin agreed to address the 126th Annual Meeting of the Naval Institute. His remarks likely will appear in the next volume of *History Makers*—if there is one.

Robert Ballard

COURTESY OF WOODS HOLE OCEANOGRAPHIC INSTITUTION

Dr. Ballard is president of the Institute for Exploration in Mystic, Connecticut, and former director of the Center for Marine Exploration at Woods Hole, Massachusetts. He has participated in more than one hundred deep-sea expeditions, is the author of several best-selling books, and has assisted in the production of several specials for National Geographic Television. The interview appeared in the October 1996 issue of *Naval History.*

■

USNI: As the leader of the expedition that discovered the wreck of the *Titanic*, how do you feel about private efforts to raise a section of the ship's hull?

Ballard: Pretty sad. It's a carnival, that's what it is. What more can you say? It's as if the *Titanic*'s tragedy continues. We tried to put it to rest, but this perpetuates the tragedy.

USNI: The people who are doing it obviously see it differently. They see value in preserving artifacts from the wreck and in offering something tangible for the public to see and experience.

Ballard: Yes, they see it very differently.

USNI: What governs the claim on the ship and her artifacts?

Ballard: Admiralty law—ancient, ancient admiralty law. There's no law in the deep sea, because the law has not caught up with the times.

USNI: If you are so much against all this, why did you publish the coordinates of the *Titanic* wreck in your book?

Ballard: The French were already aware of the coordinates, because the first expedition to the *Titanic* was a joint operation conducted by the French and U.S. governments, sponsored in my case by the Office of Naval Research and the Chief of Naval Operations for Submarine Warfare. I was on board a Navy research vessel, the *Knorr* [AGOR-15], using Navy assets. That's about as Navy as you can make it.

The French expedition was not a French Navy operation. Even though the organization sponsoring this latest operation refers to the French Navy in its literature, the French organization supporting it, IFREMER [France's national institute of oceanography], is not the French Navy. It's like us calling NOAA [the National Oceanographic and Atmospheric Administration] the U.S. Navy.

The French scientists, Jean-Louis Michel, Jean Jarry, and Bernard Pillaud, were standing next to me when we found the *Titanic*. Jean-Louis wrote down the coordinates and plotted them on his chart to see how close he had come. He missed it on his first run by three hundred yards, and he banged his fist on the table. When I asked him why he was upset, he said, "They're going to kill me." I reminded him that we discovered the ship together, but he said it was on my watch, not his. The truth was, we had done this together.

So who first carried the sponsor of this hull-raising down to the *Titanic*? The French. They had the coordinates. Of course they did, because we were on the same expedition. And they had all the rights to have those coordinates. The idea that I published the coordinates so the French could look them up in my book is absurd. My book wasn't even published until after the French had already done subsequent dives on the *Titanic*. So what would have been the sense in not publishing the coordinates?

Have you found the coordinates of the *Bismarck* in my book on that subject? No. Why? Because I'm the only one who knows them. Have you found the coordinates of all the ships in Iron Bottom Sound [Guadalcanal] in my books? No. Why? Because I'm the only one who knows them. I just found a Roman fleet; have you found its coordinates? No. I can protect that. But I cannot protect coordinates that are already known to the public.

USNI: What will happen when this expedition returns to the United States with a piece of the ship?

Ballard: That will be the first time that the *Titanic* has actually, officially, come into the country, and I'm not sure—if you read the Titanic Memorial Act of 1986—that that won't present a legal problem for this organization. The gentleman in charge of this expedition may be testing the law. The Titanic Memorial Act of 1986 leaves a lot to be interpreted. It's interesting that the hull is coming in, and not the artifacts.

What did they say five years ago? Didn't they say they were not going to take anything from the ship? The ship's crow's nest has been destroyed. They acted astounded: "You're kidding. It's been destroyed? Then it must be serious; serious decay has set in," they said. Well, I have photographs of their first expedition, one with a crow's nest and one taken later in the same expedition without the crow's nest.

USNI: Have you ever confronted the people involved?

Ballard: Yes, but most journalists have not. They won't check up; they're lazy. I told the story to *The Boston Globe*, but they didn't check it. I told it to anyone who cared to listen, but none of them ran the checks. A number of historians associated with the *Titanic* have verified that the crow's nest was destroyed.

They claim that severe decay has set in on the ship, and they're doing this out of a fear that something awful is going to happen if they let the ship sit there just another day. To illustrate this, they say that the ship's gymnasium has collapsed.

Well, isn't it odd that our discovery pictures show a collapsed gymnasium? The gymnasium probably collapsed on impact just after the ship sank. It was a weak structure. Yes, it did, indeed, collapse. Do you want to see a photograph of it? Now, they say that all these changes are taking place at a rapid pace and that they must do what they said they weren't going to do, because they need to save the ship.

They'll tell you that Bob Ballard picked up some artifacts from the bottom of the ocean and the Mediterranean. But there's a huge difference. I did it under the direction of archaeologists and only at their request.

Does the world of history and archaeology need specialists? They do have a conservationist/preservationist on board for the expedition, but there's a huge difference between a conservationist and a historian or archaeologist.

USNI: It seems that all this points back to the admiralty law.

Ballard: It's a free-for-all law. And not until we destroy enough pyramids, I guess, will we finally realize that this is antiquated. How many destroyed *Titanic*s will it take?

USNI: Let's get back to those who say that raising these artifacts makes them more easily accessible to the public.

Ballard: I'm looking beyond that now. I've actually been practicing this for thirty-some years. I see the day coming when it will be technologically easy to visit the *Titanic* on the information highway.

Imagine you're accompanying the British explorers who found King Tut's tomb, when some guy says, "Box it!" You ask what he means. "Get it out of here," he says. "No one would ever come to this place to see it. Get it back to London." You try to stop him, saying that someone will be standing here someday, the tomb won't be here, and they're going to ask why. It's the whole Elgin Marble issue. Why are the Elgin Marbles in London? They should be hanging on the Acropolis. But they are in London—beautifully presented, but completely out of context.

Imagine twelve thousand feet down, driving along the bottom of the ocean and finding two shoes, side by side, toes pointed upward. A few feet farther up is a belt, and farther up still a hat, with a wristwatch off to one side. Would you pick those up?

USNI: No.

Ballard: Why?

USNI: It seems obvious.

Ballard: If you were to go into a museum and see one shoe and someone said it's from the *Titanic*, would that have the same power?

USNI: No.

Ballard: Of course not. Then, what right does anyone have to destroy that future experience? Those shoes have been there for eighty years. Are they all of a sudden going to go somewhere? It's like the difference between walking the battlefield at Gettysburg and having Disney show it to you.

USNI: Why do you think relatively few people have expressed an opinion on this?

Ballard: Because we're McDonald's. We devour things fast and throw the paper and the Styrofoam cups away. Another reason is that we haven't been able to get out and document what has been done. We haven't been able to go back and show you the before and after pictures.

USNI: You've said that there is no debate on this issue. Would you participate in one?

Ballard: What's the point? The question is, in the end, whether it matters. I think it's important to have a debate, but this would not be a debate. The people at the *Globe* said that the American people are enjoying this. And I said, yeah, and they used to enjoy public executions, too.

USNI: Does this organization need to do this to maintain its claim?

Ballard: Admiralty law requires you to bring it home. You can't say "I found something and left it"—which is what I did—and still claim it. I put a plaque on it and said leave it alone. But it's not mine. I didn't bring it home.

So here's a guy who's claimed it, who's brought back items from it, but hasn't brought back any of the actual ship. Ninety-nine point nine percent of the ship is still there, but he maintains his claim. He has excursions. Did you get your invitation from Burt Reynolds? I have mine. Did you know "The Unsinkable Molly Brown" will be there? Yes, Debbie Reynolds is going, too. The selling of the coal on the Internet was just too much.

USNI: The selling of what?

Ballard: You can buy *Titanic* coal through the Internet. You didn't know that? They're selling coal right now for twenty-five bucks. Didn't you catch the *USA Today* ad for Christmas?

So someone else is paying this time. It's the little old lady from Pasadena who wants to see Debbie Reynolds. People are going on a "love boat" to watch it on closed-circuit television, which I think is a kick. It's a carnival.

USNI: We've heard much about your dives on the ships of Iron Bottom Sound at Guadalcanal. What are your plans there?

Ballard: One of the reasons for doing Iron Bottom Sound was, again, trying to project into the future. One of the reasons we were out on the *Britannic*—sister of the *Titanic*—last summer was to look at ways to learn more about maritime history and even ancient history, where it becomes archaeological history. The deep sea is a preserver of history.

That began to unfold in my life when I found the *Titanic* and then when I found chilling swastikas still painted on the deck of the *Bismarck* fifty years after she sank.

And then we went to Guadalcanal and saw the shine on the guns and went up to the bridge of the *Quincy* [CA-39], and all the camouflage paint was still there, perfectly preserved. Torpedoes were in their launchers and depth charges in their racks. The guns were aimed at the last salvo, locked in combat. There was a battlefield. Guadalcanal was a battlefield.

More recently, during our work in the Mediterranean, we found a fleet of Roman ships that got caught in a storm. In a desperate attempt to save themselves, the crews began throwing their cargo overboard, leaving trails of debris leading to the ships. So there is a maritime disaster preserved from two millennia ago.

If you begin to look at the deep sea's ability to preserve our history, you realize that a battlefield or the site of a maritime disaster places the artifacts in context.

When we went back to the *Lusitania*, we were able to resolve the issue of whether the magazine was full or not, because the magazine was still there. We were able to show that it did not explode. It was not because of war materials being struck by a torpedo. It had struck a coal bunker, an empty coal bunker, and it ignited coal dust that exploded and sank the ship.

The ability to go back and do forensic science, that's what's exciting. In the case of Guadalcanal, we have the capability of letting people visit it. When the *Arizona* went down, did anyone ever think we would build a memorial over the top of her and that visitors would actually be able to go out there and watch oil bubbles rise to the surface? I'm sure when they buried [Gen. George A.] Custer they never thought there would be tourism, that people would come and walk the battlefield of the Little Big Horn.

So why aren't we going to be able to examine the battlefield of Guadalcanal in infinite detail by walking it electronically? And why are we not preserving these sites? We must protect these sites, because they are our history.

USNI: As more sites are found, how are you going to keep people from making claims under admiralty law?

Ballard: Well, how do you keep people from destroying Yosemite National Park? You finally convince the powers that be. But you have to show those people the place about to be destroyed. So it's a question of getting it to that point.

We have made some progress, from Clive Cussler's book, *Raise the Titanic!* to people actually thinking that maybe it's not a good idea. The *Titanic* may be the sacrificial lamb that does it. People may get disgusted with the carnival, because it will only get worse.

USNI: Did you ever have any desire to find Amelia Earhart's airplane?

Ballard: I've done a lot of homework on it, and there's so much uncertainty. From what I can see, she probably ditched.

If the plane landed in shallow water, it would be so well oxygenated in the sunlight that it would be practically gone by now. The only way you're ever going to have an Amelia Earhart airplane is if she ditched in deep water. But that would be by accident, I think.

USNI: What are the major differences between working in the Atlantic and the Pacific oceans, if any?

Ballard: The Pacific is so big. It costs more money, generally, because you have to go greater distances. Guadalcanal was a lot of work. We sat in port waiting for parts that were being flown in from San Diego. There are no stores, nothing except malaria. It's a jungle.

So it's a logistics issue. But it turns out that most history is in the Northern Hemisphere. And most of the ocean is in the Southern Hemisphere.

USNI: What most interests you at the moment?

Ballard: I'm very interested in the Black Sea because of its anaerobic conditions. That's where I really want to work, because it would preserve Bronze Age history in beautiful condition. There's no oxygen; there are no wood borers. The ships would be preserved, mummified. No one has ever done anything comprehensive in there because of the Cold War. So I know what I want to do, and it isn't Amelia Earhart.

USNI: In the 1960s, Sea Lab was very much a point of discussion. What role do you see a permanently manned underwater sea station playing in the future?

Ballard: I'm an advocate of presence on the ocean floor, but I don't think that ambient living is going to be pervasive. We just finished the Jason Project in Florida, where we were working with the Aquarius Habitat,

NOAA's saturation facility. There we saturated scientists for two weeks, living under ambient conditions.

The United States has a long history of saturation facilities for research, and I think there will always be a place for that. I don't think there will be a pervasive use of it by the public. I don't think it has a commercial viability, even for entertainment, and certainly not for living, as far as it concerns moving large numbers of people under the ocean and having them live in ambient conditions.

I do see value in establishing presence in the ocean, particularly mobile presence. I worked for a long time during the Cold War trying to convince the Navy that it should build another kind of submarine. Naturally, no one wanted to hear that.

But I am an advocate of terrain-involved submarines. In fact, when I first came into the Navy thirty years ago, I came as a former Army officer. My original commission was in Army intelligence and terrain analysis, and my background as an earth scientist was in topography and terrain. I was amazed to find that the Navy's attitude toward the bottom of the ocean was to avoid it at all risks, and not use it to your tactical advantage.

For some naive reason, I thought nuclear-powered submarines could land on the ocean bottom. The only one that could in the early days was the *Nautilus*—not [Adm. Hyman] Rickover's *Nautilus* [SSN-571], but Jules Verne's *Nautilus.*

I was an advocate of modifying a submarine like the *NR-1*—the only deep-diving nuclear-powered submarine the Navy has ever built—into a combatant that could work in rugged terrain. That would make more sense than trying to make a big 688 [*Los Angeles*–class] or 637 [*Sturgeon*-class] boat into a terrain-involved submarine.

I've had no luck with that yet. And I have done a lot of work with MIT [Massachusetts Institute of Technology] and naval nuclear officers at MIT in looking at terrain-involved combatant submarines.

USNI: The Navy's new attack submarine, the NSSN, seems to be still undergoing a very fluid design process.

Ballard: We called it the NRX. In times of relative peace, I think we should experiment and not just continue to be preparing for the last war. We should make sure we have a model.

USNI: What different design changes do you have in mind?

Ballard: A small sub. The wave length of the terrain in the ocean is about 200 to 220 feet. If you get much bigger than that, you can't fit into the landscape. You have to remember that a lot of submarines are designed around their power plants. They're designed to go great distances, shoot their bullets, and go great distances to get more bullets.

So the power plant dominates, which is no surprise. Look who was in charge: Admiral Rickover. What if you think of these as forward-deployed assets that are put into the field and resupplied in the field? They would not require long transits. They could even be towed into the field.

USNI: Towed with what?

Ballard: A nuclear-powered submarine, or even a conventional one. I mean, either a ballistic-missile submarine or a fast-attack boat could carry these assets into the field.

USNI: It would be a throwback to the Japanese midget submarines of World War II, right?

Ballard: Not that small. I remember when Vice Adm. Ron Thunman was deputy chief of naval operations for submarine warfare, and I went into his office with a model of the Reykjanes Ridge that a group of graduate students had built based on Navy classified data of that area. I laid it on his office table in the Pentagon, and he said, "What's this?" I said, "It's your battlefield of the future." I wondered why we positioned our submarines up at the choke points between Greenland and Iceland and Iceland and Norway and the British Isles. Why weren't they in the terrain? I reminded him that it's all magnetic, volcanic rock. It's hard, it's reverberating, it's noisy, and it's a perfect place to conceal forces. I told him I'd like to take the *NR-1* into this battlefield and demonstrate its viability, operating with a traditional Navy crew. They gave me a cruise.

I published an article on it in *National Geographic.* We scaled seventeen volcanoes and were never more than a few feet from the meanest, nastiest terrain you could ever hope to have on the face of the earth—primitive, volcanic terrain, no roads, caves, overhangs, lava tubes. And we worked comfortably, bottoming the submarine at various spots.

This began to make the Navy aware that there is a bottom to the ocean instead of only a three-dimensional fluid space, which, quite honestly, isn't very thick. If you take a basketball and call it the earth, put it in a bathtub and lift it up, the water clinging to the basketball would represent the oceans of the world, in scale. That is close, hand-to-hand combat. The Navy needs to realize that there is a battlefield there. The Russians did it well, because the Russians were an army first, a navy second.

That's the kind of thing I think we should be looking at now. In any future conflict, we will be trying to penetrate an adversary's frontiers. And the best way to do that is from the sea.

Ernest Borgnine

GREG MATHIESON / MAI

Mr. Borgnine won a Best Actor Oscar for his performance in *Marty* (1955), and his many screen roles include Sergeant "Fatso" Judson in *From Here to Eternity* (1953), General Worden in *The Dirty Dozen* (1967), and Dutch Engstrom in *The Wild Bunch* (1969). But he is perhaps best remembered as Lt. Cdr. Quinton McHale, the title character in television's madcap sitcom, *McHale's Navy* (1962–66). He served two enlistments in the U.S. Navy, spanning a total of ten years. The interview appeared in the February 1998 issue of *Naval History.*

■

USNI: What made you decide to enlist in the Navy rather than any of the other services?

Borgnine: I'm what you call a Depression sailor. I got a job immediately after leaving high school; I was lucky—three dollars a week and all I could eat, working on a vegetable truck. I had never thought of it as a career, but that was all I could find in those days. You were lucky to get off the streets. One day while riding on the truck, I saw a sign that said: "Join the Navy, See the World." So I went to the recruiter, unbeknownst to my mother and dad, and said I'd like to join the Navy. They put me on a waiting list and asked if I'd be ready to come when they called. I said, "Absolutely!" So I got the call and, believe it or not, got in on another fellow's case of the piles. He failed, and I made it.

I believe at that time only eleven or twelve of us made it out of twelve thousand; that many people were ready to go into the service, simply because they wanted to get off the streets. It wasn't that we were bums. We just wanted to help our families, as I did, and also wanted to get out there and learn something.

So I joined the Navy and went to the Newport, Rhode Island, Training Station in September of 1935. It was a whole new experience. I'll never forget the advice my dad gave me the morning I left. He said, "You know, son, you're not going to be tied down by your mother's apron strings any more." He said, "You're going to have to go out and do it on your own."

I remember one day—I still get a little choked up about it—I was on board a ship, the four-stacker destroyer *Lamberton* [DD-119], and the crew was celebrating Mother's Day by listening to a program about it on the radio. That hit me in such a way that I sat under a ladder and cried. You can't imagine how hard I cried. And after it was over, I suddenly realized I had cut the apron strings. But it made a man out of me. And I have never regretted one day, not ever.

USNI: What was your most memorable experience in the Navy?

Borgnine: I'll never forget the day in San Diego I was put in charge of the captain's gig. I polished that thing until it gleamed. And then word came that we were going to take the captain ashore. Well, I brought the gig alongside smartly, with my engineer down below, handling the controls. I put one foot on the gangway and one foot holding the boat. The captain came on board and said, "128th Street Landing!" I said, "Yes, sir!" and started to push off. As I pushed, my foot slipped on the deck of the boat, because I had polished it to such a high degree. My other foot slipped off the gangway, and I went straight down into the water, between the boat and the gangway—straight down. Then I came straight back up. As I was getting my hat back on my head, he looked down at me and said, "No, 128th Street!"

That was in the *Lamberton*, when we were towing target ships. I remember one day, instead of firing at the targets, somehow or other one plane miscalculated and began firing at us. You could hear the shots whistling between the stacks. And the only thing that saved us was the chief radioman, who got on the radio and told the pilot to stop. I also remember vividly having to go out and resurface some of the tows. Sometimes they'd turn over, and we would have to go and try to turn them back up again.

At that time the Navy didn't want you to get your feet wet, so they would put boots on you—not small boots, but big hip boots. I said, "Wait a minute. If those boots fill up with water, we're going to sink like lead." We were informed that this was the way the Navy was going to do it. Well, the first chance we got, we cast them off, threw them away.

We also towed paravanes for minesweeping. That was a risky job, because paravane wire could cut metal. It was really something to watch those things work. Unfortunately, on another ship one time, the wire broke as an ensign was straddling it and cut him right in half.

USNI: What was the biggest difference between the four-stacker destroyer and the converted yacht you served in during the war?

Borgnine: The yacht, the *Sylph* [PY-12], had been owned by old man Murphy, who made Murphy Beds—the ones that folded out of the wall. I had my own private stateroom. I was a first-class gunner's mate, but the captain used to knock on my door before entering. Talk about having it made! We really did.

Of course, we weren't supposed to bring booze aboard, but in this certain ship, it seemed we always got our share. How? Several of us would go ashore at night and buy milk. We would then paint the bottles white and fill them up with booze. When we came back, the watch officer would meet us at the gangway and ask, "What do you have there, men?" We would say, "Milk, sir, and hamburgers. Would you like one?" He'd let us by and we'd go down below and get roaring. Talk about *McHale's Navy*, this was it!

So there was all the difference in the world. The destroyer was a fighting ship, built for war. The *Sylph* was a fighting ship, too, but there weren't very many things that you could do with a yacht. We had a 3-inch/50-caliber gun that we were afraid to shoot because of the wooden decks. We also had six .30-caliber air-cooled Brownings, but they were like mosquito bites against the skin of a submarine. We had a Y-gun to shoot off the depth charges because we couldn't go fast enough to let them roll off the stern if we met up with a submarine.

USNI: Did you ever encounter any U-boats?

Borgnine: Yes, we did. We met up with one, and according to the skipper, we had him dead to rights. We were guarding an oiler, and he was going like crazy. We just couldn't keep up. Our propulsion was sufficient just for going in and out of harbors slowly. But there we were, out to sea, trying to keep up; but we just couldn't. That day, we did manage to snag onto a German submarine; there were a lot of them out there. We were like sitting ducks, though. Only three ships were guarding the entire Atlantic coastline when the war started. The others were the *Zircon* [PY-16] and the *Sapphire* [PYC-2].

When we made contact with the U-boat, the old man said, "Gunner, when I blow the whistle, you let that Y-gun go." I said, "Yes, sir!" So we got all set, and he blew the whistle. I pulled the lanyard, and boom! Off she went. Everybody said, "Ooh" and "Ahh" as they watched the things go. It was the first time they had ever heard an explosion. I started kicking them in the behind, saying, "Come on, come on! Get it reloaded!" And we'd load it up again, pull the lanyard, and off she'd go. The whole time, I was listening for detonations—there were no detonations. We shot off twenty depth charges—no detonations. Finally one did go off.

I was standing there with the lanyards in my hand and said to myself, "I know I set them right—seventy-five feet, just what the skipper ordered." Because they didn't go off, I could envision my carcass hanging from the yardarm. Believe me, I was scared stiff. Well, we came back into port, and sailors came aboard and started taking off the depth charges, when one fellow said, "You got a chippin' hammer, gunner?" I said, "Yeah, I got a chippin' hammer." We took off about 147 coats of paint from one of the depth charges, and it said, right there on a nice little brass plaque: "Manufactured in 1917." That's how we went to war.

USNI: What is the difference between your Navy and the Navy of today?

Borgnine: I've been to a number of places and seen for myself the caliber of people who are in the Navy today—in all the services, for that matter. This is an altogether different bunch. These people of today are really bright, young, good people.

We had bright young men in our day, too, but we did not have the equipment they have today, either. Even radar was unheard of when I first went into the service. Then suddenly, they started putting bedsprings up on the tops of ships. We wondered what the devil they were doing, as these great big bedsprings were rolling around. We wondered what they did. Finally, the word came out: "It's a secret. These can pick up and find all sorts of things floating through the air." I said, "Come on, you're crazy. Nothing can do that." But they did!

USNI: What experiences from the Navy did you borrow for some of your screen roles?

Borgnine: I had occasion once to make a picture called *The Vikings* [1958]. The Navy stood me in good stead at that time, because, unbeknownst to anyone, I had pulled a bow oar in my whaleboat crew on the *Lamberton.* That's one of the hardest places in the boat to pull an oar, because you're sitting up forward and you're almost a down-stroke. It was tough.

When we went to Norway to shoot this picture, the very first thing they asked me to do was to go out on the boat. I was dressed up in my civilian clothes, but I jumped right in. We were pulling fourteen-foot oars and going along pretty good. Then, up went the beat, a little higher, a little more. Well, when we finished, I had impressed the rest of the fellows there so much that they would have killed for me, because I proved I was one of them. I became their man. It was marvelous, thanks to the Navy for having me pull that bow oar in the whaleboat.

I'll tell you what I did with *McHale's Navy.* I wanted to do everything that I couldn't do in the real Navy—like ski behind my ship. I did everything that you could possibly imagine, while always maintaining a good rapport with my troops. I made up my mind I was going to run this navy the right way. You see, Quinton McHale had been captain of his own tramp steamer before the war. Nobody knew this, of course, but it was written in the screenplay before we started. And they don't reveal that in the show. As an old tramp steamer captain, McHale was a lieutenant commander in the Naval Reserve, so when the war started, naturally he went into the Navy. They had no other place for him, except to put him in a PT [torpedo patrol] boat.

I wanted to continue *McHale's Navy* as a series and had some people at Universal interested in it, too. My idea was to have him wandering around New York after the war, when suddenly he hears, "Hey, skip!" from one of his old sailors. They eventually get the whole crew back together and seek out McHale's old ship, which is owned by a woman who turns out to be another Captain Binghamton [played by Joe Flynn in the original series]. McHale becomes the skipper of the ship, which carries passengers but turns out to be a spy ship for the CIA.

Universal said, "Let's do it!" But nothing ever happened, and they let it go by the board. But it was fun to think about, and I thought it could have made a heck of a good series.

USNI: Nothing ever came of it?

Borgnine: The man at Universal said, "This is the best thing I've seen since cut bread." But he never did a thing.

USNI: So it's written down somewhere?

Borgnine: Oh sure, I have it at home, all written down. It would probably have made a good picture, too.

USNI: Do you think the Navy might be a little better off today if it had more McHales and fewer Binghamtons?

Borgnine: Absolutely. But I don't think too many Binghamtons are around anymore. The Navy has changed a great deal. Not that the officers of my day were bad, because I served under a lot of good officers, believe me. But there were a few bad ones, too.

I remember one gentleman, a lieutenant commander, when I first reported to the *Sylph.* He was captain of the ship. The morning I was brought to him to be introduced, he was still in bed, in his cabin. The fellow who brought me down knocked on his door and said, "I have the new gunner's mate aboard." The captain opened the door, and he had his hand underneath his pillow. I thought that was odd, and I said, "Good morning, Captain. How are you, sir? I'm reporting aboard for duty." As we left, he made a move, and I saw that his hand was holding a pistol. Very odd, indeed.

Now, this gentleman used to have the hardest time docking that yacht that you ever saw in your life. The tugboat captain in New York would come down and watch him land, just for the laughs. Two of our fellows always came up out of the engine room to watch, too.

One chief carpenter's mate on board hated this captain. And every time he went ashore, he'd get drunk and abusive, come back to the ship, and yell down the pipe: "You no good so and so!" He kept on putting in chits for a transfer and finally got one. Two weeks later, the captain got one, too—to the same ship. As I understand it, they went to a huge transport ship that was getting ready to go overseas to Britain. Just before they took off, this carpenter's mate threw his sea bag over the side and followed it. He said, "I'm damned if I'm going with you." I heard later that the ship and all hands were lost in a hundred-mile-an-hour hurricane off Nova Scotia.

USNI: How do you think *McHale's Navy* would play on TV today?

Borgnine: Are you kidding? People love it. It's always playing somewhere in the world. Universal owns it, so it plays only occasionally in this country. They'll put out shows like *Gilligan's Island*, but they hold off on *McHale*. On Labor Day in Oakland, California, they had a big "McHale" to-do, and it went over tremendously well. It's crazy, but I've had people come up to me and say, "You know, Mr. Borgnine, you're the best baby-sitter in the world." I say, "How do you figure that?" And they say, "When our children are watching *McHale's Navy*, we always know where they are."

USNI: What was the better duty station—Taratupa or Voltafiore?

Borgnine: Actually, I didn't want *McHale's Navy* to move to Italy. Our producer had tried to do it with *Sergeant Bilko*, but the *Bilko* people said they didn't want to go to Italy. So he took it out on us, and we went to Voltafiore. Unfortunately, it didn't last very long. I think the show could still be going if it had been left on Taratupa.

I'll tell you something. Secretary of the Navy [John] Warner called me one time when I was in Washington. He wanted to see me. He said, "I want to tell you, Mr. Borgnine, that you have done more for the U.S. Navy with *McHale's Navy* than I've ever seen any recruiter do. People want to come into the Navy just to join McHale's Navy." That was quite a tribute to me and my troupe.

USNI: What was a typical day of shooting like on the *McHale's Navy* set?

Borgnine: We had a lot of fun doing it. In those days we used to start, anxiously, at eight o'clock in the morning. Well, by a quarter of eight, we were ready to go, all hands. And I guess we broke the mold, because now they start shooting at six-thirty. By noontime, we would have at least twelve to fourteen pages of dialogue and action in the can. Then we'd take it easy, laze around, blow up a few fireworks, and scare a few tourists coming through.

USNI: Do you keep in touch with the old cast?

Borgnine: Oh, sure. A few of them have died, you know. But I see Tim Conway [Ensign Charles Parker], and Carl Ballantine [Torpedoman Lester Gruber] is still around. He's older than the hills, but he's still around.

USNI: How would you rate Hollywood's portrayal of the military in general, and the Navy in particular, past and present?

Borgnine: I've found that in the past they were quite good. Of course they always took liberties. They had to put in the love interest and how it affected the man in his work and all that pertained to it. The majority of the time, though, they were quite good.

We had a naval advisor on *McHale's Navy*. After the first day of shooting, he said, "Ernie, what the devil are they shooting here?" I told him it was *McHale's Navy*. He went storming off and said, "Don't call us, we'll call you." He really left us in the lurch. He wouldn't have anything to do with us, because we weren't portraying the real Navy, his Navy. Then, the show suddenly began to blossom, and he started bringing people around to show them his *McHale's Navy*. From that point, the Navy began treating us well.

USNI: Do you think today's films on military subjects may suffer a bit because fewer filmmakers actually served in the military?

Borgnine: Definitely, yes. There is always something lacking. But they try to get it as best they can.

USNI: What were some good naval-oriented films?

Borgnine: Away All Boats [1956] was a pretty good naval picture. And I did a submariner picture with Glenn Ford [*Torpedo Run*, 1958] that was quite good. One thing we found while making that picture is that you can't go horizontally with a Momsen Lung [an early underwater breathing device]. You have to go vertically, straight up, or straight down. And they wanted us to go horizontally because of the camera angle. You can't do it. You'll fill up with water.

USNI: We hear a lot today about too much violence on television and the movies. As one of the stars of *The Wild Bunch*, which came in for some criticism to that effect, where do you think we should we draw the line?

Borgnine: They asked the same question in Jamaica when the picture was first shown. And I kind of got up on my high horse, because if ever anyone knew the West, it was [director] Sam Peckinpah. He told it like he saw it and like he knew it. Of course, he hadn't been alive in the days of the Old West, but based on what he had worked on and knew from past experience and reading, this was a hard, hard time. If you didn't keep your wits about you, you were dead. It was that kind of a violence. And he tried to show the violence. What I said at the time was, "Would you rather have the violence on your screen, or would you rather see it on your city streets?"

The key lies in the people who do not teach their children properly by saying, "Look, this is a violent picture, and it's violent because man is violent, and people do violent things to other people. This is what you must not do." But people don't train their children that way anymore.

USNI: So you're saying it's not the fault of movies and TV—it's the parents' fault?

Borgnine: Partly. It's also the fact that they'll do and redo anything that sells on TV or in the motion pictures. So we have rape, violence, explosions, and everything else, and kids sit back and say, "Man, isn't that great? It must be, because we see it so often." But is it? It sells. That's the thing. And as long as it sells, they're going to do it. I thought that *The Wild Bunch*, which later went on to become a classic, was done in a way that showed the terribleness of the situation, what these men lived through and died for—which was no good, because they died. Period.

USNI: How important is history?

Borgnine: Very important, I think. They say history repeats itself. I think everybody should know their history. Unfortunately, a lot of people don't. I had a line in a show I was doing not too long ago. I was to say, "I was playing tennis in Corregidor," and so on. I had a college graduate come up to me and ask, "Ernie, what's a 'corregidor'?"

Ben Bradlee

B. O'LEARY / *THE WASHINGTON POST*

Mr. Bradlee is the retired executive editor and present vice president at large of *The Washington Post.* He served in destroyers during World War II and wrote about his Navy service in *A Good Life,* his autobiography. The interview appeared in the December 1995 issue of *Naval History.*

■

USNI: When I told some people what I was doing, they wondered why in the world I was interviewing Ben Bradlee for *Naval History.*

Bradlee: I'll tell you a great story. A guy once wrote a letter to me that started off, "Dear Communist." He impugned my patriotism and certainly impugned my war. I promptly wrote back, "Dear Asshole. This is what I did during the war, so don't give me any shit."

It turned out that he had been in the Marine Corps during the war. We had taken his division to Bougainville and then to Saipan. We had been in some of the same battles. He wrote back, saying I wasn't such a bad guy after all, and we started a great correspondence.

USNI: In your new book, you mention prominently that your two years in the destroyer *Philip* [DD-498] were the two most important years of your life, then and maybe now.

Bradlee: The fact of the matter is that the war, and the Navy in particular, played such important roles in my life. I was on active duty for more than three years, not counting ROTC, which started for me in 1939.

It was a terrific experience. I was twenty years old, for God's sake, and I made officer of the deck in about eight months. When I was twenty-one, I was driving a ship around the Pacific Ocean. That was a wonderful chance for a kid to grow up fast. Where else do you get that kind of responsibility? The captain who ran ROTC at Harvard made a fantastic deal with BuPers [Bureau of Personnel]. He said, "If you can guarantee me that these reserve officers will be assigned to destroyers or cruisers, I'll get you the best in the college." And they made him that deal. We all went to destroyers or cruisers. And I think we all went to the Pacific, but I'm not sure of that.

USNI: Why did you choose the Navy?

Bradlee: That was such a "good war," and serving in the Navy was such a guarantee of action. You weren't going out to the Pacific Ocean in a destroyer or cruiser without being in the middle of it all. I learned things in the Navy. Some people have read the book and told me that what I described as the job of a CIC [combat information center] officer is what an editor is, too. That's what editors do. They find out information, they get the best people they can find to do the heavy lifting, and then—instead of passing information to the skipper—they present information to the people. There's something to that.

Of course, in 1942 the CIC concept had not been developed very well. The *Fletcher*-class destroyers went to sea with the CICs in the bridge instead of the captain's stateroom. And they took the captain's stateroom, eventually. But that must have been why they asked me to write the CIC manual, because CIC operations all developed in Destroyer Squadrons 22 and 23.

USNI: You wrote that you certainly did not want to be a GI in Europe.

Bradlee: No, I didn't want to be a GI. In those days, every year or two they gave you a form to fill out, asking you where you would rather be. I wrote that I'd rather be a naval attaché in Paris, because I spoke French. What a dreamer!

USNI: Of the various World War II incidents you cover in the book, you sarcastically point out that Lyndon Johnson got a Bronze Star for one flight. According to some of our staff, it was actually a Silver Star.

Bradlee: Well, I've already got a little book here called *Corrections.* He got a Silver Star for one flight over Rabaul? That's even worse!

USNI: Tell us what you think might have happened if the *Philip* had shot down the Betty that you later heard was transporting a Japanese admiral. Might that have got you a medal?

Bradlee: No, you didn't get medals, usually, unless you did something flamboyant. This was a big, lumbering, plane that came down like an eighteen-wheel truck, flying at about five hundred feet—if that—in the opposite direction. And it was flying at a slightly faster closing speed. IFF [identification, friend or foe] was not the most reliable system at that time, so you always were told to confirm a contact visually.

It was early in the morning—first light. The first two destroyers in the column did not fire. So, because we weren't at general quarters, and I was officer of the deck—which meant acting captain—I gave the order to commence firing. The flames from the 5-inch guns blew old Willie Groverman's [captain of the ship] eyebrows right off. He was just coming up out of his stateroom at the beginning of the day. The number two gun was trained aft and, bang! But we missed the airplane.

USNI: Why do you devote so much space to war stories in your book? Some would say that you were only one of thousands of reserve officers in World War II.

Bradlee: Yeah, 183735. I'm telling you, I did it because it was important to me. We went to college in September 1939, which was an important month in the history of the world. We were in ROTC in twenty minutes, and we stayed there. In August of '42 I had a degree and a commission—in less than three years.

I'm proud of what we did, because we preppies took such a lot of shit from everybody. There were twelve preppies in my graduating class who were the first guys to go to war.

USNI: Tell me more details about the Japanese air attack that turned back while you were fiddling around and calling in your own imaginary deceptive counterattack of squadrons of U.S. fighter planes.

Bradlee: It was someplace in the chain of islands going up either side of the Slot. We just heard that a mess of Japanese planes—bogeys—was heading our way. That's all they told me. I think the reason we never got the Medal of Honor for that was that we didn't know why they turned back. They could have turned back because they saw a U.S. submarine or a battleship. They just stopped heading for us and went away.

USNI: You were recommended for a Bronze Star.

Bradlee: My skipper did that, yes.

USNI: You never heard anything more about it?

Bradlee: No. I heard that I didn't get it. But that's all right. We didn't want anything. The only medal I came close to getting was a Purple Heart—for being hit in the ass with a piece of Japanese shrapnel. It must have hit the deck first or maybe even the stack, then the deck, and then bounced up and hit me in the ass. It was hot when I picked it up. I had it here on my desk, but one of the kids took it to school for show-and-tell and never brought it back.

USNI: You kept it?

Bradlee: Oh yeah, I did. The thing just nicked me. I was a squash player in college, and I felt like I'd been stung in the ass with a squash ball. It made me jump. I felt my ass to see if there was blood. There wasn't. Bob Lee was the gunnery officer, and he had wheeled the 5-inch guns back and aimed at the battery that hit us, while the guys operating the phones were broadcasting that Mr. Bradlee got hit in the ass. Lee and I were sort of special buddies, and he had visions that I was really hurt, which I wasn't.

I did ultimately have a purple heart sewn to the seat of my pants. When I was first examined, the doctor nicked me in the ass with a scalpel to draw blood right after it happened, and Wild Bill Groverman drew blood again when he pinned a big velvet purple heart to my rear end during a ship's party after R&R.

USNI: You compare the command styles of Adms. [William] Halsey and [Raymond] Spruance. Why did the men like Spruance so much more?

Bradlee: I left out one great Halsey story from the book, because I couldn't prove it. North and east of the Philippines, a great typhoon caught up with the Navy and Halsey. I was about forty miles away when this incident occurred, so I heard all about it. The destroyers in the screen under Halsey were ordered to pump ballast at night in order to fuel in the morning.

Of course, if you pump ballast in a destroyer and you're in a typhoon, it's a terrible experience. You're bouncing around like a cork. One of the destroyer skippers requested permission to cease pumping ballast and was told by Halsey—whether in person or not, I don't know—to obey the order, and he did. Then he came on again and told Halsey that he was stopping, that his ship was in danger. Eventually, that ship capsized. It went over 80 degrees, water came down the stack, and it blew up.

Halsey was supposedly looking for the Japanese fleet, but the impression we all got was that he was looking for that typhoon. He couldn't get out of it. Every time he turned, the storm followed him.

USNI: What about Admiral Spruance?

Bradlee: Any destroyer skipper or officer involved at that time will tell you that Spruance was the class of the outfit. He didn't blow his own horn, and he didn't have a PR guy blocking for him. My all-time favorite story about Spruance is in the book—the day he came up on deck while I was officer of the deck. I had been ordered to take the ship to Tinian, while the captain entertained a lot of other brass in the wardroom. I had decided to take her to thirty knots that day. The admiral paged through a file of fleetwide-distributed ALNav directives, stopped at one, and left. It was one he had issued months before, restricting the speed of all ships at fifteen knots. He never said a word. We slowed her down, a knot at a time.

USNI: That's very much in character, from everything I've read about him.

Bradlee: It's funny. I have a learning-disabled child who goes to a special school, and damned if his teacher wasn't Ms. Spruance. Turns out it was the admiral's granddaughter-in-law. One of his grandsons had married her.

That trip from Saipan to Tinian was unforgettable. In the destroyer Navy you hardly ever saw a high-ranking officer—a four-striper maybe. But you saw admirals even less. We had more brass on board that day than I had ever seen. In the last analysis, we loved Spruance, and we didn't like Halsey, which in my life is not all that important.

USNI: You include a fair amount of detail in the chapter on your naval service. Did it all come off the top of your head?

Bradlee: No. I had my orders from day one. The time I was on the *Philip* came out of my head, because I didn't have any orders. When I got transferred the last year of the war to be the forward area representative of Adm. [Arthur] Radford, I had orders with endorsements on them.

So I could remember pretty much each one. I think I was on nineteen destroyers in a year, and I remembered where I was. I haven't tried to forget, but it's not easy to forget.

USNI: Have you kept track of any of the men who served with you?

Bradlee: The destroyers have had reunions, but I got to miss them all for various newspaper reasons. I haven't been to one.

USNI: You didn't catch any of the fiftieth anniversary commemorations?

Bradlee: I was deeply involved in the fiftieth anniversary in my own mind, but this is the first time I've talked about it for years. I just don't talk about it, here or at home. My wife is twenty years younger than I am. She's an Army brat, and her dad is a retired general. My kids used to tease me and say, "Look out, here comes WWII, The Big Two."

Three of us officers on the *Philip* are still alive and working in Washington—a guy named Bill Flather, who runs an insurance agency here, and Bob Lee. He was a journalist for a long time, and he's still around.

USNI: When I inquired about this interview, your secretary said that you would probably find it refreshing. You were tired of talking about the Kennedys, she said. Well, I do have one Kennedy question for you: Did you and President Kennedy ever trade war stories?

Bradlee: Sure, a little bit. We were stationed for a long time on Tulagi, just north of Guadalcanal across that strait, and we operated out of there for months. Nights we'd go up the Slot and then alternate the next night. Another cruiser division would go up with another bunch of destroyers, and we'd come back and refuel. But Tulagi was where Kennedy's PT-boat squadron was based. I never saw him there. I didn't even know him. But God knows we saw PT boats a lot, and we must have seen each other.

He and I often mused on the fact that we were on the same piece of real estate but didn't know it. We'd see the PTs, and they'd see us, but we didn't much understand what they were doing. I think they knew more about us, because every so often one of our cruisers or destroyers would limp home, having taken a terrible shellacking during the night—ships like the *Honolulu*, the *St. Louis*, the *O'Bannon*, the *Nicholas*, the *Fletcher;* they all got hit.

USNI: You and most of your peers served in the armed services.

Bradlee: Yeah. There aren't any more World War II vets on the newspaper. Dick Howard and I were the last two. There are still some Korean War guys, but not many.

USNI: You're saying how important your war experience was to you. Is anything comparable to it?

Bradlee: Well, Vietnam must have been comparable in certain respects. It was not comparable, in the sense that Vietnam was a lousy war, and this was a great war.

There was something else, too. We had no great qualifications. I was a Greek major, for God's sake. I wasn't supposed to be able to navigate or know what an engine room was or how a gun worked. And yet we were just as good as anybody who went to Annapolis.

USNI: What about Naval Academy graduates? You say in the book that some of the reserve officers were better than the Naval Academy guys, because they were nothing but electrical engineers.

Bradlee: That's probably bragging. We weren't encumbered with knowledge that we didn't need to have. That passage in the book was just a compliment to a liberal arts education which, I think, is a very good education.

Everybody got along just fine. I don't mean to suggest there was any tension. The people I know learned great respect for the military from their military service. That seems to me the funny thing about criticism of the press for being anti-Vietnam, which I think they were. But nobody was anti–Army officer, or anti-grunt, or anti–Navy officer. Those guys were fantastic.

USNI: What do you think of the switch from the draft to the all-volunteer military? Do you think it would be a good thing if everybody served?

Bradlee: Oh, I've long thought that—to serve their country in some way. I'm not sure they'd have to be drafted into the armed services.

I had a kid in the Peace Corps, and he had a wonderful experience in Afghanistan. I think it would be great for everybody to serve the country—putting out forest fires, serving in a Civilian Conservation Corps—for no money, or virtually no money.

USNI: Does the "growing up fast" element come into play here?

Bradlee: Well, it's that, but it's also filling a need for your country. Serving in the war was a great thing for us to do. And it was good to feel needed, too.

USNI: Some of the Navy leadership today—after several controversies—say that today's naval officer is so much different from what he or she used to be because of a different value system, character differences, based on upbringing, television, and other factors. What character differences do you see between today and thirty years ago when you were hiring people?

Bradlee: I think the quality of the younger journalists is a lot higher than it was when I was starting. I wouldn't like to compete against some of these people. They're awfully well educated and they write very well, especially the women. The counterculture in this country, which came along in the early sixties as a result of Vietnam and was fueled by Watergate—where the government was forced to resign in disgrace—created a totally different person.

I mean, they're much less respectful of authority. They are more cynical. It's harder for them to believe in authority. Authority has proved to be wrong in quite a few major instances. So they started a reexamination of all institutions, including journalism, God knows. But it also included the military and the Church. There isn't a church in the world whose foundations weren't shaken. And it's still going on.

I think it must have been terribly hard for the superintendents of the service academies to bring their perspective to bear on new people. My heart just grieves for the recent problems of the Naval Academy. It's a sort of alma mater. I'm not an alumnus of the Naval Academy, but those are my people. I wouldn't like to be superintendent of those places, to have to change the way instructors as well as students believe and think.

You know, the first people discussing racism and sexism in the service academies didn't get it, just as I didn't get it when I confronted it here. You had to relearn it. You had to learn it and keep learning it.

USNI: You did have to be converted?

Bradlee: Oh, sure. Just think of the blacks. I mean, the Navy's record was just terrible. The only blacks you saw in the Navy were mess attendants, and they'd all been falsely lured into the services with promises that they'd be machine gunners—which they were for twenty minutes in the battle. That was my black experience. There just weren't many around. I think there were three blacks in my class at Harvard College out of twelve hundred. There weren't many blacks in New England, as far as that goes.

And when I was at *Newsweek*, the blacks that I saw were black leaders. I didn't know anything about it. Although I would have taken an oath that I wasn't racist, I'm sure I was unsensitized to the issue. If you don't know about racism, you're not going to be able to correct it.

And that's true for the women's movement, too. Incredible behavior by men toward women produced embarrassing incidents. Chaining women midshipmen to urinals?

USNI: Were you a hard sell on the women's movement?

Bradlee: No. I've been married more than once, and I've always married strong women who regularly beat me upside the head, telling me what a male chauvinist pig I was. And I worked hard to learn about it. My father was a parole commissioner in Massachusetts, and the chairman was a wonderful man named Matthew Bullock—a black man. So we had a perfectly modern education about tolerance and understanding, but we didn't practice it, because we never had a chance to. I wasn't a hard sell.

USNI: The Washington Post and other newspapers have taken some heat in military circles for having sent reporters to cover the Pentagon with insufficient knowledge of the military. And then, some say, about the time they have learned enough to file intelligent reports, they're transferred to another assignment.

Bradlee: You know, that was not true for the longest time. When I got to *The Washington Post*, the Pentagon correspondent here was a reserve captain in the Navy, and being paid by the Navy. I mean, that's unthinkable. He was a good guy, but the idea that you could have somebody covering the Navy who was so expert [because] he was in the pay of the Navy was not acceptable. He sure as hell knew a lot about the armed services.

Later, a guy named Lloyd Norman became a legend in the Pentagon. Lloyd Norman knew so much they built the Pentagon around him. He had been *The Chicago Tribune*'s correspondent, and then we hired Lloyd for *Newsweek*. We eventually turned that beat over to kids. There was a turnover.

Warriors became scarce. They began to grow old. I think the services have asked for a certain amount of trouble, with waste stories, for example—six-hundred-dollar toilet seats and stuff like that—which got a lot of public attention. I thought coverage of [Robert] McNamara's Whiz Kids was better than it should have been. We were so bulldozed by that, we didn't realize he was lying as bad as he was. I myself have never covered the Pentagon.

USNI: One particular reporter—Fred Hiatt—has been scorned by military types.

Bradlee: Fred Hiatt is an awfully good reporter.

USNI: But he had a predisposition against the military.

Bradlee: You can't prove it by me.

USNI: One of my colleagues remembers him actually admitting it.

Bradlee: I will make you a bet and warn you not to take it—you would have trouble proving that by reading his clips. He was there during Vietnam, and I think a lot of journalists were trying to make the case that we were not going to win that war. That must have rubbed the people in the Pentagon and in the Army and the Navy the wrong way. But the journalists weren't wrong.

I just know Hiatt too well. He's been our correspondent subsequently in Moscow and in Japan. Saying that he's anti-Pentagon just is not true. It just isn't true. For every story you can show me that you think is unfair, I'll show you five or six that cast a good light on the military. This is a really good reporter and a wonderfully educated guy.

USNI: Some people questioned the qualifications of Molly Moore during the Gulf War. Then, she went out with [Marine] Gen. [Walter] Boomer.

Bradlee: Boomer! God knows what she did to Boomer.

USNI: Was that a brilliant PR move, or what?

Bradlee: On Boomer's part?

USNI: On Boomer's part.

Bradlee: Well, she assigned herself. She went with Boomer's Marine group, and they were out of touch with the world for two or three days. So she went around with Boomer, who said, "I can't get hurt by this because she can't file anything." And they became buddies.

USNI: And so she got to know more of what she was talking about, wrote a book on the war, then changed jobs and moved to India.

Bradlee: Yeah, she's still there.

USNI: So there's another instance. Is it the Peter Principle?

Bradlee: I don't know. But you can't keep people on the same assignment for a very long time anymore. People who cover the State Department used to be sixty years old. Same for people who covered the Congress and the Pentagon.

USNI: Is that bad?

Bradlee: No! But today there's tremendous pressure for the younger people to get a piece of the action. And there is less and less desire by reporters to be sixty-year-old correspondents in the Pentagon or schlepping the halls of the Hill. They don't want to do it, and I don't blame them. I wouldn't want to do it, either. I think if you're a reporter, you ought to do it for a while and then move on.

Tom Brokaw

COLIN BABB / U.S. NAVAL INSTITUTE

Since joining NBC News in 1966, Mr. Brokaw has won every major award in broadcast journalism, including the Emmy, the Peabody, and the Du Pont. The current anchor and managing editor of *NBC Nightly News with Tom Brokaw* is the author of *The Greatest Generation,* his tribute to the people who emerged from the Great Depression and World War II to build today's modern society. The interview appeared in the April 1999 issue of *Naval History.*

■

USNI: Since you've never served in the military, some people might wonder why you wrote a book like this.

Brokaw: I had grown up in military or quasi-military environments. During the war, my dad was working in southwestern South Dakota at an ordnance depot on an Army base that held a garrison of Italian prisoners of war. The Army was testing ammunition out on the prairie and storing it there. Those are my earliest memories of the military.

My father was drafted, but then the base commander called him back because my dad had been keeping the place going. He was one of the crew of men who built the roads and plowed them out in the wintertime. After that, he went to work on civilian projects for the Corps of Engineers, building dams in South Dakota. Those dams were built by guys who were fresh out of the service, engineers and construction laborers and heavy equipment operators, as my father was. So I was always surrounded by it. If you were born in 1940, the men who were your coaches and schoolteachers and people in your community had been in that war.

When I graduated from the University of South Dakota, I wanted to go into the Navy. So I applied to the OCS [officer candidate school] program. I was accepted, and I was looking forward to it. I didn't have a job and I needed one, among other things, and that's what I had always wanted to do. But I had flat feet. In the last station of the physical, they said, "We can't take you, you've got flat feet."

USNI: Why did you want to go into the Navy?

Brokaw: I think a lot of people from the prairie have a calling to the sea. It's a kind of foreign environment for us and I think an unusually high incidence of people from that part of the country are drawn to it. I had grown up on boats on the Missouri River, and I wanted to go into the Navy and run boats.

Most of my father's brothers who went into the service went into the Navy, for example. So that's what I wanted to do, and I was really disappointed when I couldn't do it. The man who recruited me, and who had spent a long time doing it, said, "We can get you in if we can get some political intervention." But I said, "Why don't I find out where I stand in the draft first, with these feet?"

I went to the draft board and volunteered, but the same regulation applied. It was crazy, but in 1962 Vietnam had not yet heated up, so they said, "You've got flat feet. We'll make you 1-Y." In the meantime, I would be out of a job. So I missed my opportunity. I think it would have been good for me, frankly.

USNI: Why do you say that?

Brokaw: I think that one of the lessons in this book and one of the lessons of my own life is that discipline in military training is a helpful thing in those formative years. During my first couple of years in college I wasn't as focused as I needed to be. So maybe I could have used some military training.

A number of my oldest and closest friends are people who either made a career out of the military or who had memorable times in the military.

USNI: Many of our legislators and business executives have no military experience. How important is the military?

Brokaw: Everyone ought to have some understanding that how we defend the country is vitally important. The military is in charge of national security. History is replete with examples in which this country survived because it had a strong military and a commitment to it. The relationship between the military and the political community has been in balance, by and large, which I think has been critical. The military people in this large and complex society always have known that they are subject to the political will of the people, broadly speaking, and to the Congress and to the commander in chief, all of whom are civilian.

So I think the military is vitally important. I do think that public people without the benefit of military experience have to work a little harder to understand what it is all about.

USNI: Do you think some sort of mandatory national service would do the country any good?

Brokaw: You know, I've always believed in it, and I've always said it was a good idea. I think it should be both men and women, but then the costs become prohibitive. That's a big part of the problem.

I've thought about this a fair amount. I do think that it would be useful to have some kind of interim step, if you will—summer programs for young people who want to have some military experience. It may not have to be a full, uniformed experience. In between college years, there ought to be some program where young people can make contributions and learn about various aspects of American life, including the military.

USNI: People in this country seem to be starving for heroes these days. How do you feel about that?

Brokaw: I think, especially right now, that three or four factors are feeding this. One is that we've been through the past year with no heroes on either side of this [the Lewinski] scandal—or in any part of it. Nobody has emerged who is heroic—the prosecutor, the president, the women involved, the people on the Hill. All have seemed less than heroic to the American public.

Another factor is that at the end of the twentieth century, people are reviewing what this nation has been through, what they've personally been through. And when they look back on World War II, they think, "My God, look at all we have accomplished, at home and abroad." It really is breathtaking when you think about it—the scope, the mobilization, the retooling of American industry to produce armaments, the training that went on in a short time, yet was done so skillfully. Look at the magnitude of the military challenges set before these people: the terrible blow at Pearl Harbor, for example. But they recovered from it and prevailed, east and west, and came back and built the country.

I think that there often is a longing for simpler times. The World War II generation will tell you that no one should want to go back to those times because they were so hard. The Depression was an era of great deprivation. The war was a horror, with separation and death and maiming and great sacrifice and great anxiety. What these people say is that they've made it possible for this current generation to create its own era, which is what I believe.

USNI: In publishing, as I'm sure it is in television, you always take a gamble when you use superlatives and absolutes. How did you arrive at your title, *The Greatest Generation*?

Brokaw: Well, I thought about it; it wasn't just a whim. I said to Tim Russert on the *Today* show during the fiftieth anniversary of D-Day, "I think that this is the greatest generation any society ever produced." Then I went back through it and argued with some contemporaries of mine, older historians and others. I must say, I have not found a great deal of resistance to it. And I have measured this generation against others in this country.

Our founding fathers were part of a great generation. But there were people who sided with the Brits at that time. And, although the example we set here was one of democracy and the age of enlightenment, it didn't have a ripple effect around the world. We didn't export it in our own way.

The Civil War generation was an astonishing one. We went to war against each other and then healed the nation in a common way. But, you know, we really didn't deal with institutionalized racism. There were still deep divisions in this country along racial lines.

USNI: There still are.

Brokaw: Yes, and there still are. And that experience is confined largely to this country.

This "greatest" generation lived through great economic deprivations. Expectations were low because of the hardships they were experiencing in getting jobs, keeping farms and businesses, of going to college and trying to pay for it. Just when they began to have some hope, they were lifted up out of their small communities or off city streets, and sent thousands of miles across the Pacific, thousands of miles across the Atlantic, to fight wars in the most primitive conditions for years at a time. Then they came back, rebuilt their enemies, built this country into the most powerful industrial economy in the history of civilization, stared down communism, took advantage of the GI Bill, spread out across America and built communities and families and schools, and never whined, never whimpered, and never asked for attention.

So those are the markers for me in terms of determining that this was the greatest generation.

USNI: Often in your book you say that the people who saw combat generally didn't want to talk about it much. How did you get them to open up?

Brokaw: I think they opened up in part because they are now in the mortality zone and they want people to know what they went through. And they want the rest of society to understand the lessons of that.

This book had many beginnings in my mind. One of them came when I was at my little house in the far northwestern corner of Connecticut in a wonderful little town called Litchfield, a real picturesque Yankee community that goes back to the early seventeen hundreds.

I read an obituary in the paper one day about a man who had been the first citizen of Litchfield. He was a lawyer and the first selectman, which is the equivalent of the mayor. He had been active in his church and school and in the town's cultural affairs, and he was widely regarded. But no one knew about his war experience. He had been diagnosed, as I remember now, with brain cancer, and he was going to die. He knew that.

As the paper recounted it later in his obituary, about three months into his diagnosis he said to his wife, "There are some parts of my life I've never talked about. You should hear them." He was a real heroic figure. He had done great brave things and had been instrumental in operations to liberate Europe. How many stories are out there just like this one? How many of these people have never told their stories? We had better get them down on paper before they die.

On the fiftieth anniversary of D-Day I remember telling my wife to ask these guys where they were that day. Almost uniformly, their response was, "Oh, I was at Omaha, but I didn't do anything more than anybody else did." Then we would say, "We understand that. But what did you do that day?" We finally got them to talk about it. These were kids eighteen to twenty-two years of age in the greatest military invasion in the history of mankind. They faced withering fire from Germans dug in along that coastline. And they walked into a storm front of 88-mm and small-arms fire and grenades and bombs and land mines and obstacles of all kinds. And they were determined to liberate Europe. It still takes my breath away.

USNI: What about the Pacific landings and invasions?

Brokaw: I wrote about those, as well. I do think that there's been almost an undue concentration on Europe. Obviously, the Marines and the Navy in the Pacific were equally important.

One of the subjects in the book was a Pacific war veteran from my hometown. After one Halloween, he was complaining about the high school kids the night before. My mother said to him—kind of in a jocular way, because he was a guy who was well-known for his sense of humor—"Oh, come on, Gordon. Where were you when you were seventeen?" He looked at her and said, "I was landing on Guadalcanal." That's as good a sound bite as I've ever heard, by the way.

It's now been probably forty-five years since my mother came home from the post office that day and told me that story. So I found Gordon Larsen. He landed at Guadalcanal and at Bougainville and at Okinawa. He lost his brother at Bougainville, saw him killed in front of him. He went through all that and had the canteen shot off his hip. He was a Browning automatic rifleman, in the thick of it all the time. And he had never, ever talked about it.

USNI: How do you switch gears from talking and writing about the moral high ground of World War II veterans to reporting on events in Washington on the nightly news?

Brokaw: I have to do that all that time. It's not just unique to this current experience. You have to come home from Beirut, or the Persian Gulf War, or the earthquake in Armenia, or Tianenman Square, and get on with your life, deal with it. Journalists are famous for being able to compartmentalize.

What this book did, when I was preparing and finishing it in the midst of the current [White House] scandal, was to remind me once again that history is long-curve. It's not short-term. You know, these people came back from the war, and we had McCarthyism. That was another chilling scandal, of a different kind, but the psychological and emotional scars still remain for a lot of people.

It was a politically perilous time. We had expended a tremendous amount of effort and lives defending against such repression, but McCarthy was running rampant, falsely calling people communist and demanding investigations of the defense and state departments.

So these veterans reminded me, either directly or indirectly, that this country has been through a lot and that good people prevail—if they get involved.

USNI: I count ten Navy and Marine Corps veterans whose stories are in your book. What might set them apart from the rest? Did you see any common thread among them?

Brokaw: I think that the Marines I wrote about are like marines everywhere. My youngest brother was a Marine, and my closest friend was a Marine killed in Vietnam. And—you can print this—they had bigger balls than anybody I knew.

The navy people were quite heroic as well. I wrote about a man by the name of Hack Hagen, who was a gunnery officer on the cruiser USS *Salt Lake City.* Then I went back and read what Samuel Eliot Morison had to say about the *Salt Lake City* in the North Pacific. It was a hell of a fight, and Hack was in the thick of it the entire time. I had never heard him talk about that before.

USNI: What differences do you see in today's armed services, compared to the time you started in television?

Brokaw: They're much more educated. Volunteer services make a big difference. People really want to be there, and so for the most part you get the best and the brightest.

Certainly, the people I met in the Gulf and those I meet when I speak before colleges—I've been to the Army War College at Carlisle and I've been to the Naval War College at Newport on a couple of occasions—are like the rest of society. The educational level and technology skills are much higher.

I guess the one concern I have is that, not so much in the Navy, but maybe more in the Marine Corps and the Army—and there's no way of quantifying this—I worry that it attracts, at the lower levels, the people who want to learn not how to defend their country but how to become skilled in killing techniques for their own purposes. So I think the screening process is pretty important these days when you have a volunteer service.

USNI: What impact do you hope your book will have?

Brokaw: Well, I was mostly eager to tell the stories because I think these people are due the homage that may come out of this book, that their children and grandchildren and other family members, and the nation for that matter, will stop and reflect for a moment on all that they did.

I also did it for selfish reasons, because I came to care about these people. I think that most of them have a fair amount of pride in the fact that they are in the book. And I wanted to remind myself and everyone else about what the country can do when it decides that it should take collective action about something, that we can find common ground. It doesn't have to be a war. There are other things that we can do as well. The postwar years were a lesson in that.

It's a combination, really. I'm a journalist, so mostly I wanted to tell the stories that interested me and moved me. And I thought that others would possibly be interested and moved as well. I'm trying to do the right thing by that generation, and I hope that the veterans who read the book, and the people who subscribe to your magazine, will begin to put down on paper or in oral recordings their own experiences and what they learned, not just about the horrors of the time, but the greater lessons that came out of it. That was my real objective.

Art Buchwald

U.S. NAVAL INSTITUTE

Mr. Buchwald is a humorist and columnist syndicated to 550 newspapers worldwide, and he is the author of twenty-eight books. He served in the Marine Corps during World War II. Borrowing from his official curriculum vitae, "Mr. Buchwald is a workaholic and has no hobbies." He delivered the following address at the U.S. Naval Institute's 123d Annual Meeting and 7th Annapolis Seminar in April 1997.

■

I just can't say enough about the U.S. Naval Institute—because I had never heard of it before now.

I asked one member what a Naval Institute member does.

He said he didn't understand the question.

I said, "How do you justify your existence?"

He said, "We are the watchdogs of naval power, supporters of those who fight on the sea and in the air, and believers in a strong and healthy Naval Academy lacrosse team."

I asked him, "Is the Naval Institute bullish on America?"

He said, "We can go either way, and usually do."

Some people find it hard to believe that I was a Marine. Last year at the Gridiron Dinner, the fanciest dinner in Washington, as each service tune was played, the people from that service got up and stood at attention. When the Marine Corps Hymn was played, I stood up at attention.

One guy sitting across from me asked the guy sitting next to him, "What's Buchwald standing up for?"

The second guy said, "He was a Marine."

The first guy said, "Je-esus Chr-rist!"

As time goes on, all of us who have served in different wars come to exaggerate the role we played. When I was going to the University of Southern California in the 1940s, some people asked me what I did during the war. I told them I was a rear gunner on an F-4U fighter plane. The jerks were too dumb to know there was only one seat on an F-4U. In the 1950s, I told everyone I had shot down twenty-six Japanese airplanes. By this time my children were curious, so I decided to up it even more. I said I was commanding general of the First Marine Air Wing and was the only one willing to give Pappy Boyington a second chance. Finally, my grandchildren arrived, and I had to do something for them. So I said I was the one who dropped the bomb on Hiroshima.

What did I really do during World War II? I was assigned to an air wing when I finished boot camp. I was very infuriated about this, because I wanted to see action. So I went to the drill instructor and said, "When I enlisted in the Marine Corps, they promised that I would be a paratrooper."

He took one look at me and said, "Okay, you're a paratrooper."

So I wound up being an ordnanceman in a fighter squadron. And I wasn't a very good ordnanceman.

I was once loading a 500-pound bomb on a plane and dropped it. Everyone on the island scrambled for their lives. I pretended my foot was broken so they wouldn't kill me.

The next day, the commanding officer called me in and said, "I'm putting you in for the Navy Cross."

I asked why.

He said, "You forgot to fuse the bomb and saved the lives of five hundred Marines."

I know you're still asking what I did to win the war. The answer is simple: I got out. There are men and women who stayed in after the war and there are those of us who chose to serve our country in civilian life. Had I stayed in and loaded nuclear weapons on our naval ships, no one would be here today.

On a serious note, now more than fifty years after World War II, I wish to say a few words about the Navy and Marine Corps fliers who fought in that war and the men who took care of the planes. We are saying farewell to the men and to the planes at an unacceptable rate. Listen carefully, and you will hear the engines of the F-4Fs, the F-6Fs, the F-4Us, the SBDs, the torpedo bombers, and all the other planes flown by the military fifty years ago. They are preparing to take their pilots on their final flight. World War II's Marine and Navy squadrons produced the best fliers and ground personnel that any of the services could offer. They helped save the troops on Guadalcanal, and they fought the Japanese from one end of the Pacific to the other.

They were damned good. Listen carefully as each plane readies to take off for a target unknown. As for you young pilots flying your supersonic jets, dip your wings in tribute to the Navy and Marine pilots of World War II who loved to fly as much as you do.

Attention, everyone.

Listen to the distant drums sounding for the men with gold wings who flew three and four generations ago. They were the best of World War II. Don't forget it. We will never see their like again.

John Bulkeley

U.S. NAVAL INSTITUTE

The late Vice Adm. John Bulkeley received the Medal of Honor for his heroic evacuation of Gen. Douglas MacArthur from the Philippines early in World War II. He went on to an illustrious naval career and became famous for his refusal to cooperate with Fidel Castro. Here, he recalls a harrowing experience from World War II. The interview appeared in the August 1994 issue of the Naval Institute's *Proceedings.*

■

USNI: Many of us know about the fight between the German corvettes *Nimet Allah* and *Capriolo* and your destroyer, the *Endicott* [DD-495], in August 1944. Could you set the stage for those unfamiliar with the story?

Bulkeley: How far back do you want to go?

USNI: Why don't we start with taking command of the destroyer?

Bulkeley: On D+38 [thirty-eight days after the Normandy invasion] I was summoned to the destroyer *Endicott.* She had been in a collision, and she had also been late in getting to the invasion of Normandy. Commodore Harry Sanders said that her captain lacked the drive, the initiative, and the aggressiveness required of a destroyer captain. And he wanted to get rid of this one. So he sent for me.

We got in a whaleboat and went over to the *Endicott*, where he told me to go down in the plotting room and stay there until I heard that the officer I was to replace had left the ship. I was then to go up on the bridge and announce that I was taking command. There were no written orders or notification to the Bureau of Personnel—or anyone else. So I took command and got the ship under way. And away we went, down to the invasion of Southern France.

USNI: How long did it take you to get the ship into shape?

Bulkeley: The ship was, in my book, in poor material condition, no question about it. When I went to work with that crew, I made it very plain. I said, "Look, this is a fighting ship. She might get into action. If you're going to save your lives, you'd better work like hell, night and day. We're going to be watertight. And you're going to make damn sure all the guns are working, and the ammunition is readily available."

All these things had to be put together. And the crew did it in a relatively short time—about three days, I guess.

I did not know exactly what my task was going to be. Douglas Fairbanks Jr., the actor, was in the middle of this business for a diversionary raid to La Ciotat. The basic idea was to make a pretense of invading. We were to draw two German divisions all the way from St. Tropez east to our area of concentration.

We fired three thousand rounds continuously over two nights, which convinced the Germans that the invasion was going to take place—that this was a preinvasion bombardment. It did look real.

We also had PT boats that went in raising hell, shooting off tracers and machine guns, yelling, shouting, and screaming, and dropping depth charges in order to make it all like it was a preinvasion assault. I'm told that the Germans moved two full divisions to the east, about eighty to a hundred miles from where the real assault would take place. When Gen. Mark Clark landed his troops there on that particular D-day, only one soldier was killed; he stepped on a mine.

My work was finished after the Germans had been drawn off. Because our ship had sustained some damage, I was sent down to Sicily. There were PT boats in that area under the command of Capt. Stanley Barnes, a very fine officer and classmate of mine. On my way down to Sicily for repairs, I got a radio call from *PT-379* that two German gunboats were attacking two British ships, the *Scarab* and the *Aphis*, and that the latter two were getting the worst of it. They were river gunboats built for China duty, and they had very little fire control. Their guns were small, and their speed was not more that eight or twelve knots.

I turned around immediately when I heard they were under attack. We soon saw huge clouds of black smoke, which looked almost as though some ships were on fire. I didn't know what was on the other side, so I crashed on through.

The *Aphis* and the *Scarab* were apparently somewhere else, running like hell. Fairbanks admitted in a letter to me later that they were getting out of the way. They would have been goners otherwise, he said. I was making thirty-six knots when I started after the German ships. They were doing twenty-eight or thirty knots themselves. That is when I took a picture of them.

When you run into the enemy, you've got to attack, no question about it. Everyone was getting kind of shaky about the fact that we were running into something we didn't know. When we took a look at the armament—5-inch guns—we surmised that these boys were just as strong as we were.

Our mounts were armored with quarter-inch steel. They had theirs right out in the open. And they were quite big. I ordered our 5-inch guns to commence firing at a range about six or eight thousand yards—good hitting range. About two minutes went by, and no guns fired. I said, "What the hell is going on?" Right off the bat, we had a problem closing the breaches. We had overheated parts of the guns during the earlier shore bombardment, which caused them to seize up. The only gun we had working was mount three. A great big strapping gunner's mate first class was in charge of that turret. He was loading the shells by ramming them in by hand. The breach itself was sticking, and it wouldn't fire unless it was fully closed. So he used a sledgehammer to pound it tight. At that time we began to fire.

Apparently, we were pretty effective. We kept closing the range as fast as we possibly could. They had torpedoes in those ships, and I didn't want those guys to have a straight-line shot at us. So we did a lot of zigging and zagging as we closed the range. We swept their decks with the 40-mm and 20-mm gunfire.

By this time, we had closed to within eight hundred yards, by some accounts, and our 5-inch guns were scoring some hits. One of the ships capsized, and the other one sank later on. That was that. The fight was over as far as we were concerned. By this time, the British gunboats had started coming back.

We picked up 179 prisoners out of the water. The German captains were very bitter and nasty. They claimed they lost two hundred men drowned. I personally didn't give a damn one way or the other. We picked up everyone we could and did the right thing.

A doctor and a chiropractor—can you imagine—worked together and operated on the wardroom table from 0800 to 2400 that day. We had five Germans die, and we gave them a full military funeral. We sent both German captains down to the wardroom. I didn't know what to do with them, but according to the book, we were supposed to treat them decently, as gentlemen. They were tough birds, complete with dueling scars, and they were full captains. I was only a lieutenant commander, and I don't think they liked that very much.

USNI: Since you fought small combatants with such great effect during your war career, what do you think the future of small combatants is in today's Navy? Are they still valuable?

Bulkeley: I'm glad you asked that question. My career was not necessarily small combatants. Commodore Sanders said, "Look, you can't stay in small boats all your life. You've got to get out. I know you like them. It's great. You do fine. But you've got to get into destroyers, cruisers, and battleships; that's where it counts when it comes to the heavy hitters."

And so immediately I went to the destroyer *Endicott.* From there, we had another destroyer command. And from there I went to cruisers and finally ended up with a battleship. That was what it was all about. So you can't really tag me as a small-boat man.

Is there a future in small boats? In the *Cyclone* [PC-1] class there is. There are some patrolling off Haiti right now. Future? We have to have smaller craft to take care of peripheral problem areas, like Somalia and Haiti. These boats are far more sophisticated, are more capable, have more firepower, and are more deadly than I ever even envisioned in my PT boats. There's a future all right.

USNI: How did you feel about getting the Medal of Honor for rescuing Gen. Douglas MacArthur from the Philippines so early in the war? Was it a help or a hindrance to the way you fought later?

Bulkeley: I didn't know what the Medal of Honor was. I did not want to be treated differently. It really didn't mean a lot to me. My career rested entirely on my professional ability, as you well know, if you read the whole story.

USNI: Do you think the veterans were honored properly at the Normandy anniversary events?

Bulkeley: Absolutely. In my opinion, we were highly honored, and it was very well done. I was selected to greet the president. Then they lined us up, and he went down the line and shook hands with us all. The *George Washington* [CVN-73] hangar deck had more darned admirals than you could shake a stick at. It was very well done.

We heard no catcalls or any other derogatory statements from any of the enlisted men or the officers. It was all on the up and up. Mr. Clinton did what he was supposed to do as the president, and he did it very well. One thing they made damned sure of was that the veterans were up front during the ceremonies, and not relegated to the back, as they usually are, to make room in front for all the congressmen, senators, and other politicians. This time, the veterans had the best seats.

USNI: What do you think about the rest of the World War II anniversaries? Why do you think they don't get as much media attention as Normandy?

Bulkeley: Well, my answer to that is that all of us are so damned old. These guys are all in their late seventies and early eighties, some are in wheelchairs, some on crutches. We're just plain old—aged. And people aren't very interested in that. Who cares? I'm in my eighties.

USNI: A lot of people care.

Ken Burns

PAM TUBRIDY BAUCOM / FLORENTINE FILMS

Mr. Burns is the founder of Florentine Films, a documentary filmmaking establishment in Walpole, New Hampshire. Among his many credits are the acclaimed PBS miniseries *The Civil War, Baseball, Lewis and Clark,* and *The West.* At this writing, he is investigating the possibility of a program on ships and the sea. The interview appeared in the February 1999 issue of *Naval History.*

■

USNI: What is your favorite period of history?

Burns: The period that tells me, in this moment, who I am. We tend to think of the past as some nostalgic, bygone period, when in fact history is the present-day engagement with something that has gone before. So history is itself a great mirror of who we are now. I can never pin down one particular era that is a favorite, because I'm always interested in the history that's waking me up today.

I think we make the mistake of thinking that somehow we can influence the past. We can't. We approach the past in a variety of ways that tell us more about who we are than they do about the past. The past becomes the method. Cézanne, I suppose, could talk about oranges, but he was not interested in oranges, he was interested in what lies beyond, the luminescence that he was able to capture from those oranges. So, too, it's less the specifics of the past that ought to matter than the way in which we engage it and that extra something that comes from that engagement. The way in which history becomes present, for a moment, becomes our best teacher, our best medicine.

USNI: How did you become interested in history?

Burns: I think it's been in my blood all my life. I'm completely untrained. I'm a filmmaker who chose history the way a painter chooses watercolors or oils. But something both in personal history and in general has brought me to the sense of how positive and transforming a force history is.

USNI: So you didn't major in history in college.

Burns: I majored in filmmaking. The last time I took a formal history course was in eleventh grade. But I have spent my life in American history, and I can't imagine leaving it.

USNI: American history, mostly?

Burns: Always and only. I am interested in the mechanics of my country. The operating guide is history.

USNI: Most *Naval History* readers will know you for *The Civil War*. Many also will say that the series neglected the naval aspects of the war. Why were naval operations given such short shrift?

Burns: I agree that they were given short shrift, but certainly not through any intention on our part. A filmmaker is much like a sculptor who has a huge block of stone delivered to the studio and then works for many months, and in our case, many years, carving away. You make decisions in one day, and there's no way to change most of them.

So essentially, as we moved and listened to our own hearts, what came out necessarily made many things fall by the wayside. I would have liked to do more on women in the Civil War. I would have liked to do more on Congress—the Radical Republican Congress that was so politically important. I would have liked to do more on the social ramifications, more on emancipation. And I would have loved to cover dozens of other battles and, with great attention, naval affairs.

It was not a question of lack of interest. As this thing began to evolve and speak to us, it began to shape itself. We could do only just so much. It's not comprehensive; it was only eleven and a half hours. You can't even get through one volume of Bruce Catton's great Civil War histories in that time.

Another reason that naval operations have been given short shrift is that the ghosts don't come up to you in the same way they do, say, on Little Round Top, or in the cornfield at Antietam, or at the Bloody Angle, or in other places that have etched themselves in our minds. Yet the naval operations are no less important.

One can imagine the drama of the Battle of New Orleans, or Mobile Bay with Farragut, or even some of the smaller gunboat battles on the Mississippi and other big rivers. And of course, there was the Blockade and all that it did, or didn't do, to contribute to the successful prosecution of the war for both sides.

USNI: What impact would you say naval operations had on the outcome of the war?

Burns: I think the moment that draws me most of all is the heavy breathing that takes place after the *Monitor* and *Virginia* engagement in 1862, an event that not only gave pause to the United States and the Confederate States, but also to the world. At that moment, every other navy on earth was obsolete. That, for me, is a central moment. All of a sudden, we knew that everything in naval history was about to change—completely and utterly.

USNI: What is your take on the apparent resurgence of interest in war movies, with *Saving Private Ryan* and the film about Guadalcanal, *The Thin Red Line*?

Burns: Most of these are a part of an unanticipated zeitgeist that we can't ever predict. We need something from our stories. They help us get through. As I said before, they help us understand who we are now. So there must be something in the medicine of World War II stories that is helpful to us now, a certain kind of unambiguous heroism that, I think, needs to be at least positive, as we struggle with all of the complexities and the ambiguities and undertones of our modern political life.

And so I think that we can find in this simplicity, and I say that not in military terms but in heroic terms—the simple and self-evident sacrifice at Omaha Beach—a kind of medicine that helps us get through our own very complicated times.

USNI: How do you differ from Steven Spielberg in your approach?

Burns: I think that we are very similar in many ways and obviously very different in others. I do not wish to leave the facts. Shelby Foote once said to me that God is the greatest dramatist. I believe that it's important to stay with the facts. It does not mean that these are objective views. They're not. They're filled with subjective interpretation and emphasis and emotion. In fact, I call myself an emotional archaeologist. I'm uninterested in just the excavation of dry dates, events, and facts. I'm after something that adds a higher emotional resonance to our historical dialect.

Having said that, I think that Spielberg and I marshal forces in very similar ways. For too long, I think we have beaten to death this argument between what is made up and what is factual, because much is untrue in the merely factual, and much resonates with universal truths in the things that are made up. One need only compare reading the telephone book and a Shakespeare play to realize it.

So what we're doing is looking for a higher truth with regard to fact, because the mere assembly of facts is not enough, as Francis Parkman once said. It's imbuing the narrative with the life and spirit of the people, their motivations and their feelings. That's what I've tried to do.

USNI: It seems that your work is better known to some than your name. How do you feel about that?

Burns: Well, I think that may just be the choice of your audiences. Any documentary filmmaker takes a vow of anonymity and poverty, but neither has happened to me. In fact, I get stopped everywhere I go, and I don't know of that happening to any other documentary filmmaker. So, I think the "Q" quotient, or whatever they call it, is pretty high. But I don't kid myself that this is brain surgery, or even at the top of the pop charts. And I'm happy with that. I live in an anonymous place so that I can remind myself that any celebrity you have, plus fifty cents, gets you a cup of coffee.

USNI: To many people, the word "documentary" equates with "dull." How do you overcome that?

Burns: Yes. Say "documentary" to people, and their eyes glaze over. It's like cauliflower or brussels sprouts. It's something that they know is good for them, but hardly good tasting. I would suggest that the Hollywood model, the dramatic film model, is the one that's narrow and formulaic, that plays within very strict sets of rules. Documentary film has, particularly over the last fifteen years, come to mean a whole variety of things, ranging from dramatic docudramas, to cinéma vérité, in which there's no narrator, and nothing but the actual moment is happening. I think that what we're used to as an audience is documentaries as expressions of already arrived-upon ends. They are very neat, tied packages. And they are, of course, boring.

We approach our films as a process of discovery. We want to find out about our subject, and we place all the enthusiasm and the expectation of discovery into our process. I think that's what we share along with the facts of our film, and that's why the films have been so popular. They are the antithesis of this vaccination that comes in the form of a documentary.

USNI: If you could remake any of the films that you've done, would you, and what would it be?

Burns: I wouldn't remake them, because I think they are accurate snapshots of where I was when I made them. If you accept the idea of history as "not was, but is," as William Faulkner said, then the film is evidence of how I was when I made it. These are intensely personal films that are part of my own drama, as well as the larger drama of my fellow citizens. I look at the films and see their problems, and I see how I might have changed something, or added something, or taken something out. But that becomes meaningless. It's like looking at an old snapshot in an album and saying, "I wish I could change the way I was." There's nothing you can do about it. You can't take that paunch away. You can't shave the beard from the old photograph. You're stuck with it. That's who you were. So with these films, that's who I was.

USNI: Which film did you like doing the most?

Burns: That's a difficult question. They are all completely different. Actually, I have been making the same film over and over again, I discovered recently. They are all asking the same question: Who are we? Like my two daughters, they all have special aspects to them that make them unique. Each has had its special moments—filming the Matthew Brady photographs at the Library of Congress for *The Civil War* or being out on the Lewis and Clark Trail, trying to bring back a moment free of telephone wires and modern influences. Lots of times you feel a special kinship to a project. But I can't say that one project is my favorite.

USNI: Perhaps the biggest coup of your career was putting the voices and personalities of David McCullough, Shelby Foote, and Ed Bearss together in *The Civil War.* Was that a calculated decision?

Burns: Well, I've kidded David McCullough that I gave him his start in motion pictures. He had written a book on the building of the Brooklyn Bridge. My first major film, my first national PBS broadcast, in the early eighties—and one that I had been working on since the mid-seventies—was on the building of the Brooklyn Bridge, inspired in part by his book. It seemed logical to me that the person who knew most about the subject ought to narrate it. So I begged and twisted and cajoled until he finally came on. He narrated most of the next ten films I made, up to *The Civil War.* He was, in essence, my voice.

For *The Civil War,* I thought I would have dozens of voices. As it turned out very quickly, most of the academic historians we spoke with did not in any way help us understand the narrative story. They would always give you the punch line before you wanted to hear it.

Typically, we would ask, "What was the war like for the Southern soldier?" And they would tell you in one sentence, through to the surrender. Any good narrative historian doesn't want Lee to surrender to Grant until it's time—until the last episode, right? But Shelby Foote would say things like, "Well, they ate something that they called 'sloosh.' That is, they'd fry up some bacon and when that was done, they would take the bacon grease, and they'd add some cornmeal to it, and they'd roll it into a dough, and they would roll that dough into a snake, and they'd wrap it around their bayonet or their ramrod, and then cook it over a fire. They called that sloosh. And they ate a lot of it."

So there was an expressive quality to Shelby. It turns out that very few other people we interviewed were able to put us in the historical moment with a certain urgency and sense—which all good narrative history should have—that things may not turn out the way you think they will. That maybe Lee will make it up and through the copse of trees at Gettysburg, and Pickett's Charge will turn out differently. That maybe this time Lee won't surrender to Grant. That maybe this time John Wilkes Booth won't get off the shot in Ford's Theater.

Good history makes you sit on the edge of your seat, hoping that it might not turn out the way you know it's going to turn out. That's good storytelling. And Shelby helped rivet our attention, as did Ed Bearss. Ed

Bearss pulled us in with his rock-solid knowledge of every detail. I've heard Ed speak above backhoes. That guy could cut through fog.

USNI: Who selects the photos that you use?

Burns: I try to do it. People say, "You must have so many researchers," because of the number of images that we so clearly deal with. In fact, we have very few. We don't really have researchers, because the researcher is traditionally the lowest rung on a production hierarchy. Why would you want that person making the critical decision of not so much yes, but no? We like to say no, or yes, to photographs. We have a nucleus of two or three or four of us on a big project. The people who make decisions in my absence are people whose esthetic and historical judgments I trust. Even then, we have disagreements. They'll often make photocopies of twenty-five pictures and order ten, and then when I happen to see the other fifteen, many months later, I ask why we didn't order this or that one. Taste is so individual. In the case of *The Civil War*, I picked—and shot—every one.

USNI: Have you ever had a desire to do the Hollywood blockbuster, as opposed to what you are doing?

Burns: When I was in high school, I was in love with the Hollywood movies, and I really wanted to be Alfred Hitchcock, or Howard Hawkes, or Orson Welles, or John Ford—especially John Ford. I loved his stories in American history. I loved the fact that he did history from the top down as well as from the bottom up. That is to say, there's always a dog barking in the corner of a John Ford scene. There's always a dance. You're not only always aware of what people wore, but you also have a sense that this is really how they lived. There's mud on the streets, a sense of real lives being lived. And there's always beautiful music and a sense of a transcendent American message coming through it all.

That's what I wanted to be. I got my head turned around completely when I went to college—Hampshire College in Amherst, Massachusetts—by social documentary still photographers who reminded me, quite correctly, that there's more drama in what is and what was than in anything the imagination could make up. And so suddenly you had this head of a documentary filmmaker on the body of a John Ford–lover.

In some ways, I've had my dream, and I'm constantly being drawn back to a Hollywood situation. But I enjoy, with Public Television and the kind of support I get from General Motors and other underwriters, an absolute creative freedom. So I will never come to you and say, "The reason why you didn't like this film is because somebody made me do this," or "I didn't get enough money for that," or "Somebody wanted the ending to change," or "Somebody released it on Thursday instead of Sunday."

I will never say that to you. I will say that the reason why you didn't like it is entirely my fault. I never want to make an excuse. So when I've had opportunities to do something in Hollywood, my conscience has always pulled back, because I realized that I would not have total artistic control, and therefore, I could not take full blame for my mistakes.

USNI: Where does history begin for you? Can one do a responsible history of Operation Desert Storm, for instance?

Burns: Well, history is the great pageant of everything that has gone before this moment, but any realist understands that a certain amount of historical triangulation has to take place. That is to say, as in celestial navigation, or in any kind of mathematical equation, triangulation is fixing a specific spot by knowing the distances between a couple of other spots. And I think the key to that triangulation in history is time.

Let me give you a classic example of why you don't want to rush into something in the guise of history. For many years after Vietnam, that war seemed to be our albatross, a dark war that had taken on the same importance as the Revolutionary War, the Civil War, and World War II. And on top of this, it was a war we had lost. This was going to be the beginning of the decline of the United States. We labored under this popular sense for many years, and a lot of our fiction, our movies, and our popular culture issued from this belief, of this metaphor for the decline of America.

If you had done a history of Vietnam then, you would have been enthralled by that view. But, as Abraham Lincoln said, you need to disenthrall yourself and the one way you disenthrall yourself is through patience. You wait.

Look what happened. This relatively small military action called Desert Storm wiped out Vietnam as the albatross, that ball-and-chain we had been carrying. Vietnam still retains its significance and centrality in twentieth-century American history, but it doesn't have the historical weight it once had. And what did that take? A mere twenty-five years away from the subject. So my philosophy is that you need at least thirty years before you can actually say, "I think I understand what this was about," in even just rudimentary historical fashion. Revisionism is going on all the time. In five years, we'll have a better perspective on Vietnam, or at least a different one.

In my films, particularly those subjects like baseball, and now jazz, that come up to more or less the present, we untether ourselves from our straightforward historical narrative within thirty or forty years of the present day and become much more impressionistic. That is a quite conscious decision, so that we in no way make the mistake of a premature judgment or assumption. History is still being made.

USNI: What would you say are the largest gaps in U.S. history?

Burns: As an amateur historian and a professional filmmaker, I've got to say that the prephotographic history of our country is much neglected. This is why I sort of dove, however naively or foolishly, into that prephotographic era in films on Thomas Jefferson and Lewis and Clark. I would have to say our Colonial period is probably the least known and least reported, certainly in film. And I think also that is true in the scholarship, with some obvious notable exceptions. If I had my druthers, I would want to see more things about seventeenth- and eighteenth-century America.

USNI: What do you think of cable television and the advent of The History Channel, and The Military Channel, and Discovery, and Arts and Entertainment?

Burns: I'm disappointed. The only thing that we have in our modern life that's really our own is our attention. I would wager that the things and relationships you are proudest of are those that occur in duration, those that have benefited—the people, the things, the work you've done—by your focused attention.

And yet, for more than three generations of television, we have convinced people that they don't need to have an attention span longer than eight to ten minutes, at which point we'll sell you six to eight things, then go back to telling the story. So it's no wonder that we have a lack of attention. On public television, my film can go out and not be interrupted for an hour and a half or two hours, if that's what it takes to tell the story.

The quality of the work on The History Channel and A&E is diminished. They're more superficial. They're hardly more than journalistic considerations, because they don't have the time, and they don't have the resources, because there are so many of them. How can you develop complexity, if every eight to ten minutes you're interrupted to sell six to eight different things? It may seem obvious, but it's not trivial in any way. It is the single most important reason for the dumbing-down of the country: our refusal to develop our own attention.

And that's why I've tried to stay, though often to my financial detriment, in a place that rewards me so much better with the freedom and the control necessary to develop attention.

USNI: What projects are in the works for you currently?

Burns: Well, I'm working on two parallel tracks. After *Baseball,* I began with a series of biographies that started with Thomas Jefferson, then Lewis and Clark, then Frank Lloyd Wright. We're doing a dual biography of Elizabeth Cady Stanton and Susan B. Anthony, two very interesting women, and then in the year 2000, Mark Twain.

In the meantime, I will release the third panel on a triptych, the final leg of a trilogy that began with *The Civil War,* which defined us, as Shelby Foote said, to *Baseball,* which told us what we had become, to *Jazz,* which is a kind of redemptive promise of the country and a very interesting way of looking at twentieth-century American history. All three are great American creations, the great improvisational genius of America in jazz, in baseball, and in our Constitution, as manifested in its greatest crisis, the Civil War. Beyond that are more biographies, more series, and I'm just now beginning to pick and choose among dozens of potential projects.

USNI: What would you suggest that we do to get people more interested in naval history?

Burns: Since *The Civil War* and *Baseball,* I'm confronted constantly with people telling me what I should do next. I'm basically a freelancer at heart, so I have what I'm going to do set for the next several years. But it's very interesting what people talk about. The main suggestion is do something on railroads. The next main suggestion is immigration. And the third thing is to do something about naval history, to do something about ships.

What I need to do is to find a story, not a series of disconnected events but a complicated story with all of the stuff of drama. Then we'll have people beating a path to our door. Certainly, the success of *Titanic* reinvigorates any consideration of the drama at sea. *Titanic* is a drama in which everyone knows what's going to happen, and they are even more riveted because they know. That's the essence of good history-telling.

I think one of the undertold stories in American history is our growth to a major sea power. It is central to our position as a world power. And I think if you polled most citizens, they would have no idea that our present world standing came essentially from our bursting out as a navy, able at first to rival Britain and then others.

USNI: If ever you have a notion to do a naval history project, we hope you call the Naval Institute.

Burns: You would be the first people we talk to. One great thing about these projects is that we get to associate with historical agencies and groups that have the subjects closest to their hearts. They've spent their whole lives in it, and we come in for a few years and try to represent their enthusiasm as faithfully as we can.

The subjects choose me. So there will come a time, to be sure, when I'll be knocking on your door and begging you to lend me your beautiful photographs—and your expertise and kindness.

Dick Cheney

DEPARTMENT OF DEFENSE

Mr. Cheney was secretary of defense during the Bush administration and Operation Desert Storm. He is currently president, chairman of the board, and CEO of the Dallas-based Halliburton Company. In the 2000 election, Mr. Cheney will run as vice president on the Republican ticket with presidential candidate George W. Bush. The interview appeared in the May 1996 Naval Institute *Proceedings.*

■

USNI: As one architect of military downsizing, how would you rate its progress?

Cheney: I think we've made a fair amount of progress. I do not think that means it's finished by any means. When the Berlin Wall came down and the Warsaw Pact came apart, the Joint Chiefs and I decided that we did not want to wait and have an adjustment reacting to the end of the Cold War imposed on us from the outside. That is to say, we wanted to develop a new strategy and force structure internally.

The Defense Planning Guidance embodied some of this. It was a basic shift away from the old scenario, based on assumptions that a war would begin in Europe and quickly go nuclear and just as quickly go global. We shifted away from that to a so-called regional strategy, where we focused upon the need to deny an adversary the ability to dominate a region vital to the United States.

Underlying that, clearly, was the assumption that we would have adequate warning time to reconstitute forces before we faced a truly global threat, such as we had faced during the Cold War. From that flowed a whole series of decisions embodied in what we called the base force.

USNI: How valid now is the requirement to fight two major regional conflicts simultaneously?

Cheney: When I was secretary of defense, we felt it was. I think it is still, based on a regional outlook—the notion that if you get committed somewhere such as the Persian Gulf, for example, you still need to be able to deal with one other contingency.

USNI: Could we have fought in Korea, for example, while we were fighting the Gulf War?

Cheney: I don't know whether we can do it today, but that was the thesis. Even as we developed the base force, I think it was never with the notion that we would go below a force of sufficient size to be able to deal with two contingencies simultaneously.

USNI: Are we below that now?

Cheney: My concern now is in logistics. Even if you have enough force structure, your ability to deliver it to the battlefield in a timely fashion is what is now suspect.

USNI: What current trends do you see in defense spending, and what changes do you see for the future?

Cheney: Given the drive for a balanced federal budget, I do not expect any increase in defense spending in the near future. The only change would come in response to some fundamental shift in the international situation—a sudden, rapid run-up in the threat level.

I have been pleasantly surprised that spending has stayed relatively even in the midst of what obviously are very serious efforts to cut back all aspects of federal spending. But the only reasonable expectation is a level of nominal spending on defense, which will mean some real decline, based upon inflation.

USNI: Specifically, whom do you see taking the biggest hits?

Cheney: The impact has been enormous already. All services have experienced significant reductions in terms of force structure. I think there is a need for a fairly major restructuring in the Reserves and the National Guard, which is a very tough political problem. We attempted to make some changes there while I was secretary, and we ran into a brick wall—the combination of the Guard and Reserve lobbies and the Congress.

But those forces really do need to have a mission, and many of those units that we wanted to reduce in size and scope no longer had a mission, once the European scenario went away.

USNI: Gen. Carl Mundy, the former commandant of the Marine Corps, has challenged, in effect, the Navy's control of blue dollars that fund Marine Corps requirements—such as the V-22 Osprey. He strongly urges that the Marine Corps ought to control more of its own funding. How does that strike you?

Cheney: I guess I would not be an enthusiast of that notion. Fragmenting and pushing more authority out to more units or centers means that it just becomes more and more difficult to make the trade-offs and the judgments that need to be made. And everybody ends up with their piece of turf to defend rather than some sort of coherent policy being applied.

USNI: How would you rate the ongoing move toward jointness? Has it gone the way everyone seemed to envision when it began?

Cheney: I think significant progress has been made, looking back over the past ten years. I think Goldwater-Nichols [the 1986 Department of Defense Reorganization Act] gave it a major push. We certainly tried during my watch to promote jointness to the extent we could. I think Gen. [Colin L.] Powell's tenure as chairman of the Joint Chiefs of Staff served to nail down and solidify some of the concepts it embodied, making the Joint Staff a significant part of the operation.

USNI: So you think it's good that the chairman's role has become stronger?

Cheney: Yes. I absolutely do. Of course, I suppose I'm biased. I selected General Powell to be chairman of the Joint Chiefs and worked with him for nearly four years. I think prior to that time there was no real accountability from the civilian perspective.

You could look at the chiefs collectively, but what you got with a strengthened role for the chairman, I think, were clearer lines of authority. And because the relationship among the CinCs [commanders in chief] inside the military was better defined, it was easier for the civilians to relate to it. The chairman was authorized to function as the principal military advisor to the secretary and the president, rather than being just the lowest common denominator of whatever the [Joint] Chiefs collectively could agree upon. It was a significant improvement, and I think it made the military and the interface between civilians and the military more effective and more functional. Those lines are clearer, as established in Goldwater-Nichols.

USNI: Some critics have maintained that it gave the military too much power. Do you consider that to be a problem?

Cheney: No, I don't buy that analysis. I had fundamental disagreements with my predecessors on that. Frank Carlucci, Cap Weinberger, and I agreed on most things, but they both were adamantly opposed to Goldwater-Nichols. I really think that legislation—which I voted for as a member of Congress and came to appreciate once I got to the Department of Defense—significantly improved the way the place functions.

Among other things, the policy we established requiring service on the Joint Staff prior to moving into senior leadership positions turned out to be beneficial. We did not want anyone on the Joint Staff who did not have significant prospects back home in their own service.

USNI: It's getting more difficult to clear all those wickets to get there, though.

Cheney: It is getting hard to clear all those wickets, but the fact is that the Joint Staff is an absolutely vital part of the operation. From the standpoint of the president and the secretary of defense, what you want is an effective, smooth-functioning military operation that you can, in fact, use to promote the nation's interest.

I hear a lot of the same arguments even today against Goldwater-Nichols: too many billets, the need to fulfill all the joint requirements, or too much centralization of authority. But I know each service wants to go do its own thing, with its own authority. The fact is that the Department of Defense is difficult enough to run without going back to a system that, in my mind, served to weaken the civilian authority of the secretary and the president in terms of their ability to interact with and use that organization. I think Goldwater-Nichols helped pull it together in a coherent fashion so that it functions much better today than it ever did before.

USNI: Was Goldwater-Nichols a significant aspect of Operation Desert Storm?

Cheney: I think so, especially if you look at the way we functioned and the enormous authority that resided in [Commander-in-Chief Central Command, Gen.] Norm Schwarzkopf. It was not perfect, obviously. You can go back and always find places where you might have been able to improve performance. But I think we had clearer lines of authority in that operation, which avoided problems that had occurred previously—for example, in Grenada and in Lebanon in 1982 and, in fact, all the way back to World War II. We had a CinC, we had a unified command, and we had clear-cut lines of authority that ran from President [George] Bush to me through General Powell at my option out to the CinC in the field.

Within the Defense Department itself, many talented people were outside the chain of command. But nothing went into the theater that the CinC had not approved. None of the services could come in through the back door and urge a particular course of action, or deploy forces, or get involved in ways that violated the basic, fundamental chain of command.

Everybody, for good reason, wanted to get into the act. One of the biggest problems we faced was deciding who would go and who would not. We had a lot of very senior four-stars who were dying to have some influence on the decisions being made. There was a way for them to do that, in an advisory role, but there was never any question how the chain of command worked, who was responsible for it, or who had the authority to decide what did and did not go into the theater and how it was used.

We had one single air plan. [Air Force Lt. Gen.] Chuck Horner was, in fact, the guy running the air war. It didn't matter whether you were a Navy pilot, an Air Force pilot, or a Marine pilot; if you were not part of that air-tasking order, you did not fly. We had one well-integrated campaign plan for the use of those air assets, and my own view is that the air war was decisive in the Gulf. I think much of that goes right back to the principles embodied in Goldwater-Nichols.

USNI: Some have said that the air-tasking order was more a matter of coordination than a directive on how to fight the war on a day-by-day basis. How do you react to that criticism?

Cheney: The last time we fought a major air war was Vietnam—not a notable success. With CinCPac [commander in chief, Pacific command] out in Hawaii running the naval air war and the Air Force guy in Saigon executing his own plan, the lines of demarcation got clouded.

Again, from the civilian perspective, what we had in the Desert Storm air campaign plan was an initial package, a strategy that was pulled together and presented to the chairman and me. We took it to the president and signed off on the basic, broad outlines of the strategy. It was developed and refined extensively over a period of months, as targets were identified and plans laid out for hitting those targets. That facilitated the president's ability to pursue his strategy. At the same time, it precluded anybody outside the chain of command from trying to second-guess and interfere with target selection, for example. It gave us a much more coherent kind of approach, I think, toward how we were going to use U.S. air capabilities to pursue our objective. And it was all knitted together, all the way from the president, to me and the chairman, to the CinC and Chuck Horner out in the Gulf, and all the units that were part of it. I am sure it was not perfect, but we had never done that well before in our history, in terms of putting it all together. It may have been just "coordination," but that counts for a hell of a lot.

USNI: What do you think the late Secretary of Defense Les Aspin's "Bottom-Up Review" accomplished?

Cheney: This may not be totally fair to Les, but I felt we had already done a very good job of starting that process—moving to a post–Cold War force. The Democrats refused to recognize that. Their whole stock-in-trade for so many years had been, "You Republicans want to spend too much on defense." They could not adjust, psychologically or politically, to the fact that we had already started formulating what that new force ought to look like.

We had eliminated four hundred thousand billets on my watch, selected eight hundred bases and installations around the world to be closed, and shut down 120 production lines. There had already been a vast shift in the emphasis and the approach within the department during the Bush administration. When the Democrats came to town, there was no way from a political standpoint, I suppose, that my friend Les could say, "Well, they've already got a great start. We're going to build on it." They had to scrub all that and say they were going to start all over again with something called the "Bottom-Up Review."

From my perspective, I don't think it moved the ball that much farther down the road. I was a big fan of Les's. We were good friends and worked together closely while he was chairman of the House Armed Services Committee and I was secretary, but—I'll leave it at that.

USNI: Now that you've gone to the private sector in a big way, what would you say is the secret of maintaining public support for a strong defense?

You're seeing it from a different perspective now, obviously.

Cheney: In my time, before I ended up in the Defense Department—I had been in Congress and served in the Ford administration—we had a pretty good rationale for why we needed a strong military. It was called the Cold War. Most people could understand that. Not everybody agreed with the funding levels we wanted or how big the forces ought to be—whether we should or should not buy the MX missile, for example.

Based upon the international situation, the consensus in this country was that we needed to remain strong and maintain fairly robust military forces. Now, we've reached the point where it's difficult from a political standpoint to articulate a rationale that justifies a need to retain significant forces. I sometimes have the feeling today that the strongest impetus out there to maintain adequate military forces has less to do with any view of the international situation or our security requirements as much as it's tied to what I would say are "small p" political considerations: "Don't close my base. Don't shut down my production line. Don't demobilize my unit."

For now, this is about as good as it will get in the current political environment. I hope that over time we will be able to develop a stronger public rationale for why we still need to retain significant military forces. It's difficult. If you look at the '92 election, the '94 congressional election, and I think even the 1996 presidential election, there has been almost no discussion—this will be the third election cycle without it—of the U.S. role in the world from a security standpoint, our strategic requirements, what our military ought to be doing, or how big the defense budget ought to be.

USNI: In retrospect, what, if anything, could you have done to keep the A-12 program from being cancelled? Or do you think that was a logical course of action at the time, given the situation?

Cheney: Technically, what happened—the lawyers tell me I still need to be very precise about this; it's still in court—is that the request came for me to use my authority as secretary to modify the terms of the contract and then notify Congress that I had done it. I refused to do that.

At that point, the Navy terminated the contract for default on the part of the contractor. All of that is subject now to a lawsuit. From my standpoint, my initial take on the A-12 was that it was a system we needed, that it was important to the future of naval aviation. When we made the first pass through the major aircraft review, we reduced the total size of the buy, but we kept the A-12.

Only after I had gone back to Congress and testified that we wanted to continue the A-12 program—albeit at a lower level—were we informed by the contractors that they were not going to be able to complete that phase of the contract on time, or in effect, meet the terms of the contract. That is what then triggered the subsequent decision to terminate the program.

My conclusion, after we went through that second go-round—once the contractors came in and said they would be unable to produce it on time—was that we were a hell of a long way from being able to complete that program. We needed some fallback, so we ended up going with the modifications to the F/A-18.

USNI: Several times, the Navy put money in the budget for upgrades and modifications to the F-14, and the Office of the Secretary of Defense [OSD] consistently refused funding for it. In light of the F-14's getting older and its recent problems, what was the reasoning for this refusal from the OSD viewpoint?

Cheney: Part of the whole story revolved around the traditional debate between the F/A-18 drivers and the F-14 drivers; everybody loves his own airplane. From our standpoint, the prospect of buying new F-14s was a weak one. The production line had been pretty well shut down, and it was not really an option. It was a big airplane; it was heavy, non-stealth, and the maintenance hours were much higher than the F/A-18. The F/A-18 was cheaper and newer, production lines were still open, and to the extent that we could move in the direction of a common aircraft on the carrier deck, it was going to reduce the cost of maintenance and upkeep significantly. When we started to make those kinds of trade-offs, the idea of spending a lot of money on the F-14 was never very attractive.

We used to have this debate with advocates in the Congress. My buddy [Congressman] Duke Cunningham [R-CA] used to hammer me repeatedly on the F-14 versus the F/A-18. In the end, we went with the F/A-18, which is pretty much where we are right now and where I think we ought to be.

USNI: In your view, how are we going to pull out of Bosnia at the prescribed time and still leave an effective command-and-control structure in place for United Nations and NATO forces?

Cheney: I need to be clear on the record here that part of my company, Brown & Root, does not have a private army in Bosnia supporting the United States, contrary to what was reported recently in *Time* magazine. We have the logistics contract with the Army and had it long before I arrived here. Our job is to build and maintain the camps for the First Armored Division troops in Bosnia. So we are heavily engaged over there, providing logistics support—food service, water, bathing facilities, housing, that sort of thing. We did the same thing in Haiti and Somalia before this.

Having said that, I opposed sending U.S. troops to Bosnia while the war was still on there. Ultimately, I reached the point where I thought we would probably have to follow through on the president's pretty firm commitment to providing peacekeeping forces as a follow-on to a peace agreement. I think it would be very damaging for the United States, especially its relationship with NATO and our NATO allies, for us not to carry through on that solemn commitment.

So far, I think that has gone reasonably well. The thing I worry about is how we do get out. What is the strategy here for disengaging? What is going to happen a year from now that will allow our withdrawal without reigniting the civil war? What is going to take our place once we pull out? I do not yet have confidence that we've solved that problem.

USNI: Republican presidential candidate Pat Buchanan would pull many people home from many places, not just Bosnia. How do you feel about that?

Cheney: I would not pull any forces back from overseas. I disagree with my old friend Pat. In Europe, we have gone from about 330,000 when I took over down to roughly a hundred thousand. That is about as low as we can go and still have any significant presence in Western Europe, where U.S. presence is critical. I think we are the key to European security. We are the key to NATO. I think the ability of the Europeans to manage all of that by themselves is extremely limited, as demonstrated by what happened in Bosnia before the United States got involved.

I am also very concerned about the situation in the Pacific, because I sense that the United States and Japan are drifting apart. For the last fifty years, the cornerstone of security in the Pacific and the Western Pacific has been U.S.–Japan security arrangements, the forward deployment of U.S. forces—the Marines on Okinawa, the air base up on Misawa, the U.S. Navy at Yokosuka—and it would be a real tragedy for the United States and for our friends in the region if we were to withdraw from that relationship.

Unfortunately, the controversies in Okinawa surrounding our presence there and the alleged rape of the young girl last year have inflamed a lot of emotion. I worry that we may be at the beginning of a process that could run for several years, but that support for the U.S. presence in Japan is gradually eroding.

USNI: We now have left the Philippines. What other countries do you consider to be suitable for placing U.S. forces? Was Cam Ranh Bay ever considered?

Cheney: We used to joke about going back to Cam Ranh Bay. I went to Vietnam last August. I don't think a U.S. base at Cam Ranh is beyond the realm of possibility at some point.

In the Philippines, we had no choice; in the end, they told us they refused to renew our agreement. So we withdrew. I am less concerned about that than I am about the deployments in Japan.

Given our modern capabilities, the fact is, we can go just about anyplace in the world and project power in relatively short order. Forward bases are not quite as important as they once were from a purely military standpoint. We have arrangements with Singapore; we deploy aircraft there on a regular basis and train their aviators. If we had to get into Thailand or other places in that region, we could do it. We got into the Persian Gulf without having any significant presence there before we went.

What I worry about is that U.S. forward presence in Japan has strategic ramifications throughout the region. It is reassuring to the Japanese that we are there, and we are committed to their security. It is also reassuring to everybody else in the neighborhood, many of whom worry about the Japanese.

USNI: What about the Chinese? Are the Chinese reassured?

Cheney: The last time I talked to a senior Chinese official, which was about a year ago, he was more concerned about Japan than anything else.

The fact is that U.S. presence serves as a stabilizing factor; it discourages the development of instabilities that might lead people to pursue more aggressive courses than would otherwise be the case. There are other problems, obviously, in the area, but if the United States were to withdraw, clearly that would create a vacuum. And I think such a vacuum would sooner or later be filled. From a broad, strategic standpoint, the political statement made when the United States remains committed to the area with forward-deployed forces is as important as the military benefits.

So there are many reasons for us to want to stay there. I think that is qualitatively different from what happened in the Philippines. Subic Bay was a great facility. My guess is that, in a crisis, if we had to get back into Subic again, we probably could, depending upon the nature of the problem.

USNI: At what stage is the offshore mobile base project that your company has been developing?

Cheney: One of my good friends, [retired admiral] Bill Owens, was my senior military assistant when I arrived at the Pentagon. Bill was one of the big advocates of those systems. I inherited him, the first uniformed officer I dealt with after I got sworn in as secretary, from Frank Carlucci. He had been there with Frank for about six months, and then he stayed on for about a year and a half on my watch and did a superb job for me. Then we sent him out to the Sixth Fleet. Eventually, of course, he became vice chairman of the Joint Chiefs and did a great job.

I think the mobile offshore bases have a lot of potential. Again, it's something Brown & Root engineered over the years, and there has been some study work done on it. Whether or not it will ever get off the ground is a judgment the Department of Defense is ultimately going to have to make.

It's an interesting concept. These units offer a secure, stable operating base at sea capable of storing vast quantities of material and fuel. There are places in the world—the Persian Gulf comes immediately to mind—where that kind of facility would be very valuable.

USNI: Admiral Owens was an airship backer, too. Did you ever hear a persuasive case made for an airship while you were secretary?

Cheney: His was the most persuasive case I heard.

USNI: But we still don't have any.

Cheney: No, we still don't have any, and there is no sponsor for the airship now that Bill's departed. Bill was one of the most creative military thinkers I encountered while I was in the Pentagon. He really had a great ability to back off and think about problems and come at them in new and interesting ways. He was a great officer.

USNI: As you must know, Tailhook instigated a lot of fallout, and the former leader of the Blue Angels, Commander Robert Stumpf, is the most recent casualty. Even though he was apparently acquitted, now he cannot get promoted. How do you feel about that?

Cheney: I don't know the specifics of Commander Stumpf's case, and I would be reluctant to comment on his case in particular. Tailhook obviously was a disaster for the U.S. Navy. Some say that the standard has changed over time and that when Tailhook started, such behavior was acceptable.

In the end, the conduct that was alleged to have occurred at Tailhook certainly is no longer acceptable. The necessity was to find out what happened and to hold people accountable for inappropriate behavior. But there ought to be a way to put it behind us and move on.

I sometimes had the feeling that the Navy was going overboard in trying to demonstrate that Tailhook was atypical. Now, the pendulum has swung too far in the other direction, and the mere hint of suspicion has led to decisions that would not have been made except for the environment created by Tailhook.

USNI: The 12-12-5 policy, instituted to fill service vacancies with certain percentages of various minorities, is controversial on several fronts. How do you feel about it?

Cheney: It's a quota system, and a quota system is unacceptable to me. I think the U.S. military has done a better job than virtually any other institution in our society regarding minorities, creating opportunities, and trying to operate as an equal-opportunity employer. We're not perfect, and I don't think anybody would allege we are, but I think that if you look at the track record of the U.S. military and the Department of Defense over the last fifteen or twenty years, you would see that we've done a better job than virtually any other institution in our society.

You always come back to the proposition of trying to remind people what the military is for. The military in the end is about fighting and winning wars. You have to be very careful not to impose requirements on the military that interfere with that basic fundamental mission or, in some cases, not impose requirements on the military that you do not impose on any other segment of the society.

My personal view is that women are an extraordinarily important part of the force, but I think we've gone further than I was comfortable with in respect to combat roles for women. For example, I would not have supported putting women on aircraft carriers.

You also run into the problem of having women, in the Navy especially, who are unable to deploy as readily as the men. This places a heavier burden on the men, and they end up having to spend more time at sea. Their tours are longer, because you have to make up for the fact that you've included a significant number of women in the force who are not deployable.

These are difficult issues, and there probably is no one final right or wrong answer in many of these cases. But I do think we have in recent years often lost sight of that basic fundamental fact of life that the military is a unique institution, there specifically for the purposes of defending the nation and going to war if need be. You always have to remember to evaluate any prospective policy based upon that fundamental mission and how that policy might affect capacity to perform. Sometimes we simply do not do that.

Jean-Michel Cousteau

TOM ORDWAY / JEAN-MICHEL COUSTEAU PRODUCTIONS

Mr. Cousteau is the son of the late oceanographer Jacques-Yves Cousteau and founder of the Jean-Michel Cousteau Institute. He continues his father's work in environmental issues and produces television programs. The interview appeared in the April 1998 issue of *Naval History.*

■

USNI: Why do you think the space program gets more public attention than deep-sea exploration?

Cousteau: Because we've never made the correlation between flying and swimming, or "flying" underwater. Take the penguin and many other birds; they fly underwater. We haven't made that connection as a species. I think it also comes from the legends that nurtured us into being scared of the ocean, teaching us that everything below the surface is no-man's-land.

Fascination with space travel goes back to antiquity. Interest in going to the bottom of the ocean does not. We did have Gilgamesh, the king who went to the ocean floor to find the weed of eternity, but he was looked upon as very strange.

There's also an old conception of being able to relate more to outer space because you can see it. You can see stars. The ocean, on the other hand, is dark. You have to bring along all kinds of gear to see where you are.

People just don't understand the oceans. The U.S. Navy was giving a lot of money to ocean exploration in the 1950s and 1960s, until the SeaLab accident. Then: Boom! That was the end of it.

USNI: The Apollo program did not suffer the same loss of funding after its severe accident, nor did the shuttle.

Cousteau: That is a good example of what I am talking about. I was going through Cape Horn when the Challenger exploded in January 1986, and within minutes I knew about it. I remember who was on that shuttle. Do you remember?

USNI: I remember the teacher.

Cousteau: There you go! You don't remember anyone else. Suddenly, it got to everyone's heart. Worldwide, a billion people felt for that teacher [Christa McAuliffe]. Nobody is going to kill that program now. And it's still a memory today in the minds of people. We haven't had that with the ocean. We've lost people, but nobody related to them, because the ocean is such a hard sell.

USNI: The space program is credited with bringing us products that we use every day. Has sea technology produced enough to help sway public opinion?

Cousteau: No. To be frank, I don't know of any ocean technology used by every human being today. We have a better understanding of the sonar used by whales and dolphins, and we can apply that understanding to ships and submarines. But people relate to mammals. They don't relate to subs.

The question is, how do we get the public to relate to the people in subs? No one in subs has had the exposure and charisma that Neil Armstrong had, or someone like Scott Carpenter, who explored both sea and space.

USNI: People don't have as much of an appreciation for deep-sea pioneers like Jacques Piccard and Don Walsh.

Cousteau: Nobody does. Don Walsh is the Buzz Aldrin of the ocean. Buzz Aldrin walked on the moon just minutes behind Armstrong, but nobody remembers him. And nobody remembers Don Walsh. Nobody knows who Jacques Piccard is, either. And when people do recognize the name, they think about his father, not him.

USNI: Should artifacts from sunken ships be brought to the surface or left on the bottom and videotaped for educational purposes?

Cousteau: I wish there was a simple answer. It depends on where it is and what it is. I have mixed emotions about the *Titanic*, now that people have taken pieces from it. I think that some of the activity is borderline criminal. In this case, I don't think it's being done for anything other than commercial purposes. I don't think bringing artifacts to the surface has really brought much to our understanding.

USNI: We conducted an interview with Robert Ballard in 1996, and of course, he had strong opinions on this topic.

Cousteau: Well, I know Bob, too, and he's done some great things; I totally hand it to him. He's right. Taking up a section of the ship for the sake of displaying it is not going to teach anything to anybody.

We're talking about a ship that still contains a whole lot of people. It's like going into a graveyard and stealing jewelry. A bunch of vultures are there under the cover of history and archaeology.

Visiting a cemetery is okay. And what the Discovery Channel did last year, when its crew illuminated sections of the ship that otherwise would never be seen because of the depth and the lack of light—that's okay in my view. It's interesting to see how the ship has aged and evolved, what grows or doesn't grow, and how the ship went down and broke apart. I think this can help us understand a lot more of what happened than bringing back a piece and making a museum out of it.

Perhaps the lesson will be learned when somebody is hurt. I think we should stop taking things out. It's that simple.

This is not to say that we never did it. In 1953 we were south of France and we picked up approximately five thousand amphoras from a Greek vessel that had sunk in 240 B.C. I was a kid then, and I remember drinking wine that was two thousand years old.

USNI: How was it?

Cousteau: Horrible. It was totally disgusting—not only for me, but for everybody.

That really was a detective story. We wanted to know where the ship came from, who owned it, and where it was going. Every piece was properly identified, preserved, carried to the mainland, and put in a museum, ultimately for display.

We had brought back the amphoras and about ten thousand other pieces of pottery. This was all with very good intentions, and I think we learned a lot. The irony is that, by pure "coincidence," the hangar in which all these potteries were kept, the ones that were not on display, burned down. And everything mysteriously disappeared. We know very well that any one of these amphoras can sell for two thousand dollars in France.

Maybe we should have taken just enough to make a display and left everything else there. Now, with modern diving, people steal everything. Anyone can go down to 150 feet today. So you have people diving in the Mediterranean Sea, the crib of civilization, which probably by square mile has more ships than anywhere else in the world, because they've been sinking there for three thousand years.

USNI: What general impact have navies had on the oceans?

Cousteau: Obviously, when it comes to defense, they play a vital role. And that, too, is underestimated. What do people remember of the Gulf War? Airplanes. But where did those planes come from? Many came from ships. Navy programs are consistently poorly exposed, underestimated, and misunderstood.

Who could be a charismatic spokesperson for the Navy? That's what it needs—a person who's going to be heard. My father was in the French Navy, and he made the ocean popular in a way that the public could understand. One has to speak the language of the man on the street; if you don't, you're left behind.

We need to know what the [U.S.] Navy is doing. After all, it's our tax dollars. I always love to see what NOAA [the National Oceanic and Atmospheric Administration] is doing, for instance. And when I see a sign saying "Tax dollars at work" at a highway construction site, I feel good. It's tangible. My money is right there. Not that they couldn't do more with it; that's another issue. But I have no idea what the Navy does. And I'm not speaking as Jean-Michel Cousteau, I'm speaking as the man on the street. I probably know twenty-seven times more about what the Navy is doing than the man on the street.

When I'm in Panama City, I'll often see the U.S. Navy testing diving equipment. I know they are doing a service. But the man on the street doesn't know it. And we cannot reach the man on the street through our diving industry. It's too small. People in the Navy need to tell the story themselves. I wouldn't mind seeing a little bit of our tax dollars being put into letting the world know what's going on.

The Coast Guard has a lot more exposure, it seems, because it keeps doing things the public can relate to. They're helping. They seem more human. You see a Coast Guard vessel arrive and feel a sense of relief. The Coast Guard has a better image than the Navy, I think.

USNI: The Coast Guard will tell you they don't get enough positive publicity.

Cousteau: If they don't, it's their own fault. People like Bob Ballard don't wait for somebody else to make them popular.

USNI: What do you say to those who claim that the Bob Ballards and the Jacques Cousteaus of the world are more showmen than scientists?

Cousteau: They are cutting their own throats. The popularization of ocean activities is supporting their work. And when it's time to locate funds, the decision-makers and the public will lend support more easily. It's all a matter of perception. We live in a world where sometimes perception has nothing to do with reality. The realities are that some people can speak more eloquently on behalf of those who are doing the research and do them a service at the same time.

USNI: What do you see as being your father's greatest legacy?

Cousteau: Me. Unfortunately, my brother and my mother are no longer around, and I'm the leftover of the past. Every one of those people has brought a lot to this world. Least known is my mother. She was the real strength behind the entire Cousteau operation. She was the daughter of an admiral, and many generations of her family were naval officers. Throughout her youth, she was frustrated in knowing she couldn't be in the French Navy, because there were no women in it until recently.

I guess she thought the next-best thing was to marry a naval person. So, when she was sixteen, she met a young naval officer, my dad. I don't know under what circumstances, and I may never know. At seventeen, she was engaged; at eighteen, she was married; and at nineteen, I was born. So, she never really knew anything else.

She was frustrated until 1950, when my father asked her to move on board *Calypso.* When people asked her where she lived, she would say *Calypso.* She spent more time on the ship than my late brother, my late father, and myself together—including the time she spent ten months on *Calypso* in the Amazon without going ashore. She was the morale of the crew, a diplomat, and literally the decision-maker. She was also in charge of cuts and bruises.

USNI: What is your relationship with the Cousteau Society now?

Cousteau: Absolutely none. In 1992, when I saw what my father was allowing his new wife to do, a wife who appeared out of a hat suddenly, with two little rabbits, my half-brother and half-sister, I realized that he had found someone who could agree with him about everything. And thus, because he hated to be challenged, which I did always, she was going to be the one to take over. So, I left.

I had been living in California since 1968, when I was invited to design a museum of the sea on board the *Queen Mary* in Long Beach, California. When my brother died in 1979, my dad said, "You have to come and help me. If you don't, I quit." It was a direct threat. So, like a good sailor, I said, "Aye, aye, sir!"

By my father's side, I took over the Cousteau Society in the United States, with 128,000 members. We brought it to 264,000, and I engineered a way to get out of five million dollars in debt by selling a lot of assets that we had. I redesigned the *Calypso Log*—which at the time was a folded poster—into a real magazine. And a colleague of mine and I created the children's magazine, *Dolphin Life*, which instantly had 104,000 subscribers. So, I think we did a lot of good things. We put the Cousteau Society on the map. Shortly thereafter, in 1981, we created the Cousteau Society in France. Overall, we had more than 360,000 members worldwide. And our team takes a lot of credit for that.

Today, it is a catastrophe. When I left in 1992, membership in the United States was around 65,000; in France it was around 35,000; and it is going down and will continue to go down, because you cannot have a Cousteau Society without a Cousteau. My out-of-stepmother is a Cousteau, but she is borrowing the name. The only thing I hope is that they preserve my father's legacy, my father's work, and present it in such a way that the public will have proper access to it. But I don't think it's happening. She has launched a fundraising program, which I think is disgraceful. Four months after his death, she released a catalog that sells soap and detergents and playing cards, tea and coffee, all which my father would never have accepted. And now, she's made a deal here in the States for getting royalties on perfumes. It's so unlike my dad. So, I don't believe she can do a good job, and I'm very worried. But he elected her to be the guardian of his work, and I have to respect that.

When I saw everything was going to hell, I made good with my dad in May 1997. He had been sick from 25 January, and he died exactly five months later. She kept me away from him. She really resents me; she fears me. For four or five years, she had kept all family, friends, and colleagues at arm's length, so much so that the poor man died alone, with few people knowing that he had been sick. The wrong message had been distributed, saying that he was getting better—even that he was back home sipping coffee—when he really never left the hospital. So, I forced my way into the hospital, and I saw him in May. It was a very important moment for me and I hope for him, too, because she was not there, and thus we could be ourselves. I think we made up completely.

USNI: Let's talk about the Jean-Michel Cousteau Institute.

Cousteau: I created a not-for-profit institute in the 1970s, when I was working with Pepperdine University. And I closed it down when I joined the Cousteau Society. So I decided to revive it in 1993, after I left the Cousteau Society, because I wanted to do some charity work. I expanded that in July 1997 to a full-fledged organization, where I am now putting in a lot of my time. I want nothing out of it personally. I will give and not take.

The institute is focusing on three different fields. One is coastal management—estuaries, mangroves, and marshlands. Another is anything we dump into the ocean—metals, chemicals. And the other is fisheries management and agriculture. We're trying to help people better manage their resources at the world scale and help the transition from being hunters to becoming farmers, like we've done on land.

Because we are not experts in most of these issues, we are not a membership organization. I don't want to compete with other membership organizations for the same dollars. So, I seek support from corporate sponsors, private donations, and of course contracts.

After the institute identifies a priority, we team up with the best institution in that particular field. So, we're not going to be married to one organization. We're going to have one-night stands with many organizations. Whether they lead a particular effort or we lead, it doesn't matter. I want to see the problems resolved.

For fifty years I've witnessed the kind of damage we have done to the ocean. I've seen my own backyard in the south of France being used as a universal sewer, and there is still more sewage going into the Mediterranean, by the millions of gallons every day. We don't have to identify the problems, we know them. As I said years ago, we now have entered the era of solutions. And that's what we're doing at the institute. We're going to find solutions. And we're going to make proposals to governments and industries. They're not the enemies. They are us, and we're going to propose how to solve problems.

The army of people out there, prepared to do that, may be called the disciples of Jacques Cousteau. In many ways my dad was a pessimist. I don't think deep inside he believed that we as a species will be able to survive. I do—and that was part of our healthy argument. So that's who we are and what we're doing.

USNI: What areas of the oceans are currently at greatest risk?

Cousteau: If one would agree that everything is connected, it's really hard to identify one thing. I would say that coastal management is probably a priority, because that is where the majority of marine life forms are found, and that is where the nurseries are. It is precisely where we put the most pressure. That's also where we dump. And that's where we shape and reshape the coastline, where we dredge. From a purely economic point of view—no emotions here—we can't afford it. An acre of marshland is worth a hundred times more than we can afford. We can't afford to turn it into a parking lot, because the revenue from the parking lot will not provide the income that nature provides. Nature works for free. Anytime you fight nature, it costs you money. Nature doesn't care. It's doing it for free.

My home of Santa Barbara, California, has a dredge that pumps sand from the harbor entrance to another point close by—for four hundred thousand dollars. What does nature do? For zero, it puts it right back. Who's the winner? We're stupid. We might as well study a little more at the beginning to figure out what nature does and work with it. Often, nature will do the work for you.

USNI: What do you think of the Navy's training dolphins to seek out mines?

Cousteau: I've always been opposed to that. I think that man will never stop doing whatever it takes to be the best. And that comes at the sacrifice of a lot of creatures, including humans. I just saw a film on [the atomic bomb tests at] Bikini. When I see what we've done to those Micronesians and the way we treated them, I think we're capable of anything.

The difference between animals and us is that we know, and they don't. Animals don't do things on purpose. We do.

Walter Cronkite

COURTESY OF CBS

Mr. Cronkite is the retired Emmy Award–winning anchor of *The CBS Evening News.* A former naval correspondent for the United Press, he accepted a late offer to join the Army's Eighth Air Force for the Normandy invasion. In 1962, he won the George Foster Peabody Award for his news reporting and for his popular series, *The Twentieth Century.* Cronkite is the author of *A Reporter's Life,* his autobiography. The interview appeared in the June 1994 issue of *Naval History.*

■

USNI: We understand you were a naval correspondent early in World War II. How did that come about?

Cronkite: I think I was one of the first correspondents accredited after Pearl Harbor. I was with the United Press in Kansas City when they brought me to New York and sent me down to the Navy office at 90 Church Street to be accredited.

In about March 1942 I went out on my first convoy—at that time the biggest, fastest convoy that had ever been put together. It was a huge assemblage of all the former passenger queens that took the nucleus of the Eighth Air Force overseas. It included a battleship and a cruiser–destroyer escort force and steamed at fifteen to seventeen knots, which was much faster than any of the others at the time. All the ships were over twenty thousand tons.

On the trip over, to Greenock, Scotland, we had a couple alarms but no actual attacks. The destroyers went chasing off after various pips that came over their sonar, but we never experienced any attacks. We had one problem with an old Dutch ship. She was an old three-stacker that couldn't keep up. She was making smoke every day, and that created a lot of problems for Commodore [C. F.] Bryant.

The *Manhattan* burned on that return trip. She had an accidental fire on board. Fortunately, she had not been sabotaged as first feared. She was bringing back some casuals, Americans who had been working in Ireland establishing bases at Londonderry. That was quite a dramatic naval story. The *Brooklyn* put her nose right up against the burning *Manhattan* to take off the passengers. It was a remarkable feat. I was the only correspondent around, so I had a nice scoop on that story.

USNI: How did a naval correspondent manage to see the Normandy invasion from the air?

Cronkite: Well, I did not have a reportorial assignment. I was going to write the lead story at the UP office in London. It was a kind of compliment to get that assignment, but on the other hand, I was torn in my emotions. Obviously, it would be a lot safer in London than on the beaches, but I did want to be in on the action. I was disappointed not to get an active assignment on that historic day.

But in the middle of the night, around one-thirty in the morning, a dear friend, Hal Leyshon, who was a public relations captain in the Eighth Air Force, appeared suddenly at my door. He was an old poker-playing, drinking buddy of mine, a former advertising man from New

York. Many nights he'd appeared at my door at one-thirty, but not in the sober condition he was this night.

He was very formal about it all, and said in somber tones unlike him, "Is there anyone here besides you?" I don't know who he thought might have been there, but he came in after I assured him there was no one else. He looked in my closet, under my bed, and in the other room. I was a little offended at this inspection I was getting, after saying nobody was there. Then he said, "I've got to swear you to secrecy before I tell you anything else."

Of course, we had been expecting D-Day at any time. Our correspondents who were to accompany the troops and the ships had been disappearing one-by-one for almost a month, as the military tried to cover up what day D-Day would be. They didn't want the correspondents all leaving town at the same time.

We knew it was coming, so I knew as soon as he started that pledge-to-secrecy business that this had to be something about D-Day and that it might even be that day.

The Eighth Air Force had not planned to take correspondents on whatever its D-Day air missions might be, but when it learned that some of its planes would be bombing right behind the beaches, it was decided at the last minute that a pool of correspondents representing all of the press should go. Of those correspondents qualified for high-altitude flight, I had won the secret draw.

By good luck, I was assigned to the 303d Bomb Group, with whom I had flown on the first mission to Germany and whose activities I had covered for some time.

All this Hal didn't tell me until we were in his military car on the way to the base, safely away from listening devices or prying ears. All I knew there in the apartment was that the assignment would be dangerous, but the Eighth Air Force thought the story would be worth the risk. Although I would be going against my UP D-Day assignment, I didn't hesitate to grab the chance at least to have a look at the action, if I couldn't be on the beach itself.

As we drove toward the base, Hal also helped relieve me of any concern I had about UP reaction. I would be back, he said, perhaps even before the first stories were getting back from the beaches, and I probably would have, for a palpitating public, the first eyewitness story of the invasion.

It didn't turn out quite that way. I didn't get back from our mission until almost noon, and by that time, thanks to superb military communications—particularly by the Navy—the first dispatches from the newsmen on the ships and on the beaches were coming back.

And worse, the cloud cover was so heavy that my view of the beach had been, for the most part, obscured. I did get a look at the huge armada of forces, an incredible assembly that spread as far as we could see through the clouds. Up and down the coast were battleships and cruisers firing their big guns and landing craft assembling for the attack.

The last I saw before the clouds became impenetrable were landing craft just leaving their ships to head for the beach. But I never got a good look at the beach itself. With pathfinder aircraft accompaniment, some of the Allied air armada, including other squadrons of the 303d, were able to bomb through the clouds. Our squadron, however, was told to bomb only if we practically could see the expressions on the German faces. We were to take no chances on bombing targets of opportunity or jettisoning our bombs. Our crew was too uncertain as to where our ground forces might be by the time of the bombardment.

Led by Capt. Lew Lyle, who later became a major general, we went in at around fifteen thousand feet, a comparatively low level for the heavy bombers. With our bombs armed and ready, the flight—in close formation through heavy cloud layers—was a hair-raising experience.

Our target was shrouded under a solid blanket of cloud. The bomb bay doors were slammed shut. Lyle hoped to make another pass, playing on the small possibility that an opening would appear in the infernal clouds.

The clouds were so thick with aircraft, however, that he was forced to stick to the highly detailed flight plan dictated at the morning briefing. There literally was no way to get back into the queue of planes thundering toward their targets at every level in and above those clouds.

Then, we did the almost unthinkable. We returned to base in England with our bombs still on board. Despite terrible visibility in intensifying fog, we wended our way through the traffic jam of bombers coming and going and landed without incident. But the exercise with that load of explosives was no picnic. With the light flak and absence of enemy fighters, there were no battle casualties.

Perhaps the greatest danger I faced was returning to my office, where my boss unleashed his fury before I had a chance to explain my mission. My story, competing with those of our valiant colleagues on the beaches, understandably saw light of day in few newspapers.

USNI: A lot of people, even in high school and college history classes, forget that the Navy was even involved in the various amphibious landings of World War II. Why do you think that might be?

Cronkite: Though this isn't necessarily the most popular line to take with the U.S. Navy, the Coast Guard is the service that never got much credit, and it was very heavily involved. But you're right. The Navy doesn't get enough mention. The reason at Normandy was that the great-sea-battle aspect was missing. There were no enemy ships among the fleet. There were no Trafalgars, no great fleet actions to dramatize.

And the major feat was getting to the beach. The Navy provided that transport and lost a heck of a lot of people in landing craft that were scuttled and shot up.

But I think it was not unnatural of the press to concentrate on the men ashore, the push against the Germans, forcing them off the beach. Naval gunfire, of course, played a major role, too. Artillery never gets much credit, nor do the transport troops. The Navy was both transport and artillery at Normandy.

USNI: Your friend and colleague Andy Rooney has said he wishes we could come up with something besides a war to rally the American people as World War II did. Do you think anything will ever come along that will get everyone that excited again?

Cronkite: Oh, not to that degree. This was four years of concentrated effort against great odds at first, with a serious danger of failure that people knew existed, despite all the morale-building and drum-beating.

It took us a couple of tough years before we were able to get to the beaches of Normandy and put the German war machine to rout. For two and a half years, from December 1941 to June 1944, we suffered several setbacks. The German invention of the V1 and then the V2 rockets was especially troubling. Fortunately, they were able to launch those only at the end, as a last gasp. But if they had had those just a few months earlier, it might have made some difference in the outcome of the war.

So we weren't out of the woods for a long time, and the fact that we were in an all-out battle for the survival of our system rallied people more than anything else could.

Of course, the next great thing aside from World War II was the space program, which was a peaceful effort, but it had an underlying element of rivalry with a major contender for world dominance that united the American people.

USNI: The press played a major role in rallying people during both World

War II and the space program. Would you say it also played a role in reversing that feeling during the Vietnam War?

Cronkite: The situations were vastly different, so vastly different that I think the comparison is a specious one, really. In World War II there was no question of the nature of the enemy or the necessity of the fight. In Vietnam, there was considerable doubt—reasonable, rational doubt that we should be there.

Our presence in Vietnam was an option, not a necessity being forced upon us by enemy action. After all, by December 1941 we were still dragging our feet about being part of World War II. And we probably would have dragged our feet right on through, if the enemy had not offended us, endangered us, attacked us, threatened to invade us.

That was not the case in Vietnam.

USNI: I'm sure you know that Peter Braestrup, in his book *Big Story* [Garden City, N.Y.: Doubleday, 1978], criticized television news pretty strongly, as opposed to print journalism. To what do you attribute that criticism?

Cronkite: You mean in the Vietnam War coverage?

USNI: Yes.

Cronkite: I'm not an enthusiast for Braestrup's book for several reasons.

USNI: I'm sure you're not.

Cronkite: I think he misses a point. It seems to me that if the people of the United States are willing to vote and to support sending their young people—now women as well as men—into combat, they should be willing to look at what combat really is.

If they are unwilling to sit in their living rooms and see what the troops—the troops they sent to fight—are up against, they are somehow playing the coward themselves. And that is beyond anything I'd like to contemplate. I don't think that's what we Americans are.

Now then, does it affect the politics of conducting war? Of course it does. But that's for the good. It is well that we all are aware of what war really is—what it means—before we commit to it.

I do not say that we idly commit to war. I don't think we do. I think those who are involved in policy-making are rational people, and have been in most cases, but they might be a little bit wrong-headed sometimes in thinking that the expenditure of a few lives can save many. Maybe they'd better think about how many would be expended in the worst-case scenario before they get us involved.

USNI: You said "show people what war is." Is that the reason Braestrup criticized broadcast over print coverage? As a print journalist himself, he says they got it right, and you guys got it wrong, essentially.

Cronkite: Well, I disagree with that.

USNI: He referred to you and Frank Magee of NBC, in particular.

Cronkite: He was talking mostly about my summary for Tet. That is the only editorial I've ever done on the air, other than those in defense of freedom of the press itself.

No, I don't think I had it wrong. Admittedly, it would appear that later evidence contained in North Vietnam—now that the North Vietnamese generals have talked about the war—shows that they had suffered severely and were not capable of mounting another offensive of that nature. While that would seem to indicate that Braestrup and other critics have it right, that I was signing off a little early, it ignores the fact that General Westmoreland was asking for something over three hundred thousand more men in order to put a finish to the war.

Well, we'd been hearing about this escalation of forces from the time we first sent troops under President Kennedy to help instruct the South Vietnamese Army. Our people were there only for purposes of instruction, originally. From that we'd escalated into this terrible mauling that the Vietcong and the North Vietnamese Army planned for us. I can't see that we were wrong in reporting about that. If Westmoreland needed that many men to build his forces for an all-out attack on the enemy, then we were promised only another massive escalation in the face of crumbling support from an increasingly divided homefront.

USNI: Some reporters have complained about Desert Storm, about limited access and censorship. And some military people have complained about instant satellite television transmission. What would you say can be done to improve military and media relations?

Cronkite: I think the way the military handled the press in the Persian Gulf was a miscarriage of democratic processes. I think it was a frightful commission against the American people not to let them know what their troops were doing in combat. We send them there. They're our boys and our girls, and it's our war. And we'd better know about what they're doing—in intimate detail.

I'm not against censorship. I'm for it. I believe in censorship. Some of those in my own profession who demand live coverage from the front are simply incredibly unrealistic. It's impossible. It can't be done. It shouldn't be done. There should be no live coverage. But we should have cameras at the front recording what goes on. Then the film or the tape can pass through censors before being released. There are military secrets, clearly, and the security of our forces is the first consideration. That security should never be placed second to anything, including freedom of the press.

But you can have both, as proved in World War II. We were permitted at the front. We were aided in getting to the front in nearly every case except the most highly secret, small-unit operations. We were there, and history was recorded.

But there is no freely acquired history of the Persian Gulf War, because we weren't there. It's history as vetted by the military. And that's not adequate, not good enough. They've got a special interest. So I'm indignant about it.

USNI: It sounds that way.

Cronkite: But for good military and media relations, the essential is to understand on both sides the nature of the mission. If you understand the mission of the other guy, you've got to be sympathetic to his problems and the importance of his mission.

The military simply must realize that it is an army of a democratic nation, and a democracy demands that the people know so they can support our military actions. The public needs to know the rationale of a military action as nearly as it can be interpreted by good reporters. But there are some terrible ones. Believe me, I'm not one to defend all war reporting from the Persian Gulf or anywhere else, including World War II. An awful lot of bad reporters get out there, just like some people are promoted to lieutenancies who should not be leading troops. It happens on both sides, and we ought to understand that. Both will make mistakes.

I'll tell you, a lot of war correspondents who wear that battle patch never leave the base command quarters. And a lot of soldiers never leave headquarters but still wear the ribbons they're after. They're heroes of the war who never heard a shot fired in anger. And a lot of correspondents are in the same category.

But the guys on the line or on board the ships have a great appreciation for each other—the correspondents for the troops and vice versa. Boy, there's an appreciation. They're in the thing together, and they understand. What it takes to understand security is to be out there with the troops. Then the correspondents want a lot of security, for obvious reasons. By the same token, those guys on the front line or in the ships want to be recognized. They like having the correspondent around. They like the idea that their names might get in the papers back home.

They have a right to be recognized. And they are the first to appreciate the correspondent, even as a correspondent appreciated what the grunt goes through in the dugout by being with him.

The grunts also appreciate that those correspondents are there voluntarily. I don't know how many times I was asked during the various wars I covered, "What in the hell are you doing here? Do you have to be here? Did anybody send you here?" I would say, "Well, my office asked me if I'd come." And they then asked, "And you accepted that? You went?" They had a great appreciation for the fact that we were up there doing the job.

So the problem is not with the troops or the correspondents in the field. It's with the headquarters, perhaps of both. I think it's as much a fault of the networks to talk about live battlefield television coverage as I think it's a terrible mistake for the military to prohibit cameras at the front because somehow or other our security is going to be violated. The cameras can go without satellite dishes. So there's no reason why the war should not be recorded.

USNI: What do you think of the information superhighway we're hearing so much about? It seems to me that the urge and the demand for real-time transmissions are only going to get worse.

Cronkite: Well, the capabilities will be even more of a problem. You know, there will be a day in the not-too-distant future, when the satellite transmitter will fit right on the camera. But we can require that cameras going to the front line are not so equipped. I don't think that's so difficult to do. I can't imagine fighting a war, under present circumstances at least, with live television coverage at the front. For one thing, the transmission could presumably be captured from the satellite by the general or the major sitting five hundred yards away on the other side of the line. How can you show the deployment of troops and expect the enemy to be blind to what you're covering? The last I heard, the television industry was still making that demand of the military, that we have that privilege. I think that's a ridiculous request.

USNI: We'll wrap up with something fun. What would you say has been the most significant event that you covered as a news reporter?

Cronkite: I don't think there's any question about it—landing a man on the moon. Of course, as a reporter I've covered the wars. And those were significant events. The assassination of President Kennedy was a significant event. There were a lot of them. But for real, true historical significance, man landing on the moon is going to be the most important date in twentieth-century history. All the other things we're talking about today, in the history books five hundred years from now will be mere asterisks, compared to the moon landing.

When we think back five hundred years from now, we think of Columbus landing in 1492. But a lot of other important things happened in the fifteenth century—a Renaissance, a Black Plague, an Inquisition. But do you remember any of those dates? Can you even cite the events? The Columbus landing in 1492 is a different story, and the moon landing will be similar in stature.

USNI: We understand you are writing your autobiography. How is it progressing?

Cronkite: Don't ask. I do this instead of writing my own book.

■

After our formal interview, Mr. Cronkite related the following bonus anecdote:

You know, the Naval Institute *Proceedings* was a tipoff to one of the best shows we ever had on *The Twentieth Century.* We took the man who spied on Pearl Harbor for his first and only trip back to Pearl Harbor. And we barely got him out of town before the lynching.

We were trying to keep his visit secret. He was inclined to have a drink or two and got into a Japanese bar, where the local clientele found out who he was. Word spread to the newspaper, and we had to spirit him onto a plane and get him out of town.

A Marine lieutenant colonel had tracked him down and was interested in just whatever happened to the guy. He had found him in a successful fuel oil business in Hokkaido in northern Japan. Then the colonel had written a piece about him. Nobody else picked it up, except a bright-eyed guy who worked for us. He brought the clipping in from *Proceedings*, and we went right to Japan.

At first the fellow said he wasn't going back to Pearl Harbor. He spoke virtually no English, but we finally persuaded him and got him to come. He was curious enough, so we played on his curiosity and promised him that he wouldn't run into trouble.

And he was wonderful.

Golly, it's been thirty years since we did that. It was remarkable.

The Navy actually loaned us a boat, and we went out and he identified the ships. We took him up to the teahouse where he had spied on the Pacific Fleet.

He was sent over allegedly as an assistant to the Japanese consul in Honolulu. That was his cover. He had attended the naval command school, was a trained intelligence officer, and he was to spy on the ship movements out of Pearl Harbor. Well, he tried to get a job at the Navy yard, but failed because he didn't speak any English, among a few other problems.

So he was desperate. What was he going to do? Then he went one day to a Japanese teahouse up in the hills overlooking Pearl Harbor. As he sat there drinking tea, he realized he was looking right down on Pearl Harbor. He said he could read hull numbers without binoculars. And he said to himself, "This is the best possible view." He went up to that teahouse every day, sat there all afternoon, and observed what ships were in and what ships were out.

Of course, we were making the great mistake of being in a routine. It was absolutely hidebound. Our ships went out on Monday and came back on Friday, and he recorded the numbers and where they were docked. That was the way he spied on Pearl Harbor. There was no undercover work. Anybody could have done it.

William Crowe

DEPARTMENT OF DEFENSE

Adm. William Crowe, U.S. Navy (Retired) served with distinction in several naval commands before becoming chairman of the Joint Chiefs of Staff. Upon his retirement from military service, he served as ambassador to Great Britain during the Clinton administration. The interview appeared in the January 1992 issue of the Naval Institute's *Proceedings.*

■

USNI: In your view, what are the major indicators that the Cold War is behind us?

Crowe: The major ones, of course, are developments in the Soviet Union. Even if the Soviets were inclined to pursue the Cold War, they are in no position to do so now. They are consumed by their own political and economic problems, and they need foreign capital desperately. The most striking piece of evidence is their cooperation in Operation Desert Storm.

USNI: How can we be certain that the thirty thousand nuclear warheads still held in what used to be the Soviet Union remain under effective control?

Crowe: I don't know how you can be sure of that. I'm not sure you can be sure. We haven't been confident for the last forty years. Certainly they were under central control in the Soviet Union, as far as we knew, and I think now we think that Mr. [President Mikhail] Gorbachev still has his finger on the button. But the central question that we do not know, and we do not have the privilege of knowing, is whether in any future crisis the military organizations that oversee those weapons are going to be responsive to the political leadership.

USNI: You have considered for years that the Soviet strategic nuclear arsenal is the most dangerous military threat to the United States. What do you see as the greatest danger today?

Crowe: I'm not sure that's changed very much. I don't mean to imply that Soviet nuclear weapons will be used, because I think it is very unlikely. In fact, I think the likelihood of a nuclear war has receded to the lowest point now since the end of World War II or since the Soviets developed nuclear weapons. The reason I say it is still the most dangerous threat is because nuclear weapons are the only weapons that can reach the United States. We have been living under that specter since the mid-1950s. And we can do very little about it.

Now, if you had asked me about the most likely threat, my answer would have been different.

USNI: What is the most likely threat?

Crowe: I'm not sure there is a likely threat to the continental United States, but there are many threats to our interests. We just confronted and defeated one, and we're probably going to see more balkanization and instability around the world. We are seeing it now in Yugoslavia, Pakistan, and India. Africa and North Korea have some major problems.

The most important threat, however, would be the breakup of the Soviet Union, if it turns violent and hostile. That is not going to threaten the survival of the United States; it is, however, going to threaten our interests. The stakes are high in that part of the world, so we will be involved directly or indirectly.

USNI: With President [George] Bush's tactical nuclear weapons announcement, the "Neither confirm nor deny" policy is now no longer necessary. Is this a gain or a loss?

Crowe: I think it's a gain. I don't see how you could sustain the policy. This seems to be a logical follow-on to the decision made by President Bush. He did not make it for this reason, but certainly it will now be easier for foreign countries to approve U.S. ship visits. Our political-military relationship with Japan—where this has always been a source of considerable confusion, if not argument—should improve. "Confirm nor deny" is not the problem in North Korea, but certainly the president's policy should put us in a much better position to influence Kim Il Sung not to produce nuclear weapons.

USNI: How much confidence do you have in the verification process?

Crowe: First of all, President Bush's announcement, as I interpret it, left a considerable hedge in our own inventory. We are not eliminating all of our capability. One thing that may present a bit of a problem for the Soviets is that we are not destroying everything we have, even tactically. So I think we have some margin for error. Our ability to verify is probably pretty good. Our ability to prevent cheating a hundred percent is probably not.

USNI: Some would say your exchange visits with the Soviet Union in the late 1980s paved the way for improving relations between the two countries. At the time, what changes did you expect and which ones surprised you most?

Crowe: Number one, I'm not sure our reciprocal military visits paved the way to anything. I would never be so presumptuous. What I had hoped for was to improve the relationship sufficiently so that we could discuss at least our mutual problems and have more open disclosure between militaries. That way, we would have a better handle on what the Soviets did and did not have, and a more realistic appreciation of what we were confronting. It's done a little of that. I don't know that it's done it sufficiently to satisfy us, but I think we understand more about the Soviet Union than we did. Perhaps, now, because the Soviet Union is in so much trouble, we understand how hollow the entire system was.

But one thing we did do, I think: We changed the minds of a lot of people concerning the aggressiveness of the United States. I know we changed Marshal [Sergei] Akhromeyev's view. He started those talks with a very distorted and depressed view of United States ambitions. During the last three years of his life, he changed his mind, and told me so. In his judgment, too, the prospect of war between the Soviet Union and the United States had become the lowest it had been since World War II.

What impact that has on other events, I don't know. But I think many senior Soviet officers who have had the opportunity to visit here have had a similar awakening. And I suspect that those in the U.S. military who are having more contact with the Soviet Union are discovering that some of their deeply held convictions may not be as right as they once thought.

USNI: You developed a good working relationship with Akhromeyev. Why did he give up on the reform movement?

Crowe: He probably had a little different version of the reform movement than we did. We don't know that he participated in the coup. Several articles say that he did, but I don't know. A number of good, high-level Soviet sources have either called me directly from the Soviet Union or through intermediaries, saying their information is that he was not associated with the coup. But I cannot testify from personal knowledge.

He was closely wedded to Gorbachev and he thought—this I know for a fact from my conversations with him—there were a lot of things wrong with his society. He had matured in that society as a thinking man, and he understood that. He did not like sending people to exile in Siberia, or shooting people, or restricting their travel, or chasing out professional people. He could list at great length the things wrong with his nation.

To paraphrase, Akhromeyev wanted a kinder, gentler socialist state. But he did not want to see the socialist state disappear. He worked his whole life in the vineyards of communism. He did not want to see the republics become independent. He did not want the Warsaw Pact to erode or go away. The process that he originally encouraged was going further than what he had in mind. He wanted a better relationship with the United states, and I think he wanted that until the day he died. But he wanted a fifty-fifty relationship, and he wasn't so sure it was fifty-fifty. Everything the United States wanted was happening. Nothing he wanted was happening. And that irritated him.

He had great trouble admitting that all problems in the Soviet Union were self-generated, but that was built into his soul. The trouble with revolutions is that not everybody is satisfied after the revolution. There must be two sides or you don't have a revolution. I just finished a book about the last days of Robert E. Lee. You know, the South was pretty upset with the outcome of the Civil War. And Akhromeyev was pretty upset by the outcome of this revolution. He said to me at one point, "We're electing people to office I never even heard of, and they're lazy."

I said, "Marshal, we've been doing that for two hundred years. That's the name of the game. If you want pluralism, you've got to get used to that."

USNI: One of the side effects of President Bush's tactical nuclear weapon initiative seems to be an increase in congressional clamor for further cuts in an already sharply reduced defense budget. In your view, how much defense is enough?

Crowe: The real answer is I don't know. But I like the approach of the administration and the military right now, saying they're going to make cuts in the neighborhood of 25 percent to 30 percent in five years. That I think is about right. My fear is that if current trends continue in the Soviet Union, Western Europe, and around the world, Congress won't be satisfied with that. And as the five-year period draws to a close, they will continue to cut further and further. There must be a threshold. [Chairman of the Joint Chiefs of Staff, Gen.] Colin Powell says that this is a baseline we're moving toward and we should never go below that baseline. That makes a certain amount of sense to me. My instincts tell me we won't get away with it, that if the world continues to progress the way it is, the Congress will go deeper. And that would probably be a mistake.

Of course, it's a dynamic equation. It all depends on circumstances outside and inside and on what other demands you have on your budget. I happen to believe right now that because our domestic concerns are very grave, this is the proper time to cut the military. There has never been a better time in my adult life to draw down the military than today. However, I would do it gradually, and I would stop at a minimal level. I preach all over this country that whatever size military we decide on, it must be a healthy one.

To attract good men and women, which should be our very first priority, we must allow people to fly, to sail, and to shoot, whatever size the military is. Otherwise, young men and women who are so attracted to it now won't come into it later. And if you don't have good people, you won't have a good military. And you won't have a good cadre around which to expand when the day comes that we need larger forces. And that day will come sometime.

USNI: The recent tactical nuclear weapons action seems to be exclusively between the Soviet Union and the United States. What should be done to get other countries involved?

Crowe: Of course, if President Bush can not only reduce his own inventory, but inspire the Soviets to reduce theirs, the deeper and more sustained the cuts are, the more important this question becomes. There will be a level that nobody will want to go below until we have all the other nuclear powers participating in the process. We have not as yet taken that into consideration. In fact, in our strategic talks, we have insisted all along that nobody else should enter into the discussions—just the two of us. We will have to review that question and expand the scope of these matters if reductions are to continue below the three thousand or four thousand level. We simply cannot continue indefinitely without bringing the French, the Chinese, and the British into the debate.

USNI: Do you think it is feasible to work with the Soviet Union on the Strategic Defense Initiative (SDI)?

Crowe: The Soviet Union has neither the resources nor the talent right now to compete directly with us in SDI, if we choose to make a determined effort. I don't know if we're looking to them for anything at this point. It seems to me as though the problems in the SDI are such that we have to make some very painful decisions on our own, irrespective of what the Soviets do. Whether you're going to have a space-based SDI or not depends on how much money is going to go into defense, how deeply you want to cut the Army, Navy, and Air Force in order to build an SDI. Is the return on the investment great enough to justify it? We've got a lot of questions to ask.

The current level of debate on SDI in this country is very superficial. I think the people who want it, want it, and they ignore most of the practical problems. The people who don't want it ignore the same problems, too. The two poles of the argument are so busy advocating their own positions that they don't really treat the subject in great detail and comprehensively. It's a very serious question.

The goals of both sides are, in a certain sense, right. An effective SDI that could knock down all incoming nuclear weapons and keep the United States free from attack would be a most laudable goal. But so what? The question is, what does it cost? What do you give up? Every time you spend that kind of money, you give up something. It is frankly too early into the game to commit irrevocably to a certain kind of SDI. The fact that we have a Patriot missile does not mean we can have an SDI.

I happen to think that we can overcome the technical problems. Then, you must ask, "Is it worth the investment?" We've got to know a lot more than we know now before we can answer that question. But the advocates don't want to talk about that. They want you to make a decision right now, no matter what it costs. The people opposed to SDI don't want it, no matter how promising our research. Some are just plain antinuclear. Some are interested in domestic problems. Some just don't like the people who are advocating it. Some are politically against the people in office and want to throw them out of office.

These issues are so hard because of the motivations of the people doing the talking. They usually never say exactly what they have in mind. They might have some cause in mind they don't want to articulate. It's the old story. One rule of thumb, I think, applies to just about everything that goes on in Washington: whatever it is, it's never as good as the advocates say it is, and it's never as bad as the opponents say. SDI, I think, falls in that same category. There are strong arguments for SDI, but there are some strong caveats regarding SDI. I don't want to see the Army and Navy disappear in order to get us an SDI. If we had unlimited resources, I would be for an all-out SDI program. We don't have unlimited resources. If we do, I'm not aware of it.

USNI: Why have we seen no evidence of cutbacks in Soviet strategic weaponry?

Crowe: We have a couple of areas—naval forces being one—where we have not seen the cutbacks we anticipated. We keep predicting that the Soviets' economic situation will inevitably force drawdowns. We have seen some reductions in the Soviet ground forces, but we have not seen significant strategic reductions. Now that we are going to get a strategic arms agreement, perhaps the picture will change. But at this time, the Soviet Union is in such disarray that START is their second priority. If Mr. Gorbachev announced, "We're starting cutbacks tomorrow," I don't know if that would mean anything.

I don't think there's any question that the prospect of a protracted major war with the Soviet Union has receded dramatically. The Soviet Union could not wage war for a long period of time because of its economic and political disarray. So the fundamental threat has retreated, but whether the strategic weapons numbers are down or not, and why not, I can't say.

USNI: In 1978 you wrote the longest article in recent *Proceedings* history, "The Persian Gulf: Central or Peripheral to United States Strategy?" Much of it is very prophetic. One of the things you predicted is that with "a further depletion of the world's oil supplies Baghdad could very well turn its attentions southward." Now that such a move has been thwarted, what's your forecast for the Middle East, short-term and long-term?

Crowe: You're really trying to get me into trouble, aren't you?

USNI: Well, sure. That's what interviews are all about, right?

Crowe: You let me get myself in trouble. It seems to me that, irrespective of Desert Storm, the fundamental political problems that have plagued the region for quite some time are still there. We contained Saddam Hussein and drove him out of Kuwait, but we haven't replaced him. His radius of influence is reduced and his ability to kick everybody around probably never was very high, although we credited it to be high. In any event, he is contained and is now just a symptom of other problems in the Middle East, which are still there. The people of the Arab world, despite their big talk, are not unified. The "haves" and "have nots" are still a tremendous problem, and the "haves" don't want a new world order. They want to go back to the second of August 1990 as soon as they can. Pluralism is alive—at least the pressures for pluralism—in the Middle East. They are not so intense as they are in the Western world, but they are there.

We have to deal with all these things. Of course, the United States faces a basic conundrum, which has been there from the very outset, since the late 1920s. We have to deal with the elites who control the oil; we have no choice. On the other hand, those elites are probably going to disappear sometime.

USNI: As Commander, Middle East Force, did you meet Saddam Hussein?

Crowe: No, I did not. I was not allowed to go to Iraq. I have several friends in Bahrain who know him well. A military victory against him has not solved all our problems. Many Americans have a tendency to forget that military victories should be linked in some fashion to political agendas. We don't just defeat people for the thrill of defeating them. Iraq is a good example. We overwhelmed its forces, and yet Saddam Hussein is still in power. A lot of people in the Middle East who do not want to change are still running the Middle East.

How do you reconcile these pressures? Are you on the right side of history? In several things we've engaged in over the years, we've been on the wrong side of history. Our involvement in the Middle East is going to be protracted, it's probably going to be painful, and I don't know any way we can avoid it. That's the burden of being a great power.

USNI: Would you say we're on the right track in getting the two sides at least to sit down and talk—or shout?

Crowe: Yes. That's progress. It's minute progress, but it is progress. And it's very characteristic. You go to a lot of effort to take one small step, but there's no other way to do it. I've followed the situation very closely. You know, the hype that accompanies everything we do—instant television coverage and so forth—is very unfortunate. The reason I say unfortunate is that it is not just a matter of informing or educating the American people; it raises their hopes and expectations. The nature of our political system is that the president must come out and say certain proposals and negotiations are the greatest things since sliced bread, no matter how small the steps. In this case, there's going to be a lot of agony. But it's a necessary part of the process. The American people are constantly led to expect too much. It would be much better if the president were allowed to insulate himself from these everyday pressures. Personally, I am a born pessimist. I've discovered that it feels so good when you're wrong. I wish the American people were more guarded, but they're the opposite. As a result, they are constantly being disappointed.

Clive Cussler

COURTESY OF CLIVE CUSSLER

Mr. Cussler is the author of the best-selling "Dirk Pitt" series of novels and is the founder of the National Underwater Marine Agency, an organization responsible for locating the wrecks of many well-known sunken ships. The interview appeared in the August 1995 issue of *Naval History.*

■

USNI: We've seen practically nothing directly from you in the national press about your locating the wreck of the *Hunley.*

Cussler: Yes, I know. We kind of got buried. All this opened a real can of worms. Now, a battle is on between the State of South Carolina, the Navy, and the General Services Administration [GSA].

USNI: How did that come about?

Cussler: Not being a member of the bureaucracy, I can only speculate. Part of the problem seemed to be that the University of South Carolina's Institute of Archaeology and Anthropology put a fellow whose only credential was a degree in journalism in charge of the *Hunley* project. His staff had no qualification for such a job.

And so a big storm hit. The Navy was not happy, and it took the state to task. I know I certainly did. Our nonprofit foundation, the National Underwater Marine Agency [NUMA] had been ready to say "mission accomplished" and walk off to the next project. Then this fellow started talking about building a coffer dam—a totally ridiculous idea. So we came back into the picture and raised a little hell. I'm not sure where the Navy stands, but in talking with the GSA people, I know they're not going to give it away, they want it, and they're working now with the Smithsonian Institution.

USNI: Did this happen before the announcement that she had been found?

Cussler: It was after. I had left Charleston and had been home for a week or so when all of a sudden articles started appearing in newspapers saying that the State of South Carolina wanted to mark the site with a buoy. The Navy and I threw up our hands at that. The last thing we want is to mark the site so people can come and rip it off.

This search had been going on since 1980, and we had run over a thousand miles of bottom. The crew that made the actual discovery was not just a group of divers, as originally reported in the press. Ralph Wilbanks is a former state archaeologist; Wes Hall has been in archaeology for eighteen years and has a master's degree; and Harry Pecorelli, the first man down on the wreck, is one grade point away from his master's in archaeology.

We eliminated all the sites around Breach Inlet and the back bay and ran an extensive expedition out to the *Housatonic* [the ship sunk by the *Hunley* in 1864] and beyond. Finally, when Ralph Wilbanks was working a bit farther east than we thought the *Hunley* would be, they hit on her.

When Harry Pecorelli made that first dive, he said he didn't think it was the *Hunley*. Then Wes Hall went down. I guess they moved about a foot of silt and luckily came down on the hatch, which was raised about eighteen inches. The sub was lying on its side, so they excavated a little area where they could see the hatch, the snorkel, and one of the diving fins and made the identification. That was it.

USNI: Your organization is to be commended for not desecrating these sites.

Cussler: The agency tries to find lost ships of historic significance before they're gone forever. When we find one, we turn over all our records and walk away. People who come to my house are amazed, because I don't have one artifact—just a couple of ship models.

On only two or three occasions, when we worked with particular states, did we bring up artifacts. In Virginia, I remember when we identified the Civil War ship *Cumberland*—even brought up the ship's bell—and identified the *Florida* from other objects we brought up. We were supposed to split the cost of preservation with the state, so we soaked all the artifacts in kiddie pools, locked in warehouses. Suddenly, the state came and said, "Sorry, we're too tied up with the York River. We don't have the money to spend, so you'll have to throw the artifacts back." I said, "You're crazy." So the College of William and Mary took over the preservation work.

USNI: What is your motivation for all this—and who finances it?

Cussler: Well, my wife is an accountant, who thinks I belong in a rubber room, under restraint. I do it because I enjoy it. All the money for the expeditions comes from book royalties. Certainly, nobody would give me a dime if I said I was going after a historic wreck and there's no return. I'm sure if I said I was after treasure, I'd have people lined up at the door. I think I've spent about $130,000 finding the *Hunley*. But by God, it was worth every nickel. What can I say? Does that sound crazy?

USNI: If sky was the limit, what would you have done with the *Hunley*?

Cussler: The Smithsonian would be a great source, because millions of people would see it there. Charleston could be a good choice, if they did it right and put it in a museum. They could put the crew in a marble sarcophagus on one side, and they could dig up H. L. Hunley and his crew from Magnolia Cemetery and put them in a marble sarcophagus on the other side. But that's just wishful thinking.

If the GSA decides to keep it, I would say the odds are that it will probably wind up with the Smithsonian.

USNI: What's your next project?

Cussler: We've got two, but we haven't set dates yet. One of them is to go to Galveston looking for the *Invincible*, a Republic of Texas Navy ship. Yes, Texas really had a navy. It's the only time in history that a sailing fleet ever competed against a steamship fleet.

Then I want to take one more stab at the French World War I ace who took off from Paris to New York in 1927 and vanished. Of course, Charles Lindbergh took off a week later and made it. It's up there in Maine. It's a long shot, but I want to go for it.

USNI: So you go for aircraft, too?

Cussler: If it's lost, we'll look for it. We found the remains of the *Akron* and then we looked for a lost locomotive that vanished in a flash flood in 1876. We were looking for the *Carondelet* in the Ohio River, when the sheriff's department there had us help find a car with a woman inside who had been missing for three years. If you say it's missing, we'll go look for it.

Douglas Fairbanks Jr.

NATIONAL ARCHIVES

The late Douglas Fairbanks Jr. appeared in more than eighty motion pictures. He served as a Naval Reserve officer in the Atlantic and Mediterranean theaters of World War II. He was the author of *The Salad Days,* a Hollywood memoir, and *A Hell of a War,* a recounting of his wartime experiences. The interview appeared in the October 1993 issue of *Naval History.*

■

USNI: You took great pains not to be recognized or treated specially during your naval service. How do you feel about participating in interviews and getting attention now?

Fairbanks: Frankly, being in the theatrical world, and also the governmental, diplomatic, and political worlds, I've been at the other end of interviews since I was a boy. So there's really nothing novel about it. I try to make sense out of it, to give the right answers, and to be as honest as I can.

USNI: To put things in perspective, where would you place your naval service in the overall context of your life?

Fairbanks: That's a good question, isn't it? It's one I shouldn't answer quickly. [Pauses] I'd put it very high up, very high up indeed. But it had to be. I wasn't a boy when I went in. In fact, I was beyond draft age. I went in 1940, when I was already thirty years old. My theatrical career was fairly flourishing at the time. But I wanted to get into the Reserves and take on Adolf Hitler. Actor Robert Montgomery and I went in at the same time and did our training together. I had a difficult time getting a commission in the first place, because I didn't have a university education. I finally got one through a correspondence course in California. Franklin Roosevelt Jr. went with me the day I signed on to go to sea in Boston.

USNI: You've probably heard the various theories espoused about how in the world we could have been taken by such complete surprise at Pearl Harbor. At least one even implicated President Franklin D. Roosevelt in a conspiracy. What do you think about all of that?

Fairbanks: Nonsense. I don't believe that President Roosevelt would have been involved in any conspiracy. If that were true, evidence of it surely would have come out much earlier than this. People suspect anything they don't like or don't want to digest. It's libel and slander on the president to suggest a conspiracy. All sorts of things could have happened. Nearly everything is possible. The senior admirals and generals, I'm sure, considered it a possibility—but not a probability. And they likely gave it no more credence than a dozen other options.

USNI: We realize that you had a close relationship with President Roosevelt and his family before the war. Has your opinion of him changed since then?

Fairbanks: Not at all, except that I have even more admiration for him now. I thought he was a wonderful man, and still do.

USNI: In the book you say that, after you received an ALNav bulletin that Pearl Harbor had been attacked, you threw it in the wastebasket. Having been the first and only one on board to have seen it, what made you pull it back out?

Fairbanks: I was not certain what it meant—"Air Raid Pearl Harbor, this is no drill." What the hell was Pearl Harbor? Where was it? And what did they mean, "this is no drill?" That part made me think it might be serious and that maybe I should tell somebody about it. I was an Atlantic sailor at the time, not a Pacific one. Nobody in the Atlantic knew much about Pearl Harbor.

USNI: You acknowledge that you were luckier than most, especially those in the Navy. How would you rate your general relationship with your shipmates?

Fairbanks: Pretty good. I didn't have any special advantages. I was just lucky that the things I did came off all right and that I didn't get hurt. And I didn't break any rules, or at least I didn't get caught breaking any.

USNI: So you made a specific effort not to trade on your celebrity status?

Fairbanks: Oh, absolutely, yes. That would have been stupid—suicidal. There were always some who tried to put me in my place. "We'll teach this guy," they'd say. When I didn't pay them any attention, that sort of annoyed them. They got no fun out of it and eventually just gave up.

USNI: What do you remember about your relationships with the enlisted men?

Fairbanks: I suppose it was just the same as any other junior officer—a very junior officer. I must have been a curiosity to many of them for the first few weeks. Then the curiosity just melted into the ship's company.

USNI: Which is exactly the way you wanted it to go.

Fairbanks: Oh, of course, that's the way I tried to guide it. It would have been impossible to do the job otherwise.

USNI: When would you say you turned from being a green officer into a veteran?

Fairbanks: I suppose that happened during the first engagement we had with a German U-boat on the destroyer—the *Ludlow* [DD-438] it was—when we crossed the Atlantic. It doesn't take very long once you get a good scare. You get scared once, and you're part of the team.

USNI: You obviously had a varied Navy career, at least as far as ship types go. By our account, the only ships in which you did not serve were submarines. If you could have served in only one of those ship types, which would it have been and why?

Fairbanks: I enjoyed amphibious work best of all, because it had a little bit of everything. It had land, sea, and air, a combination that was sort of off the beaten track, not straight down the line. It was sort of special operations, and so it was more fun. It wasn't so conventional. A battleship is too big, and a destroyer in a bad sea rolls around and rocks too much. A lot of people liked the tin cans best. But I'd take cruisers. They're sort of in between. I enjoyed my time in the battleships—the *Washington* and the *Mississippi*—but they were so enormous.

USNI: If you could have done anything differently in the war, what would it have been?

Fairbanks: Stayed out. No, seriously, I've always been interested in the diplomatic and political side. I would have liked to be in the State Department or to serve in some diplomatic capacity. I enjoyed my Navy experience, but I think I would have enjoyed doing the same sorts of things I did before the war for FDR down in South America and in Europe, particularly in England and France. I found it all very interesting. I was on a much higher level than people would have imagined from somebody like me. Nobody would have suspected that I was dealing directly with the president and the secretary of state. So it was all very interesting and fascinating from my point of view.

USNI: What impressions do you retain of [Allied Combined Forces Commander] Adm. [H. Kent] Hewitt?

Fairbanks: Very fond ones, very fond. He was a gentle, nice man. When Adm. [Ernest] King gave him hell in front of the lot of us, the old man almost wept with embarrassment and humiliation. We hated Admiral King for doing that to him, because we had such affection and respect for Admiral Hewitt.

USNI: You described the frustrations you felt in the beach jumpers when you had a skipper who was not very knowledgeable or supportive. Did that situation improve once he was replaced?

Fairbanks: The man was a madman. He was absolutely impossible. He tried to conspire with me, saying "You must get more recognition. You must arrange to have somebody killed on the next operation. We haven't had enough casualties yet." That's when I got around to reporting it. I was on friendly terms with some senior officers. I didn't want to go through proper channels. This was too dangerous. He was widely disliked, widely hated, widely feared, and finally sent out to the Pacific.

USNI: How did the term "beach jumper" come about?

Fairbanks: It was a code name given by Mountbatten, I think. We had training up in Inverary, Scotland. The idea was for it to be a kind of cover name—partly descriptive—and a code name at the same time.

USNI: Do you feel that the beach jumpers really fulfilled their potential?

Fairbanks: I thought we could have done even more. Today, this type of operation is an integral part of the force.

USNI: In the book, why did you spotlight operations in the south of France over Normandy, which usually gets most of the attention?

Fairbanks: They didn't do too much of my sort of fighting at Normandy. At Normandy we were experimenting with new things, like the Dieppe operation. Normandy was pretty much all power, not much deception. And we were later involved in strategic planning. It was called London Control—just a cover name. That was an interesting group. They had supervision over that sort of operation all around the world.

USNI: From the looks of your walls, it's almost as if people were standing in line to give you medals.

Fairbanks: A lot of them don't mean a thing. They're just routine. Two or three of them mean something, and I received them gratefully. The others are all just automatic.

USNI: Some of the action summaries that you wrote during the war and then quoted in the book certainly display a flair for writing. Do you enjoy writing?

Fairbanks: Yes. I probably should have done more. I've always enjoyed writing, and I still do. That is the art I most respect.

USNI: What type of writing do you prefer—newspapers? Or novels? Or what you're doing now?

Fairbanks: Different kinds. I wrote articles and poetry when I was sixteen and seventeen. Two poems of mine were published in *Vanity Fair*, and I had some short stories printed in *Esquire*. I've been scribbling a long time. I didn't win any prizes, but I did get published.

USNI: What are you working on now? Is it a follow-on to *A Hell of a War*?

Fairbanks: Oh yes. I'm not working very hard on it, though. There's no rush.

USNI: Are you going to bring us up to the present in your next book?

Fairbanks: I won't really know until it happens. I'll see what the publisher wants. You might say I just scribble for the sake of the family now.

USNI: How much did you rely on memory, how much on notes, and how much on research?

Fairbanks: It's a little mélange of everything. I found some diaries and notes, and letters to the family.

USNI: The research is the fun part, and the writing is the hard part.

Fairbanks: You're absolutely right. It is fun to get it all assembled. Then you find one bit of research that upsets everything else before it, and it contradicts what you've already concluded.

USNI: As historians, we wish everyone had as keen a sense of history as you obviously do. What does history mean to you? How important is it?

Fairbanks: I've always enjoyed it—the stories, the excitement, how things developed, the origin of everything. I'm not only fascinated with natural history—the sun and the stars—but also political history, language, and culture. I've been interested in how things began ever since I was a boy.

USNI: Today's history teachers try to instill this interest in young people, but it's become more and more challenging.

Fairbanks: My children aren't in the least interested in history, so I understand the situation.

USNI: In your opinion, how has World War II been depicted in films? How would you rate it?

Fairbanks: Do you know, I haven't seen very many of them. I'm trying to think of one. *The Longest Day* is one. I remember seeing the play, *The Caine Mutiny*, but I didn't see the movie. *In Which We Serve*, with Noel Coward, I thought was great. That was all about Mountbatten, of course.

USNI: What we are driving at here is that one of the big criticisms of movies, at least these days—and you must have heard it before—is that historical accuracy often suffers in favor of romanticism.

Fairbanks: Sure! And why shouldn't it? Films and theatrical productions are not meant to be documentaries. Shakespeare wrote a lot of history, but I doubt if much of it was historically accurate. He made Richard III a famous hunchback villain. But there's no evidence at all in any history showing that Richard III was deformed, that his right shoulder was higher than his left. Somebody else wrote that his left shoulder was higher than his right. This was the only contemporary mention that Richard III was crippled at all. Yet Shakespeare made Richard III famous as a hunchback villain.

USNI: Do you have any stories or anecdotes that you'd like to share with our readers but didn't include in the book?

Fairbanks: I doubt it. Nothing that I could say out loud, anyway.

Shelby Foote

CHARLES MUSSI / U.S. NAVAL INSTITUTE

Mr. Foote became an overnight sensation for his homespun commentary on Ken Burns's Emmy Award–winning PBS miniseries, *The Civil War.* He is best known in literary circles as a popular historian, novelist, poet, and playwright and is the author of a classic three-volume history of the War Between the States, twenty years in the making. The interview appeared in the October 1994 issue of *Naval History.*

■

USNI: Why do you think that naval and maritime matters have been overshadowed, if not neglected completely, throughout history?

Foote: I strongly suspect it's because historians, and especially good writers, haven't paid enough attention to it. It's probably just that simple.

More attention ought to be paid to it. The only Civil War naval stories that attract any real attention are the *Monitor* and the *Merrimac* fight, and maybe [Rear Adm. David G.] Farragut's busting into Mobile Bay. They were colorful and dramatic.

But to my mind, [Rear Adm. Samuel F.] Du Pont's attack at Hilton Head on Forts Walker and Beauregard was also an important part of naval history. That expanding ellipse attack he made on those forts was the first definite proof that any time the Navy wanted to take a place, it could do it.

Of course, that was disproved later at Charleston. Both Fort Walker and Fort Beauregard were practically defenseless against those steam-driven machines that did not depend on the wind. Expanding ellipses brought them right past the batteries and enabled them to fire end-on. They won an easy naval victory against men who were presumably well trained in old-style defense.

USNI: The western rivers get hardly any play in Civil War history.

Foote: Well, the whole western theater gets hardly any play. I sometimes think that the people in this country who know less about the Civil War than any other one group of people are Virginians. They may know a little more than South Dakotans, but that's about all.

They think that the war was fought in Virginia, while various widespread skirmishes were going on out West. The opposite is closer to the truth.

Confederate general Robert E. Lee and his six or seven opponents skirmished back and forth between Washington and Richmond for three years. But out West, whole states were falling at once. Fort Donelson, for instance, was the first real battle of the war—including Bull Run, because it wasn't much of a battle. But at Donelson all of Kentucky and most of Tennessee was lost, and it marked the emergence of U. S. Grant as a leader.

A lot of people who call themselves Civil War buffs don't know anything about Fort Donelson. Nor do they know anything about Murfreesboro, another of the great battles of the war.

It's a misconception encouraged by the fact that much more material exists about the eastern theater, especially photographs and newspapers. And because there's more historical material, there's more history. It's a serious mistake. But this has been corrected a good deal in recent years.

USNI: I know that the Battle of Shiloh is near and dear to your heart. Why is that?

Foote: For one thing, the Shiloh battlefield is within a hundred miles of me. The other reason is even better. Shiloh is, to my mind, unquestionably the best-preserved Civil War battlefield of them all.

It has been singularly fortunate in many ways. It's not close to a large city or populated area, so it is not clogged with tourists all the time. But the main thing is, it has had only five or six superintendents, I believe, and each one has been thoroughly conscientious about keeping the place the way it was when the battle was fought. It's not surrounded by hot-dog stands the way Gettysburg is. In the *Official Records*, Pat Cleburne's report of the attack on what had been [Maj. Gen. William T.] Sherman's headquarters describes going through a blackjack thicket and then across marshy ground and up a hill. You can go there today, and the blackjack thicket, the marshy ground, and the hill are still there. It's a beautiful experience.

USNI: Back to naval matters; what impact do you think the Civil War navies had on the outcome of the war?

Foote: A huge impact, especially in the West, where the ironclads took the rivers. The blockade, tenuous and penetrable as it was, still had an enormous effect on little things. Nobody really knows the effect the blockade had on the people of the Confederacy.

The rarity of little items that you don't ordinarily think of was hugely important. They didn't have needles for sewing; they had to improvise thorns to use for needles. They didn't have nails to repair their ramshackle houses. By the time the war was over, after four years of being without nails, half the houses in the South were being shaken to pieces. Things like that you don't normally think about, but the North's naval blockade caused it.

USNI: The Civil War, as you know, is the most written-about period in American history. In your research, have you found any gaps that need to be filled?

Foote: Not really. You always wish you knew more about anything. I think the gaps are filled. I don't think at this late date we're going to find out much more. I did find out from a biography of A. P. Hill that he was ill and often indisposed. He frequently rode in an ambulance. From looking at his photograph and reading descriptions of him, I thought he'd probably had tuberculosis. Thank God I didn't say so. I read that what he had was severe prostate trouble caused by having got clapped up when he was on his way from New York to West Point one time. He stopped by New York and contracted gonorrhea and had prostate trouble the rest of his life. That's not all that illuminating, but it shows that new information can come to light.

USNI: Should anything be done to preserve identified historic sunken ships? Should they be disturbed at all?

Foote: Have you been to Vicksburg?

USNI: I never have, but I certainly want to go sometime.

Foote: Well, you've got a great treat in store for you. It was to me. I'm thoroughly familiar with that place, and I've looked at all the photographs available on naval and river warfare. But when you see the *Cairo* sitting there, you get a whole different notion. That thing is three times as big as I thought it would be. I can't conceive now how they got those boats down Yazoo Pass. It's about as wide as a bed. It's incredible. The amazing thing about naval engagements is the accounts of men firing 8-inch guns at each other from a range of eight feet. I'm afraid that is beyond my understanding. But they did it all the time in naval battles. It was a very strange business.

Getting back to preserving sunken ships, certainly the raising of the *Cairo* was a splendid thing to do because she went down so fast. Everything about her is the way she was. Unfortunately, when they brought her up they didn't do a skillful job. She broke in two and they lost parts of her. But her guns are there, and they've rebuilt those parts that were broken. It's worked out well. They have part of her broken down in sections so you can really see how she was built.

I can't recommend too strongly that you go and see her. Having spent all that time reading about her, I had absolutely no idea of the size of the thing. I knew the dimensions, but when I saw her it was absolutely amazing.

USNI: Many regimental histories were written for Army units in the Civil War. Why was that apparently not the case for the Navy?

Foote: I really don't know. No big Navy man even wrote his memoirs, did he? *Guns on the Western Waters* was one of my main sources. And I used the naval *Official Records.* But I have found a shortage of naval material.

USNI: As much as any other historians, you and David McCullough are responsible recently for popularizing history, as opposed to doing formal academic studies. How would you defend the way you approach your renditions of history to an academic?

Foote: I wouldn't defend it to an academic. I'd tell him, read it! If you find something wrong, tell me! Just because I'm a narrative historian doesn't mean for an instant that I have any less regard for the facts than he does. The difference is that he thinks the facts are the story, and they're not. The story is in the way you put the facts together.

The average academic has no notion of how a story is told. Too many of them have no notion of how to write a sentence. And they'd better get to work if what they want is to have their research last. Take a look at historians. Go all the way back to Herodotus and Thucydides, up through Tacitus, and even Francis Parkman, for that matter. There were damn few academics in that bunch.

What the academics have done to history, equating facts with truth, is a murderous thing. Facts are not the truth. The truth is how the facts came into being, what effect the facts had, not the facts themselves. Academic historians have no sense of plot. But all life has a plot. Anytime a man dies, you've got a beginning and a middle and an end. You don't know the plot until he dies.

Strangely enough, it's life imitating art, because once he dies, you understand his youth. When my best friend died at the age of twenty-four over at Ploesti in World War II, I understood why his youth had been so reckless. It was just as if he knew he was going to die young. But academics don't comprehend that. Narrative history helps readers understand things better.

Having said all this, I think something ought to be made clear. The academic historians can get along very well without me. I can't get along without them. They're the ones who do the necessary hard digging in dry documents. And so I'm not scorning them as much as it sounds. I scorn them for argumentative purposes. There doesn't need to be any war between us. They just have one notion about writing history and I have another. I'm actually indebted to all the academics.

USNI: How can we make history more popular in the classroom?

Foote: You know, I'm not interested in popularity, being popular, or even selling a lot of books. I like to do it, but that's not why I write. I'm trying to understand the damned thing and make other people understand it. Calling it popular makes it sound as though I did something to history to make it more palatable. I never want to do that. What I want to do is tell as forceful a story as I know how, as true as I know how to make it. There's nothing popular about it in conception. If it turns out to be popular, fine.

USNI: Teachers often have a tough time persuading their students to study history.

Foote: Absolutely. What I had to do when I took history in school—a very long time ago—was memorize dates and things. I still remember I had to memorize the thirteen steps to the Treaty of Utrecht. I don't remember them by a long shot, but that's the way history was taught. I think it was taught that way because you can grade that kind of testing easily. If I missed two of the thirteen steps I knew what my grade would be.

Teaching history is influenced strongly by teachers. Most of them are damned poor, and it's a great shame. History should be the most exciting course in school. As it is, it's probably the dullest.

When I got to school at the University of North Carolina, I took whatever I wanted. I still don't quite know why I took a course on medieval history, but it was the best course I had in school. I had a good teacher, and it was fascinating to see how many things about the modern world began in what's called the Dark Ages.

It was a fascinating subject, and it was well taught. It was a lecture course. We didn't have any of these happy-go-lucky discussions. The man stood up there to the lectern, delivered a lecture for one hour, said "Thank you, gentlemen," and walked out of the room. He was great.

USNI: I'm sure you know about the controversy surrounding the use of the Confederate battle flag in some of the state flags of the South. Is it really a symbol of evil, or is it an essential part of our history?

Foote: It is an essential part of our history that ought not be neglected or forgotten. It is also a symbol of evil. The reason it's a symbol of evil is that people who knew better sat back and let some yahoos use it as a symbol of resistance to integration.

But the blame is not with the latter. The blame is with people like me. When there began to be freedom marches and civil rights workers down South, responsible and educated Southern people looked at these people and said, "They're sending their riffraff down here, let our riffraff take care of it."

So what you got was a bunch of yahoos carrying a Confederate flag around opposing these people who were trying to get what the Constitution guarantees everybody. The Confederacy stood for the very opposite, and it should have been made clear at the time. But responsible people—and shame on them—left it up to the riffraff.

When three people were lynched in Meridian, the common comment was that they came looking for trouble and they found it. It was a shameful, shameful thing to say. It was like approving of lynching. But that was the feeling about it in those days. It's most regrettable, but that's what happened.

As for Senator Carol Moseley Braun [D-IL] not letting the Daughters of the Confederacy use the Confederate emblem on their stationery—not the battle flag, just an emblem of the Confederacy—she is a benighted creature. She wants no sign that the Confederacy ever existed. She hates it and everything it symbolizes. She doesn't want to be reminded that anybody was ever in slavery. She's hiding from history when she does that.

I regret that in a U.S. Senator, but what I resent most is that she wants to hide history from us. That I don't forgive. How she persuaded the rest of the Senate to go with her on that, I'm not sure, unless they were after whatever votes she could rally for other things. It's shameful.

USNI: Back to historians. Are today's historians as good as the ones you read when you started?

Foote: Yes, they are.

USNI: Should we be watching for any particular younger ones who have impressed you?

Foote: I don't know the very young ones. James McPherson is a fairly young historian, as far as I'm concerned, and he measures up to Bruce Catton. He's every bit as good a Civil War historian as Catton was.

What I'm calling young historians are people at least in their forties or fifties. You have to reach that age before you have enough life experience to be a historian. I don't think you can have a twenty-two-year-old historian. You can have a twenty-two-year-old mathematical genius. You can have a twenty-two-year-old poet. But I doubt you can have a twenty-two-year-old historian.

USNI: I understand you joined the Mississippi National Guard and went into World War II. Where did you serve?

Foote: I dropped out of school in 1938, because I saw the war was coming and I wanted to spend some time at home. Then in 1939, when Adolf Hitler's Germans invaded Poland, I joined the Mississippi National Guard, and we mobilized in November of 1940.

Right after Pearl Harbor, I went to Officer Candidate School. I was in the field artillery the whole time. I was cadred out to the Fifth Division in Patton's Army, which had been in Iceland for two years. We trained in Northern Ireland, south of Belfast. I got into a personal squabble with a colonel on the artillery division staff, and that man then set out to get me in every way possible.

A brigade ruling stated that you couldn't use an army vehicle for recreation beyond a range of fifty miles. Our battalion was fifty-four miles from Belfast, and the other battalions were within the fifty miles. So we had the common habit of putting forty-nine miles down on the trip ticket.

I would go to Belfast to see my girl and routinely put down forty-nine miles. I'll be damned if he didn't have me up on a court-martial charge of falsifying government documents. And he made it stick!

I was court-martialed and sent home. I came back to the States and worked for the Associated Press on a local desk in Manhattan for about four months. I couldn't stand it any longer, so I joined the Marine Corps and went through boot camp at Parris Island. They had a lot of fun with me, saying, "You used to be a captain in the Army. You might make a pretty good Marine private."

I had been court-martialed practically on the eve of D-Day. When I was getting ready to go overseas as a Marine, we dropped the atomic bomb. So the war was over, and I came back home.

USNI: What was your function on the U.S. Naval Academy Advisory Board when you served on it in the late 1980s?

Foote: My function was pretty close to nothing. They showed us how they were doing this and that, but I didn't speak out. I didn't think it would do much good. It seemed to me that the Naval Academy was concentrating almost entirely on two things—athletics and mathematics.

Vice Adm. Jim Stockdale was on the board, too. He told me a story about the long time he was a prisoner of war. There was another Annapolis man there, a younger man who was absolutely crazy. The North Vietnamese couldn't do a damn thing with him. He'd spit in their eye and say, "Hell no, I won't do it." He just stood up to them every time. Stockdale said that man did more to hold them together than anybody there. Well, that man obviously couldn't get into the Naval Academy today. The admissions policy was what I objected to. They have too many football players and mathematicians. I want them to have a little of everything. I wish they had a few truck drivers, myself.

I've heard about some of the troubles they had with cheating. Some of them were football players. The idea that a naval officer must be an athlete seemed to me at the time a serious mistake, and I said so, but only in passing. There wasn't anything I could do about it.

USNI: The controversy over the proposed "Disney's America" theme park in northern Virginia brings up the age-old conflict between historical integrity and commercial freedom. Aside from all the physical encroachment, how do you feel about the project?

Foote: Physical encroachment is the strongest point against it. It's the one most people empathize with to the most effect. My objection is simple. Anything that Disney has ever touched—whether it's fantasy or fact, whether it's Davey Crockett or whoever—has always been sentimentalized. And every good historian, every great artist, knows that sentimentality is the greatest enemy of truth.

In sentimental things, good always prevails, evil always suffers. The tears shed aren't even salty. No one suffers, and everyone knows everything's going to be all right in the end.

That is a false picture to plant in people's minds. Disney asks, "Wouldn't you rather have that than nothing at all?" No, I wouldn't. Nothing is something you can build on. A false picture is something that's going to be distorted for the rest of your life. So I'm against Disney for that reason.

Some say they're not against the Disney Company if they'll just put the park somewhere else. I'm against Disney down the line. When they called to ask me to be an adviser, I thought what a good thing it would be to get young people interested in history. What a splendid thing. Then a little red flag started waving, and I said, "Wait a minute, this is Disney."

They said they wanted me to help get it authentic. Personally, I think what they wanted was my name. In any case, I do know they want to do what they want to do. If I were to say a certain event didn't happen, they'd argue that it would be very attractive to kids.

I remember when I was a boy, they used to have a Wild West show after the circus. They always had a ceremony in which Lee and Grant appeared in resplendent blue and gray uniforms. Lee turned his sword over to Grant; Grant received it and handed it back to Lee, to great applause. Everybody was clapping and happy. But Lee never gave his sword to Grant. What dramatic value it had was based on an absolute fabrication. Therefore, it was worse than worthless. It was a lie.
How much of that kind of stuff would go on at Disney?

Gene Hackman and Daniel Lenihan

PHOTOS DAVID HOFELING / U.S. NAVAL INSTITUTE

Gene Hackman has appeared in more than seventy motion pictures. He has won two Academy Awards—Best Actor for *The French Connection* (1971), Best Supporting Actor for *Unforgiven* (1992)—and he has been nominated three times (Best Actor for *Mississippi Burning,* 1988; Best Supporting Actor for *Bonnie and Clyde,* 1967, and *I Never Sang for My Father,* 1970). His acting career did not take shape, however, until he finished an enlistment in the U.S. Marine Corps, which he joined at age sixteen after lying about his age. He is coauthor of the seafaring novel, *Wake of the Perdido Star,* with veteran U.S. National Park Service underwater archaeologist and historian Daniel Lenihan. The interview appeared in the February 2000 issue of *Naval History.*

■

USNI: Why did you choose to enlist in the Marine Corps?

Hackman: It was probably because of Lowell Ford. His sister was my girlfriend. This was when I was fourteen or fifteen, at a time when young men don't quite know who they're in love with. Her brother had been killed on Guam. A year and a half or so later, when I wasn't quite seventeen, I thought it would be very heroic of me if I joined the Marine Corps. I wanted to show her that I was proud not only of her, but of her brother, too. When you are a young man, sometimes your motives are pretty obscure and complicated.

USNI: Did your military experience affect your career in any way?

Hackman: Yes, I think it did. I think it gave me a kind of a discipline that I wouldn't have had; a tack on things that would have been different if I hadn't been in the Corps.

USNI: Do you think military service is worthwhile?

Hackman: I think it's good for some people. It depends on who you are and what you need. I grew up somewhat without a father. I mean, my father was in and out a lot, and my mother and father divorced when I was young. So I probably didn't have the discipline that I needed as a young man. And the Corps brought me back to reality about what I could do and what I couldn't do, in terms of authority.

USNI: Do you keep in touch with any of your old acquaintances from the Marine Corps?

Hackman: I run into some of them once in a while. Somebody occasionally will come up behind me and say, "Semper Fi!" A couple of years ago, I was walking down the street in New York, and I heard a voice behind me. He said, "Have you been to Ping Kong Tung Lee's lately?" This got my attention; that was a whorehouse in Tsingtao, China.

USNI: Did you know what your mission was when you were in Tsingtao?

Hackman: I was so young, I had no idea what I was doing there. I didn't understand why the Marines were there. I was just looking to have a good time. I played on all the sports teams that I could try out for. And I ended up also working for the Armed Forces Radio Service in Tsingtao.

I guess our mission was to guard whatever interest the United States had in that town. Exactly what that was, I had no idea.

USNI: We've heard a story that your former company commander once dressed you down as "a sorry son of a bitch," when he saw you working as a hotel doorman after your discharge from the Marine Corps. Is that true?

Hackman: Well, it was something like that. He was actually my recruiting sergeant. Why he remembered me, I don't know. I had been given a job as a doorman at the Howard Johnson's restaurant in New York City, during a Shriners' convention. This was a little, tiny Howard Johnson's. But it did a tremendous business, because it was right on Times Square. And they wanted even more business. So they rented white uniforms with green piping and hats to match. I had been standing there opening the door dressed like that for a week.

Then along comes this Marine in dress blues. He stopped momentarily, then he came close to me. And as he walked by me, he said, "Hackman, you are a sorry son of a bitch."

USNI: And what did that mean to you?

Hackman: It just meant that I looked terrible, that I was never a great Marine. I suppose people who end up making the Marine Corps a career—and I'm sure that this man did—would see somebody like myself as a traitor to the Corps, because I diminished the look of a Marine by wearing this tatty-looking uniform. It did give me pause for a while.

USNI: Your new book certainly seems to lend itself to a movie. Which part are you going to play?

Hackman: Hmm. There really isn't a part for me in it, other than maybe a small part—the sea captain [the oft-besotted Captain Deploy]. If somebody wanted me to, I'd probably do that.

USNI: Is a movie in the offing?

Hackman: The book is in the hands of a theatrical agent now, who is shopping it around, as they say in the parlance. It's only been out there a short time, so we haven't heard anything yet.

It would be a difficult movie, a big, sprawling production. Anytime you're working on the water, it adds a whole new dimension. I'd guess it all would be shot in the Caribbean. You could doll things up there to look like the South Pacific and parts of Cuba.

USNI: Besides being neighbors in Santa Fe, New Mexico, how did you two get connected?

Hackman: Through diving. My wife and I wanted to be certified, so we asked around Santa Fe, which is not the diving capital of the world, certainly. It does have a couple of dive shops, though, strangely enough. One man told us to get in touch with Dan, who has been very helpful ever since, in terms of my wife's and my diving.

USNI: Do you dive in any particular spot? We understand that you have done some diving on World War II sites at Truk Atoll.

Hackman: My wife and I were on Truk Lagoon, "Chuuk," as they prefer to call it now. We've done dives in Hawaii, the Cayman Islands, some places in the Bahamas, and at Fort Jefferson in the Dry Tortugas with Dan. That location became a scene in the book.

USNI: We understand that one of you began writing at the end, and another started at the beginning. Is that correct?

Hackman: Well, it's somewhat right. We don't like to talk specifically about what we wrote, because I suppose it kind of pushes us farther apart in some funny way. Needless to say, Dan wrote the technical things about diving, because I don't know that much about what that might have been like. Dan's great imagination filled that in.

To answer your question, I started by writing a chapter in the center of the book called "Storm." Then Dan and I talked about the arc of the story. Later, we exchanged pages and chapters back and forth, and it just developed. We were in the middle, and then we were at the beginning. And then we went from the middle on. It worked for us, because we had a solid idea about where we wanted to go.

Lenihan: Perhaps there is a bit more emphasis in the second half of the writing, because that's where most of the diving scenes take place. I wrote chapters in the beginning and Gene wrote a number of the chapters in the end. And together we worked closely on the last chapter. So it's very hard to distinguish.

Some people have assumed that I must have been the one working on the technical maritime aspects. That's not true. Actually, Gene was involved heavily in writing several of the scenes that have to do with the men at sea on the ships—and how the ships are both being wrecked and then being rebuilt.

Hackman: I think our literary agent is the only one who really knows what Dan wrote and what I wrote, because he was much more aware of Dan's previous writing in scientific circles. But our publisher says that she doesn't know.

Lenihan: When Gene was doing a film, I would often work with Betsy, his wife, who was extremely critical to this book's being done, logistically and in every other way. She was a real driving force. After a while, Gene and I had merged sections and chapters to such an extent that we were a little confused ourselves about who had written what. If we disagreed on an edit, the final decision would go to the person who wrote the pages in question. I remember discussing edits with Betsy, and after about the fourth page, I said, "Betsy, I didn't write this." I think that was an indication that maybe it had been fairly well merged.

Hackman: All this was over a span of more than three years, and we were both doing other things.

USNI: You've talked about the technical aspects of the story. Did you ever consider that you might be running a risk of turning somebody off with all the arcana?

Lenihan: I suppose you always run that risk, if the reader isn't going to care about how these characters reestablish themselves. The book wouldn't be for them, anyway. There's a bit of the Robinson Crusoe element at play here. And if someone doesn't care about ships, the sea, and diving it might be enough to dissuade them. Only a very few people have had that reaction.

Hackman: One of the most satisfying things we've heard about the book is the fact that women enjoy it, which we never thought would happen. Several have said exactly the same thing: that in reading the book, it taught them something about what men dream of, what men find interesting.

Lenihan: It was a real unexpected education for us. In fact, some women have used almost the same words to describe their reactions.

USNI: Your main character, Jack O'Reilly, seems to be a rather sensitive guy for a seventeen-year-old in the early nineteenth century. Through him, you deal with issues like slavery and religious persecution—even animal rights. Was that a conscious effort?

Hackman: Yes, it was. I happened to write most of those parts. What I wanted him to be was a sensitive guy who was pushed into violence. And that in the back of his mind, in the back of his soul, there would be some kind of redemption. That there would be kind of a salvation for him; that he wouldn't end up being a pirate, a barbarian, a buccaneer. That he was better than that.

Lenihan: The one thing we both agreed on with him was his personality. Jack is a decent person. He's a young, highly energetic, physical guy, who has the capability of extreme violence. That's part of his makeup. He's basically a tough kid. But he's also, basically, a decent one.

As he's deprived of his family and develops a new shipboard family, he finds that in defending them—maybe defending his new family better than he did his old one—his proclivity for violence works for him, maybe too well. And by the end, he's taken up on it.

I think it's a complicated ending, because what happens is, you see him find other ways to solve his problems. He knows he's gone too far.

USNI: Did you base the *Perdido Star* on a particular ship?

Hackman: The one pictured on the title page of the book is a hermaphrodite brig, I think. It looks like it's gaff-rigged on the main.

Lenihan: This would pass muster as a brigantine. The ship at the end, which is also the *Star*, is a barkentine. It was important to Gene, in the reclamation process, to get it right. I think this is something that comes partly from theater, but words are strong, especially to him. He pointed out that you can't really run a mizzen on a brigantine. So at the end, we made the *Star* a barkentine, which would be easier for that small complement of men to operate. So as the ship is reborn, it's one that's three-masted; the main and after-mast are fore-and-aft rigged.

USNI: Dan, as a writer of mostly nonfiction in the past, what was it like to delve into fiction?

Lenihan: I think it's exciting. It's really liberating in a lot of ways. There's such a powerful sense of freedom of expression that comes from the ability to change the world to the way you want it. It's just not as constraining as nonfiction. That's the way it struck me. I found it exciting and took to it pretty happily.

Hackman: It was wonderful for me. I had the exact opposite process that Dan did. I had never had anything published until this. And just the other day we had a piece appear in *National Geographic Traveler*, a nonfiction article about the dives on Truk, which Dan helped to write.

USNI: What are your favorite maritime and nautical authors?

Hackman: Well, I suppose Jack London would come to mind first, and Herman Melville. I think we probably stole a little bit from Robert Louis Stevenson and *Treasure Island*, in terms of ambiance.

Lenihan: I think those three motivated us the most. You pattern yourself after the things that grabbed you when you were younger. Part of what we were trying to do was to reach back to a different genre. Interestingly enough, people occasionally ask, "What about Patrick O'Brian?" Others have asked about the *Hornblower* television series. We were actually oblivious most of the time to O'Brian. Toward the end of this process, we looked at one of the O'Brian books. Once we realized that it covered the same time period, we didn't want to look at it.

Hackman: Some have intimated that we are jumping on the popularity bandwagon of the *Hornblower* television series and Patrick O'Brian. We started this project three and a half years ago. I don't believe the *Hornblower* series had even started.

USNI: Obviously, you could have chosen any period of history. How did you arrive at 1805 as the book's starting point?

Hackman: We wanted it to occur outside of any specific event. Lewis and Clark was about the most publicized story at the time. Enough years had passed since the Constitution had been signed, and there was still turmoil in the country. It's twenty-five or thirty years after the Declaration of Independence and just prior to the War of 1812. We wanted it set so we wouldn't be obliged to have to deal with momentous historic events. And yet there was still an ambiance of the Napoleonic wars and the coming of the War of 1812.

Lenihan: We wanted to have that sense of turmoil and unrest in the nation, some of which you see come out in the interaction between Jack and his father. We wanted that to be a background so that we could isolate the characters. The plot could take place without having to be too dependent on events that were going on in the real world. It was a vehicle for this story of coming of age in these times.

The Dutch East India Company had collapsed; the government had taken it over. And literally, the crews in ships sailing at that time, in most parts of the world, didn't know who they might be at war with, or what port they could go into, with what flag raised. We wanted that sense of chaos, that the world was an unstable place at the time. The characters were playing out their own drama in that context.

Hackman: Also at that time, Eli Whitney was just getting under way with his mass production of rifles. And that played a bit of a role early in the story.

USNI: What do you both think of treasure hunting, for the lack of a better term, and the people who are less scrupulous than others when diving on wrecks?

Lenihan: Well, it's our history. Patrimony is a fleeting thing. I don't see the big problem being the treasure hunters themselves, as much as society's—sometimes American society's—willingness to let that past become a commodity, letting it dribble through the hands of people for profit.

Hackman: I don't have the same philosophical leanings about treasure. I don't quite understand the big deal. I don't mean to be insensitive about it. I think I would tend to agree with Dan that somebody who goes down and absolutely devastates a wreck with big suction blowers is irresponsible. But I think it's okay if people pick up a coin if they dive a site by themselves. I must say that I pick them up, or I would if I found one.

When we were diving Truk, they were saying that the amount of artifacts that have disappeared over the years is astonishing. But to me it looked very rich. There were machine-gun bullets all over the place. And I think it's very tough to tell somebody they can't pick one of those up and take it home. There's a lot of ordnance on those ships that the locals take. They take the powder out and they use it to fish. They make dynamite explosions, and the fish come to the surface. That's wrong, yeah. That is definitely wrong.

But when I'm diving, I can't keep my hands off of things. I had my hands on a Japanese Zero at Truk.

USNI: Most first-time authors dedicate their books to loved ones. You've dedicated this to the sea and the people who've navigated it. Why?

Lenihan: It comes from the heart. We both have very strong feelings about the sea and seamen, the whole class of society who grew up around the sea and live by it. It's the great unknown. Three quarters of the world is covered by it, and those who ply its surface and plumb its depths deserve some recognition.

Kaoru Hasegawa

COURTESY OF KAORU HASEGAWA

Mr. Hasegawa was a Japanese World War II naval aviator—the rare survivor of a kamikaze mission because he was shot down and rescued by the crew of a U.S. destroyer in 1945. He is the current president of the Rengo Company, Ltd., an international corrugated packaging producer.

At 1015 the morning of 25 May 1945, after dodging antiaircraft fire from the battleship USS *West Virginia* (BB-48), Hasegawa's bomber took a hit from the USS *Callaghan* (DD-792) and crashed into the sea. The destroyer crew in turn rescued the severely injured aviator (the aircraft's other two crew members did not survive). Ironically, a later kamikaze attack sank the *Callaghan* on 29 July 1945.

In July 1995, as part of a wreath-laying ceremony and reception at the U.S. Navy Memorial in Washington, Hasegawa remembered the dead and honored the survivors of the *Callaghan* and later attended the ship's anniversary reunion at Pigeon Forge, Tennessee, where he was treated as a *Callaghan* survivor himself. The interview appeared in the October 1995 issue of *Naval History.*

■

USNI: What motivated your visit to the United States and to the U.S. Naval Institute?

Hasegawa: I had asked my friend, Capt. William Horn, U.S. Navy (Retired), to confirm the records about my encounter with the U.S. destroyer *Callaghan*. I have therefore come here to reconfirm my recollection of the past. I am here also for the fiftieth anniversary of the date—25 May 1945—when I was shot down by the *Callaghan*.

USNI: Many U.S. servicemen have died for their country, but seldom was death a virtual certainty. Given that consequence, how did you feel before your Special Attack mission?

Hasegawa: Of course, the psychological pressure was tremendous when I got into the airplane, because the success of the mission meant my ultimate death. It is difficult, however, to measure the pressure that I encountered as a military officer during that war against standards in peaceful times.

USNI: So the philosophy was a "war-fever" of sorts?

Hasegawa: I think it was a "war-fever." During the war, not only Japanese servicemen, but also American, British, and French soldiers, were dying every day around me. Everybody had pressure. But since Special Attack meant death when successful, we felt another significant pressure in addition to that felt in an ordinary attack. It was a totally different kind of pressure, however, than we would feel during peacetime.

USNI: Where were you at the time of the Pearl Harbor attack, and what was your attitude toward that attack?

Hasegawa: I was at the Imperial Naval Academy at that time. I had heard the news in the morning of the day when the attack occurred, but I did not know any of the details.

USNI: What were your thoughts about it?

Hasegawa: I am not in a position to express my opinions as to whether that attack could be justified or not. I heard many things about it afterward. I knew that many of my seniors, such as Adm. [Isoroku] Yamamoto, participated in the attack. Many factors related to it. For me to answer this question would take a very long time. There were many considerations—strategic, national, political, military. The judgments or views of a military officer would be separate from that of a private Japanese citizen.

USNI: How did you happen to volunteer for the Special Attack Corps?

Hasegawa: The approach to form the Special Naval Attack might have been different between the Navy and the Army at that time. I was assigned to the 405 "Ginga" (Galaxy) Corps. It was a natural or normal procedure that, as a lieutenant in the Navy, I would be selected to command the Tenth Ginga subunit, which was assigned to the Special Attack on 25 May.

USNI: Was this simply your duty as a naval officer?

Hasegawa: Normally, there were about twenty officers in a flying unit. Somebody had to be named to command an attack mission. If I had died as a result of a kamikaze attack, somebody else would have assumed command of the next aircraft. So in that sense, it was a normal duty as a naval officer.

We had only thirty airplanes, when we should have had forty-eight bomber aircraft in our corps. It was a losing war. We were conducting many ordinary attacks. In an ordinary attack, you came back after you completed your mission. In a Special Attack, if you were successful, you did not come back. There was no special sensational feeling that came with our service in the Special Naval Attack Corps, because we had both types of missions. Every day and night we were attacking, and many people were dying. A few days before 25 May, it was decided that the forthcoming mission would follow the Special Attack method.

The 405 Corps had been assigned to carry out many ordinary attacks against Okinawa, Iwo Jima, and the American naval fleet. Some died during the missions. That method or mission procedure was the same as that used by the United States or other countries. Some days before the twenty-fifth, we were informed that that day's attack would be a Special Attack mission. It was not a decision made after special deliberation. One day we would employ the ordinary attack method; the next day we would be alerted for a Special Attack mission.

I must emphasize here that the Special Attack mission was not something we regarded as extraordinary. Of course, they were extraordinary tactics. Military men, however, had to follow whatever orders were given to them and believed that they should do their best to complete assignments.

USNI: Did you receive any special training for such missions?

Hasegawa: There was no special training for Special Attack operations. It was not necessary. Any pilot with high skills could perform the mission.

USNI: What was the general condition of the aircraft used for these missions?

Hasegawa: The airplanes of our corps were in very good condition.

USNI: Even for Special Attack missions?

Hasegawa: Yes. As a matter of fact, we thought Franceses were too good for kamikaze missions. I remember that we often talked about how wasteful it was to use these good airplanes for Special Attack missions. They could fly at high speeds and for long ranges. Also, they could carry a lot of ammunition. They even had radar equipment.

USNI: Recount, if you will, your 1945 mission.

Hasegawa: At that time, we were divided into four small groups, each group having three airplanes and having been ordered to approach an enemy fleet from different directions. After the groups were deployed, every one of the aircraft—except mine and another airplane—returned because of bad weather. The other pilot joined me and together we found the battleship *West Virginia* at about 1000. The battleship began shooting at us at 1002. The records of those times are all recorded in the official account of battle. I was hit by guns from the nearby *Callaghan* and crashed into the sea.

USNI: According to books written about the kamikaze, you and your comrades were afforded a "spiritual guarantee," if your missions were successful. How did you deal with the fact that you survived?

Hasegawa: At that time, I thought it was dishonorable not to have succeeded in attacking the U.S. ships. I should mention, however, that now I do not think that way. When I was captured, I was badly injured and did not see any reason to live. I tried to commit suicide in the battleship *New Mexico* [BB-40] while being transferred to Guam. I attempted to kill myself in a toilet. I became unconscious, but somehow survived. The U.S. sailor who had been assigned as a guard to watch my behavior was later scolded by his superiors.

USNI: How were you treated by your rescuers?

Hasegawa: The crew of the *Callaghan* rescued me from the sea. As they were involved in a heavy air and sea battle, they were very busy, and there was much commotion. I remember somebody looking into my eyes to see if I was alive or not. After they discovered that I was alive, I was left to lie on the deck while the crews went on fighting. In general, the crews of the *Callaghan* and later the *New Mexico* were very polite and treated me very decently.

USNI: What was the extent of your injury?

Hasegawa: I suffered contusions over most of my body. Several of my teeth were broken, and I also had a fracture in my leg. The contusions were all on the left side of my body, from my hip to my ear. I remember it hurt very much.

USNI: Why were kamikaze tactics not used earlier in the war, if they were considered to be so effective?

Hasegawa: One can rationalize many ways to fight a war. The specific tactics that are used vary, and any one tactic might be effective on a certain occasion. But from a broad point of view, I cannot say that an attack succeeded just because it was a kamikaze attack. An ordinary attack could be just as effective. I do not think that kamikaze tactics were so effective, considering the ultimate sacrifice of a human being and an airplane for each "successful" mission.

USNI: How are World War II kamikaze survivors treated or regarded today?

Hasegawa: There are technically no kamikaze survivors. If you were deployed as a kamikaze and you succeeded, you died. Some survivors who participated in the Special Attack Corps missions are the ones who had turned back while on the way to the original mission because of bad weather, engine failures, or other reasons, or those who had made a forced landing before reaching a destination. My case, in which I was shot down over an enemy ship and returned, is very rare.

USNI: Are you saying that you were not a kamikaze?

Hasegawa: It depends on how you define kamikaze. If you were deployed to attack as a kamikaze, you are dead. Precisely speaking, I was assigned to a kamikaze mission, but returned alive.

USNI: If Japan had been in the position of the United States in 1945 with an atomic bomb, what do you think the Japanese would have done?

Hasegawa: I cannot take that kind of question very lightly, because any response, particularly today, will only lead to misinterpretation, controversy, or misunderstanding. Fifty years have passed since the war. From a historical perspective, many critics have evaluated the warfighting decisions and actions of both sides, have they not?

USNI: Some of the World War II fiftieth-anniversary commemorations have met with difficulties and controversies. What recommendations do you have for such events in the future?

Hasegawa: War is part of the history of human interaction. It is important that we judge and evaluate the war at the fiftieth, sixtieth, one hundredth anniversaries and so on. The reason for my being here is to fill the void in my own memory, not to condemn or judge the past at the national level. I do not have any particular recommendations for future commemoration, but I do think we should make every effort to judge the war in a fair manner.

I would like to preserve the historical record related to the war in memory of those who died. I am planning to visit the families of the dead and explain the condition to them. As a result of our plane's having been shot down, both of the other men in my crew that day are dead. Warrant Officer Yoshida's older brother is living in Kyushu, as is the family of Mr. Koyama, the pilot of the airplane. I plan to visit them to explain what happened, based upon the confirmation of the past using your official historical records.

USNI: Do you have any particular message for readers of *Naval History*?

Hasegawa: I believe that the U.S. Navy, Royal British Navy, and Japanese Navy have always had a kind of comradeship toward each other. Whenever I visit the U.S. Naval Academy or the Royal British Naval Academy, the people there always treat me with warm friendship. Because Japan does not have a formal navy any more, I feel a sense of nostalgia toward the U.S. and Royal British navies. I would like you to know that I have very close friendly feelings toward you. I want to send my warmest regards to the U.S. Navy.

Jim Lovell

SUSAN TODD BROOK / U.S. NAVAL INSTITUTE

Capt. James A. Lovell Jr., U.S. Navy (Retired), was an astronaut in the Mercury, Gemini, and Apollo programs and is best known as the commanding officer of the ill-fated Apollo 13 mission to the Moon. The interview appeared in the December 1995 issue of the Naval Institute's *Proceedings.*

■

USNI: As a Naval Academy graduate, what advice do you give future naval officers who want to go into the space program?

Lovell: When I entered the program, we all had questions about being sidetracked into a quasi-government program that would have nothing to do with naval traditions or naval promotions. I think naval officers ought to have certain experiences and foundations to be career officers, especially if they are going to defend their country.

Having said that, quite frankly, I didn't have many of those, because I went into the space program. But naval officers tend to go into varied fields—more so, I think, than Army officers. And many naval officers are in government or some aspects of government, and do other things besides command ships. NASA has expanded into several disciplines now. You don't have to be a test pilot anymore. In fact, only two people command the space shuttle itself. All other people are mission specialists of some sort. Several of our astronauts were really not pilots, per se, but were mission specialists. We've even had civilians come in as payload specialists. So I think the space program is still a very viable field and a great career.

I think people who choose naval aviation take on a certain amount of risk, and there is certainly an element of risk in the space program. I don't think it's as great as it once was. The shuttle today is much like getting on an airliner. Occasionally, though, accidents do happen.

USNI: What do you think the space program could do differently to attract young people?

Lovell: I think NASA has consistently been accused of doing a poor marketing job. People ask, "Why are we still sending people into space? What benefit did we get from the Apollo program? Why did we spend all that money away from the earth?" Well, in actuality, we spent all the money on the earth. But that message has not come across well. I think NASA should emphasize the advantages of having an active U.S. space program.

Right now, we are no longer threatened by the great Evil Empire, and to some degree that's bad news for us who try to justify space travel. Keeping up with the Soviets was a great incentive. It was intense competition, and we love competition. As a matter of fact, we were underdogs for a long time. In reality, that was a good thing, because it spurred our Apollo program.

But we don't have that now. What we do have, however, is cooperation. Several countries are knitted together with the common goal of an international space station. We have a method of communication among countries on a subject surrounded by little or no controversy. Many questions remain, of course—how big it should be and who should spend the money—but it's not that controversial. And such exchanges create rapport and lay the groundwork for interaction between countries in other fields, because a camaraderie has already been established, without boundaries. Those are intangible benefits of an active space program that Congress sometimes misses when the time comes to appropriate funds year by year. Our lawmakers fluctuate, depending on which way the winds are blowing politically, without really looking at the big picture. The space program yields intangible benefits, and that story needs to be told.

USNI: It seems that our new relationship with Russia has not been publicized as much as some of the other aspects of the space program. Why would you say that is?

Lovell: Certainly, docking with the *Mir* was a very important milestone for NASA, but it was not a milestone in the eyes of the American public like landing on the Moon. This is Earth orbital. We've been doing Earth orbital stuff since Mercury and Gemini, and we've had more than seventy shuttle missions now.

We have to realize that this program, like most programs, has matured. The Russians have a tremendous amount of talent. They spent most of their money in the past either in space or on the military, to the detriment of everything else. So it would be foolish not to tap their experience and knowledge. And if we're going to spend a lot of money to help them, we ought to get something back for it.

As for publicity and exposure, it's just a matter of time. The more things we do together, the more stories about them will find their way into the papers. Knowledge will ultimately get back to the public, which I think will be more responsive.

Because of the book [*Lost Moon* (New York: Houghton Mifflin, 1994)] and, more so, the movie [*Apollo 13*], I found out just recently that the silent majority in this country, the people who obviously don't write to their congressmen, are in favor of the space program.

A lot of people I talk to now weren't even born when I flew. Anybody younger than twenty-five years old wasn't around for Apollo 13. But I find they still are interested. They learn about it in school. A perfect and very visible example is a guy by the name of Tom Hanks. He was a closet astronaut. He really wanted to get into space, knew the names of all the astronauts, all the space flights. When he finally got in the acting business, he wanted to play an astronaut. He finally got his chance.

USNI: President John F. Kennedy's rallying cry to land on the Moon seemed to unite all Americans in that pursuit. If the same challenge were set forth today regarding Mars, for example, what do you think the ultimate response would be?

Lovell: Well, in reality, it was set forth. Back on the twentieth anniversary of Apollo 11 in Washington, President [George] Bush did set somewhat of a goal for going to Mars. But it was not the same rallying cry that President Kennedy had made. I'm fully convinced Kennedy made that statement because of the political situation he faced at that particular time. The Soviet Union obviously had an edge on us scientifically, and we were asking ourselves why we didn't have an educational system that produced people who could do what the Russians were doing.

So President Kennedy had to make a very bold move, and this was one way he saw that he could do it. It really is a shame that he did not live to see his goal accomplished. I think he probably had doubts that this would actually come to pass, but in 1961 he had to give Americans something to look forward to, a goal that would be unique.

USNI: It may take a political competitor to get us in that mind-set again.

Lovell: We also need a Congress and public that say this is what we ought to do. Nothing today would prevent us from going to Mars, nothing technical, at least. The Russians have had people in space now for well over a year, working out the procedures to keep the people healthy, but not so much to go to Mars; it's to come back to the earth and live under the influence of gravity again.

But all it takes is effort, time, and money to do the job. All the systems active today can be used to go to Mars.

USNI: We just need the check.

Lovell: Yes, we need the money and the will to do it. Right now, we're concentrating on the space station, which has, I think, important applications in the diplomatic as well as the technical arena.

USNI: Two schools of thought seem to prevail concerning the future of space exploration. Some say that, since we've been to the Moon, we should focus our efforts more outward to other planets. Others say there is more to do on the Moon, specifically, that we should land on the Moon again to gain public support to go elsewhere. We have also heard discussions of colonizing the Moon. What are your thoughts on that?

Lovell: The studies I've seen indicate that the Moon can possibly be used as a training base for a Martian mission. Which of the two schools of thought has more merit depends on what set of scientists you listen to. Geologists were very disappointed when Apollo 18 and 19 were canceled. Some people in NASA, basically the engineering types, wanted to cancel the program after Apollo 11.

Then there are the scientists who say that we have to find out more about the solar system and do probes to the other planets, and to the satellites of other planets. These two groups are at odds, and many of the differing opinions involve robotics. "We don't need people for these missions," some say. "Let's concentrate our existing funds on unmanned, robotic systems. Then if we lose them, it's not a traumatic situation."

That argument will continue. We'll probably reach a compromise at some point. I think we will go back to the moon, but not before the next century. Right now, the only way we can sell Congress is to show a return on the investment. This is how the shuttle came into being. Originally, it was only one part of a two-pronged space effort; one was the shuttle and the other was the space station. The shuttle was merely the transportation device to travel to the space station. At that time, Congress was not about to fund two programs, so our lawmakers elected to build the shuttle first and the space station later.

The time for the space station has come. From a macro position in space, we will learn more about the earth and bring a quicker return on the investment. A lot of people cannot understand the point of going to the Moon. We brought back moon rocks, and twenty-some years later we are still examining them, trying to figure out what we have. They probably raised as many questions as they answered. It's amazing.

USNI: During the Apollo 13 mission, you must have experienced a feeling of detachment from Earth, which would certainly be inevitable on a mission to Mars. Do you think the phenomenon will be a factor in such far-flung missions?

Lovell: I don't really believe that to be as much of a problem as a lot of people have surmised. I recall flying an F8U before I got to NASA. For the very first time we were wearing the early Navy pressure suits that would inflate if we lost pressure above fifty thousand feet. The Navy psychiatrists at that time started doing studies on detachment. They concentrated on what happens above fifty to sixty thousand feet. Would you suddenly feel detached from the earth, much like a diver who experiences rapture of the depth and doesn't realize how long he's been down—or which way is up—and suddenly either doesn't care or gets so enamored with what's going on that he forgets the situation?

Well, nothing like that ever happened flying airplanes. Then we started going into earth orbit. NASA, among other things, had a lot of faith in psychiatrists. They invited several to interview us after we came back from our flights. They would send the psychiatrists out to the ship, and as soon as we came on board they would start interviewing us subtly to see if we had any problems.

I can recall one instance after Gemini 12, when I was in the wardroom having lunch. A psychiatrist was sitting directly across from me. By this time, with my two flights, I had logged 440 hours, which was more time in space than anybody in the world. So I happened to know why this fellow was watching me. Myself, I was just happy to be back on earth. As I was explaining some of the things we did and saw, I had one of those heavy Navy wardroom forks in my hand. I waved it up in the air—and left it up there. I had done that for 440 hours.

USNI: It didn't stay there, did it?

Lovell: No! It came crashing down onto the table. You should have the seen the eyes of the psychiatrist. Boy, they really lit up. But he had a smile on his face. He'd finally found something to report.

We never really experienced anything I would refer to as detachment in earth orbit. We never felt any detachment in my two flights to the Moon. On Apollo 8, up to when we cut the engine and were anchored to the Moon, we did hope, in the back of our minds, that the engine would fire again. Otherwise, we would have been a satellite of the Moon—permanently. But that's the risk you take. It's no different from being launched off an aircraft carrier and you get a cold cat shot.

I don't think detachment will be a factor in going to Mars. Based on time, the size of the ships, and how acclimated one can get to life in space, missions to Mars or Venus and other solar system trips will be possible. Of course, you can't land on Venus, but you can go around it. You'd never be able to get to the nearest star, which is Alpha Centauri—four light years away. If ever we can figure out how to travel 186,000 miles a second, it would take us four years to get there.

USNI: We're not at Star Trek yet.

Lovell: That's right. Einstein said that, as time slows down, mass increases. If we ever got a chance to come back, the earth would have changed millions of years. Nothing would be the same. So I think we're anchored here in the solar system.

USNI: Getting back to robotics, what role will humans play in the future? Can we do it all with robotics?

Lovell: We can do a lot with robotics, no doubt about it. In fact, I think the Naval Research Lab is making a very simple, inexpensive probe for either the Moon or Mars. But I don't think anyone has developed a computer as inexpensive and as complicated as the human brain. When things don't work as they're supposed to work, as happened on Apollo 13, human beings are still part of the loop and are very, very important.

I don't think we'll ever lose the human desire for adventure and exploration into the Last Frontier—space. People are going to be there whether it's financially expedient or not or whether it's worthwhile or not.

USNI: Without that excitement, getting public support will be a challenge.

Lovell: Yes, without people involved, the public doesn't get much enamored with the program.

USNI: Were you aware that people on earth were hanging on every word of every report on what you guys were doing in Apollo 13?

Lovell: No. We got our communications strictly through the capsule communicator. Even when we landed, the recovery ship had been out to sea for about a week. Not until we got back to Hawaii did the tremendous impact of this flight begin to dawn on us. Of course, I made one of the traditional goofs. We were on vox-hot mike—when I said, "It will be a long time before we have another moon mission," or something to that effect.

Of course, it took the poor administrator a couple of days to convince the news media that "what he really means is. . . ." When I got back, I was confronted with the same thing; that was always the first question.

USNI: The film *Apollo 13* should impel a lot of excitement—not short-lived excitement, let's hope—with the public.

Lovell: Even though I was worried at first, I was happy with the way it turned out. Ron Howard did a great job of directing. When he approached me about doing a movie based on the book, I told him that the ABC television network produced a docudrama in 1971 called, "Houston, We Have a Problem." They used Apollo 13 as a backdrop, but they focused on four fictitious flight controllers. That was the main story. One of them had marital troubles, one of them had child-support problems, one of them had a heart attack, and the fourth one's grandfather died.

I told them they ruined a good story. It had nothing to do with Apollo 13, even though the real story had all the drama required to make a good TV program. They didn't have to make up that stuff. I wrote scathing letters to ABC and to NASA for allowing them to use the facilities. When Ron Howard approached me, I told him to look at the ABC program first. "If you're going to do the same thing," I said, "forget me, because I don't want to be any part of it."

USNI: The big question for many viewers was, "If I know how it ends, how can I stay interested?"

Lovell: He did a great job of keeping the suspense going, and all the incidents in that movie are true. He didn't have to hype anything. His main job, his main concern, was, "What do I throw out?" When he did the first edit, he had a four-hour movie. Universal said, "No way are we going to have a four-hour movie." So he got it all down to a two-hour-and-fifteen-minute movie. That's why I tell people that they'll appreciate the movie more if they read the book first.

USNI: As far as the general public is concerned, do you have any concern that the movie itself will become the historical record?

Lovell: Well, there's always that chance, just like the movie *Patton.* When you think of that movie and you think of Gen. George Patton, what image comes to mind? George C. Scott, right? I've kidded Tom Hanks, saying, "Look, you'd better start learning how to write my name, because when all these photographs come for signatures, I'm sending them to you."

To answer your question, if it has positive results, a positive influence, I couldn't care less.

USNI: At least the story is out there.

Lovell: The true story is out there. That's the reason why I wrote the book. I was very fortunate to get a great co-author, Jeff Kluger, who had never written a book before. I had never written one, either. We both wrote technical journals, but he worked for *Discover* magazine and had a degree in journalism. He wrote me to say he wanted to write a book on Apollo 13. I said that I wanted to do it, too, and that we should do it together. That's how it came to pass.

USNI: In the book, you and Mr. Kluger give high praise to Jules Bergman at ABC News for going through some of the training that the astronauts went through and for being sympathetic with what you were doing. What did you think of the general news coverage back then, and what do you think of it now in comparison?

Lovell: I thought the news coverage in those days was very positive. My wife Marilyn won't give the same accolades to Jules Bergman, only because he was, after all, a newsman. Apollo 13 was Doomsday for Jules—only a 10 percent chance of getting back, the whole business. But he did go through all the training to be fully up to speed. Marilyn would much rather have listened to Walter Cronkite, who had a more fatherly approach to everything.

I think they're covering it pretty well today, too. But you have to realize that human nature says that repetition means people get complacent, and people got complacent about Apollo 13. This was the third lunar-landing mission, but none of the networks carried it. The movie showed some of the subtle things—guys yawning, one of the guys looking at the baseball game on the side. They were all waiting to shut down for the night, because we were going to go to sleep. It was just another day at the office.

Today, with more than seventy shuttle flights, I don't think one network carries shuttle launches. Maybe CNN does, because they think they have an "in" if something goes wrong. For the *Challenger* accident, they were right there. If something unique happens, like the *Mir* docking, they will cover it. And that was, I think, adequately covered. The Hubbell telescope repair also got some coverage. These are all great events. The public just doesn't understand. It was the same way with Apollo 13. For many years people did not appreciate what really went on to get the spacecraft back home again.

I think a lot of people don't understand the successful docking between an ancient space station and a shuttle, or the repair of a telescope out in space, or the capture of a satellite. Again, these are good examples of humans taking over when robots were incapable of getting the job done.

USNI: Do you think we have too many scientists and not enough aviator types? Do the astronauts today, pardon the phrase, have the "right stuff?"

Lovell: I wouldn't want to discriminate between scientists and aviators. I think the people who go into the program—whether they are geologists, physicists, doctors, or pilots—all need a certain amount of adventuresome, risk-taking spirit. They've got to be pioneers, regardless of what their discipline is. We don't need people who know just how to fly airplanes. We do need people who can adapt to an ancient *Mir* space station and to eating Russian food. They've got to learn to be survivors.

USNI: It's often our custom to give our interviewees a parting shot. Here's your chance to address anything we have not covered.

Lovell: I have a couple of things. Number one is the fact that I am very proud to be part of the naval establishment. I think the Navy in all aspects has provided a foundation for space activities in this country. I think our space program, however it forms in the future, will be an important factor in the overall operation of this country.

NASA has the ability to create new technologies. It creates new industries and new products. And it is very much a diplomatic tool.

I recall vividly, when *Sputnik* was launched, the great outcry questioning why we did not have an adequate system to do the same thing. It was that way for a long time. I think the majority of the people today feel that NASA still plays an important role in the U.S. government's efforts to keep this country a leader. So I hope Congress realizes that, and the administration realizes that, so they can stop quibbling year in and year out and vacillating so much that we don't have a clear direction for what we should be doing in the future.

David McCullough

COURTESY OF PBS

Mr. McCullough won the Pulitzer Prize and the National Book Award for his biography of Harry Truman. He hosts the PBS series *The American Experience,* won an Emmy Award for *Smithsonian World,* and lent his unmistakable voice to Ken Burns's *The Civil War.* He is the author of *The Johnstown Flood, The Great Bridge* (the story of the Brooklyn Bridge), *The Path Between the Seas* (about the Panama Canal), *Mornings on Horseback* (a profile of the young Theodore Roosevelt), and *Brave Companions* (essays on historic figures). He is currently finishing a book about John and Abigail Adams. The interview appeared in the February 1994 issue of *Naval History.*

■

USNI: What role do you see *Naval History* magazine playing in the education of the American people?

McCullough: Publications of this kind are fundamental to improving the teaching and the understanding of American history, which is in seriously bad shape right now.

USNI: Could you be specific, as far as naval history goes?

McCullough: I don't think you can understand the history of the country if you don't understand naval history. The Navy is often a barometer of how technology is changing our way of life. The shift from a wooden to an all-steel Navy between the Civil War and World War I, for instance, was one of the major events in the history of this country, not just because it changed the Navy, but also because of what it did to the steel industry. Naval history is always about our place in the world.

USNI: Our place in the world, both physical and philosophical?

McCullough: Exactly. Some of the best books ever written have been about the Navy and naval history. I love *The Caine Mutiny* and Adm. [Samuel Eliot] Morison's marvelous histories of World War II. I love everything from the *Hornblower* series up to and including *The Cruel Sea,* Monsarrat's wonderful book.

One of the things you get in good books about the Navy is the intensity of human relations, because they're all in the same boat, literally and figuratively. It's a writer's and a dramatist's dream, because the stage is defined and confined, and relationships are accentuated in a way that they aren't necessarily on land. It is uncertain, timeless. Something about the sea always spells adventure.

In my view, our country has given too little attention to the sea and to the importance of our merchant fleet. The great days of the clipper ships and American seafaring were some of the most wonderful chapters in our whole story.

You're talking to a guy who wrote a book about the Panama Canal. It's much of our identity. Our sense of who we were at the turn of the century was tied up in creating that canal. Why? Because of our dream of sea power, all that Adm. [Alfred Thayer] Mahan had been writing about and all that Theodore Roosevelt was brimful of. You can't be around ships and not have a sense of history. I don't see how you can. Anywhere you have ships you are going to have stories. Even the great storied cities are seaports.

USNI: Of all the periods in American history, which most interests you?

McCullough: Until I began work on the Truman book, I would have said the period between the end of the Civil War and the start of World War I. It's been my beat for most of my writing life. But I imagine myself being pulled kicking and screaming into the twentieth century by Mr. Truman. The fact that he was in so many ways a nineteenth-century person was chief among his most appealing qualities for me. But having written about his part of the twentieth century, I'm torn.

I love that time after the Civil War, because it was so protean, so productive, so expansive, and in the main positive and creative. That's not to say there weren't tremendous problems, discontent, and anguish.

USNI: Would you say the Industrial Revolution had anything to do with that?

McCullough: That time was both the light and the shadow of the Industrial Revolution. I don't think anyone could have grown up in Pittsburgh as I did and not feel both the exhilaration of all that industry and productivity, but also find something fearful and dehumanizing about it.

History is really about change, and change is the rule of life. So history is about life, if you take it logically. And that was a period of such dramatic as well as fundamental change. Civil engineers were at the forefront of a tremendous shift in emphasis toward science and technology and a romantic aura that Jules Verne made so much of. Science and technology were conferring on mere mortals the powers of the gods. There seemed no end to the possibilities up until World War I, when suddenly all those powers were creating mechanized slaughter—scientific, technological slaughter. We saw the tank, poison gas, and the machine gun used for the first time. Barbed wire no longer just fenced off cattle—it was tearing bodies apart. The dream went sour. But no one knew that in the 1870s, eighties, and nineties. All this was still over the horizon.

It was in a way our adolescence. We were discovering how strong and virile we were and how exciting our life was going to be as a consequence. I don't think there was doubt in anyone's mind then that tomorrow was going to be better than today. That's powerful medicine. It's a tonic for a nation to think things are going to be better for its children.

USNI: Which would you say is the most neglected in time period in American history?

McCullough: I think that period is. It's still wide open. There was a time when many historians dispensed with it as an era of putrid, corrupt politics, gingerbread architecture, and general Gilded-Age hypocrisy throughout. But now, we see it differently. Its painting, its music, and its literature must be taken seriously.

USNI: Do you think oral history tends to get more to the truth than diaries, letters, and memoirs?

McCullough: A historian working in the twentieth century can often gain more from interviews with those who were there than from hours of conventional archival or library research.

Many academic historians disparage and dispense with interviews. Their argument is that we're all inclined to deceive ourselves about what happened, or to put a better shine on our own part in some event.

USNI: It seems the temptation might be greater if one had time to think about it before writing it down, rather than responding off-the-cuff in an interview.

McCullough: The academics say that subjects of an interview will tell you a lot of baloney, a lot of nonsense. That's all quite true, but if you've done the homework, if you've done the necessary preparation before you go into the interview, you can spot that when it comes along. Once in a while you can be taken in, as others could be, but that's a minor risk compared to the enormous gains to be had. I was talking about this point with [historian] Walter Lord, who went on at some length about the need to prepare yourself before an interview. *A Night to Remember*, his excellent book about the *Titanic*, drew praise especially for its wonderful first-person accounts. He told me that, in order to prepare himself for those interviews, he wrote the whole book before he conducted them. Then he took what was valuable or pertinent or useful from the interview and put it into what he had already written.

USNI: Have you done that yourself?

McCullough: I've never gone that far. Before I wrote about the entire course of Harry Truman's war in France, I did go to all the battlefields and the bases where he had been. And I wrote that particular chapter before I went to France for that very reason—so I'd have it in my head.

As you know, nothing fixes things in your mind quite the way writing does. I was an English major. When I started out, I thought that the way you go about it is to do all the research, then write the book. But I haven't worked that way since finishing my first book. I do maybe 60 percent of the research, then I start writing, because it's then that you find out what you don't know and need to know. I think it's a much more effective way to target your research. So I'm researching and writing the whole way through the book. I'm still doing research when the book's in galley.

USNI: Wow!

McCullough: That's what my editor says.

USNI: How can historians and educators get young people interested in history?

McCullough: I think Barbara Tuchman was the one who put it best. She said, "Tell stories." Do everything possible to convey that these were real people, with all the strengths, weaknesses, ambitions, talents, failings, and emotions that we have. What's more interesting than people? I don't know of anything. Who they were and what they did bears directly on who we are, what we do, what we believe, and what we stand for. We walk the same ground, we look up at the same sun, moon, and stars. Even the food we eat tastes no different, really, than it did to them. We have far more in common with them than we have differences.

If you want to convey the reality of the past, do not look upon history as just social issues, politics, and the military. It's everything. And it's essential to understand how everything affected everything else. We can't possibly understand our own time without understanding the impact of science and technology on earlier times. How many history courses even mention, let's say, the advent of the skyscraper, an entirely American phenomenon that completely changed our cities, how we work, where we work, and our notion of American accomplishment?

USNI: Young people tend more and more to expect instant gratification and visual support. If you were confronted with that sort of attitude, how would you handle it?

McCullough: I think if you look back on your own experience, you'll find that the courses and subjects you liked best were taught by the teachers you liked best. And the teachers you liked best were those who were the most enthusiastic and knowledgeable about the subject they were teaching. If the teacher conveys that the subject is interesting, exciting, and worthwhile, the student feels that, too.

If I were to recommend a way by which we could solve this problem nationwide—and it is a nationwide problem in which we are becoming historically illiterate—I would teach the teachers. I would organize two- or three-week seminars all over the country for teachers to hear first-rate lectures and speakers—and other teachers. I think we've got to do much more of what you might call the lab technique in the teaching of humanities. We can learn a lot from the teaching of science and technology. If the student is to learn about something that involves research, by definition that student is going to have to learn a great deal about a lot of other things, too.

I wrote a book about the building of the Brooklyn Bridge. To learn about the bridge, you have to learn about why they built it, the mood of the era in which it was built, what is cost, where the money came from, what happened on each side of the bridge as a consequence of its having been built, and so forth. That's the way you get inoculated. That's the way you catch it.

For a term paper in the course I taught at Cornell I gave every student a photograph—just a simple photograph. No two students got the same one. Each had a simple caption. One might say "American Oil Tanker Being Sunk by German Submarine off the Coast of Florida, February 22, 1942." Whatever it was, that was your photograph and that was your term paper subject. Since no two people had the same photograph, every student was working on an individual, original project. There was no right or wrong answer. They loved it.

USNI: But that still would not work with many of today's younger students. The pictures must move and speak.

McCullough: There's nothing wrong with the students. They have certain expectations of the kind you're talking about, but I think it's relatively easy to go beyond that. Too many teachers are assigned to teach history and have no interest in it. Many schools turn teaching history over to the athletic coaches. Now five states in the country do not require the teaching of American history at all. I'm involved with an organization set up to confront this problem. We have a distinguished group of people assembled.

USNI: What is the name of the group?

McCullough: It's the National Council for History Education. We've gathered material on the current state of history in education that'll make your hair stand on end. This movement began with high school teachers in Ohio. My feeling is that the real progress, the real dramatic change, has to be made at the grade-school level.

USNI: Is there a place for television and other electronic media in teaching history?

McCullough: Of course. I wouldn't be involved with the *American Experience* series if I didn't feel strongly about it. The programs we've been doing have been used extensively around the country. I think we—or somebody—should be doing shorter programs. Ours are an hour. I would like to see half-hour and even fifteen-minute programs. I think someone could do a great deal with what you might call one-person plays, in which a character from the past tells about his life or her experience. I would also like to see a publisher develop a series of plays that children can put on themselves in school, historic plays with maybe ten or fifteen parts. If you're cast as George Washington or Frederick Douglass at age nine, you're never going to forget it.

USNI: How would you describe the general state of popular—as opposed to academic—history today?

McCullough: I think it's very good. I have to say that, because that's what I do. I feel that I work in a school with a long tradition of nonacademic writers who write history. People like Margaret Leech, Bruce Catton, Shelby Foote, obviously Barbara Tuchman, Paul Horgan, Wallace Stegner, and, more recently, Robert Massie, Jean Strouse, Robert Caro, and William Manchester, are almost without exception people who began as writers. Many started as journalists who later found their territory, so to speak, in the past. They tend to write very well and their research is as good as or better than the rest. And they reach a large audience. One way to interest more Americans in history is for historians to start talking to the people—not just to other historians. They have more of a public responsibility to fulfill, in my view. Their duty is not just to themselves.

I can't understand how anyone could not be interested in history. And I don't think it ought to be strictly the franchise or the territory of a select priesthood. It belongs to all of us, and the more we understand it, the more we communicate it, the better for everybody. The system of academic life does not reward the academic historian for reaching the general public. In fact, in some quarters the attitude is that if it's popular, it can't be very good.

I hope I write for everyone. I try to write the kind of book that I, as a reader, would like to read. After all, we were all readers before we were writers, and we like to think we're pretty discriminating. So I struggled and found it not only possible, but enormously stimulating and invigorating. I loved it. And I was hooked. Now, the pull of our country's story is irresistible to me.

The people involved were what drew me to each of my subjects. I am convinced that if you don't understand the people, then you don't understand why things happen the way they happen.

To me, it was thrilling to discover how much I could learn about people who, even when they were alive, were not well known, or were not figures in history, with a capital H.

USNI: You discovered those people just by the trail they left behind?

McCullough: Yes. Their wonderful letters and diaries give you the thrill of holding the original letters in your hand and of sorting through the memorabilia, the scrapbooks, the field notes, and the remnants of a life.

The subject matter is inexhaustible. Once having written about a subject, I never lose interest in it. I'm still very interested in new material about Panama or the Brooklyn Bridge, and I know I will always be interested in new material that turns up about Truman. And it will turn up. Things will come to light that I don't know about, that maybe nobody knows about right now.

USNI: It seems as though the reputations of historical figures go through cycles. When he first left the presidency, Truman was considered a failure by many, a well-meaning man who just didn't measure up. Even you said at one time that many people took him as a sort of cosmic hick—a sort of Will Rogers in the White House. Then, in the mid-1970s, he suddenly became a cult figure. And after John F. Kennedy was killed, he was practically deified. Now, suddenly, a recent biography paints a rather unpleasant portrait. What would you say contributes to those cycles in a figure's historical reputation?

McCullough: Part of it is the effect of comparison. We see Truman now not just as he was, but in contrast to those who have come after him in the same office. He becomes a rare commodity, in effect. I think it takes about fifty years before the dust settles and you can start to see how it looks. It's like standing back from an Impressionist painting. You have to stand back from it to appreciate it properly. It's much too soon to tell about Ronald Reagan or George Bush or Jimmy Carter. We're also building on new material and new interpretations. There is no such thing as a "definitive biography." It's like "the foreseeable future." It doesn't exist.

USNI: In your opinion, who are among the most overrated and the most underrated figures in American history?

McCullough: I think the most overrated figure is George Armstrong Custer.

USNI: He's still interesting, though.

McCullough: Oh, you bet! And he's box office, he'll always be box office. He takes the dive. He's the Evel Knievel of military history.

The most underrated would be Jimmy Carter. I think his stock will continue to rise, in part because of his exemplary conduct since he left the White House. I don't think anyone has been a more admirable former president than Jimmy Carter has been. He's an example that the others should take to heart.

Generally speaking, I've felt strongly for a long time that the civil engineers—the technicians of American life in the period after the Civil War before World War I—were greatly underrated. The most underrated person in American life, or one of the most underrated figures, is Everyman, the ordinary anonymous American citizen of the last two hundred years.

USNI: Why do you say that?

McCullough: It's hard to be celebratory in portraying someone if you have very little to work with. And we don't pile up vast quantities of historical fodder from just ordinary folks. While it's easy to rhapsodize about seeing history from the ground up, or seeing the enlisted view of life more than we have in the past, it's also very hard to do it accurately without writing from conjecture and sentiment. That's why it's so important when a great body of letters comes to light from one of the unsung people. Part of the power and appeal of what Bruce Catton did so long ago was his writing about ordinary Civil War soldiers.

But people today don't write letters and keep diaries. Future historians are going to find it virtually impossible to write about us. What are we going to leave? They're going to think we talked like business memoranda. They're going to think that's the way we talked, and worse, the way we thought. The modern Everyman could be lost to historians.

USNI: That brings to mind a quote from Herbert Hoover that went something like "When you celebrate the common man, too often you celebrate mediocrity." How do you respond to that?

McCullough: In part, Harry Truman is the argument against that thesis. If Harry Truman was an ordinary fellow, then the ordinary is extraordinary. When I was working on the Panama Canal book, I read all the reports filed by the expedition to Central America. Most of these went out during the Grant administration, led almost without exception by naval officers. I was so impressed, so in awe, not only of what the expeditions accomplished under difficult and dangerous conditions, but by the clarity and grace of the writing in what they filed. And they didn't have any public relations adviser brushing up their prose and cleaning up their syntax. These were written by relatively young Naval Academy graduates, who clearly had been well educated in the use of the language. Those were admirable people. Extraordinary people turn up in the least likely places, in all forms and in all professions.

I like a good story. That's what really draws me. It's all well and good to say something was very important or someone was very admirable, but if it isn't a story it doesn't interest me. That's number one on my list of priorities.

USNI: Speaking of good stories, can you give us a preview of any projects you're working on?

McCullough: I'm poking around in about a dozen different ideas. So far the bug hasn't bitten, but it will. It just sort of has to resolve itself. It may sound strange, but I sometimes think my subjects pick me. It can be a chance remark at lunch, or happening upon some newspaper article, or hearing something that somebody down at the Naval Institute says in passing.

Some of my friends kid me for being obsessed with water. Justin Kaplan in a review once called me the Herodotus of hydraulics, or something to that effect, because of my having written about the Johnstown Flood, the Brooklyn Bridge, and the Panama Canal—first you're inundated by it, next you go over it, then you channel it. I think I wrote the Truman book in part to prove him wrong. But I feel the old water pull at work again. It would be great fun to write a really rip-snorting sea story. If I see the right thing, it sort of clicks. The bug bites. It just happens.

William Readdy

COURTESY OF NASA

Capt. William F. Readdy, U.S. Naval Reserve, commanded several space shuttle missions and is currently heading the shuttle office at NASA headquarters in Washington, D.C. The interview appeared in the February 1997 issue of the Naval Institute's *Proceedings.*

■

USNI: Since you served on the *Forrestal* [CV-59] and *Coral Sea* [CV-43] and flew A-6s, how do you feel, now that all three have been laid to rest?

Readdy: Well, it's sad. The January [1997] issue of *Air and Space* magazine reports on turning A-6s into an artificial reef off the coast of Florida. I probably flew many of those airplanes.

The A-6 performed its intended mission in spectacular fashion, but it was getting a little bit long in the tooth. The F/A-18 series—the E and F, in particular—surpassed it. Even though the time had come to retire it, I'll always have a soft spot in my heart for the A-6.

USNI: What role did your naval service play in preparing you for a career in the space program?

Readdy: Its influence is probably as large as the entire time I spent in the Navy—the foundation I got at the Naval Academy in aeronautical engineering, the different disciplines I learned as a young officer operating in a squadron, flight training itself and growing up in the fleet, being forced to make decisions in an aircraft, and being a naval test pilot. I think that my naval career was a fantastic launching pad, if you will, for a career as an astronaut. I learned a wide variety of things in the Navy that I put directly to use as a shuttle commander.

USNI: How important is military service in becoming an astronaut? Is it as important as it used to be? It seemed as though all astronauts at one time had some sort of military background. Now, it's not necessarily so.

Readdy: No, it's not necessarily so. But if you think of how the whole business has evolved, it's not purely flight test and evaluation. It's not purely hand-eye coordination and manual piloting. So much of it now, especially as we gear up in the space-station era, is more directly like working in a laboratory. So more than half of the office is composed of PhDs and medical doctors, because much of the research we're going to do in the future will be exploration of the human body, microbiology, physics, astronomy, and other hard sciences. So I'd say that probably half or more of the astronauts from now on are going to be chosen from the scientific and the medical communities.

USNI: At one point the shuttle and the space station were poised to play major roles in military operations. For various apparent reasons, that all seems to have changed. What role will the shuttle play in future military space missions?

Readdy: For starters, the whole world has changed. The Department of Defense [DoD] was one of the original customers of the space shuttle, which has launched DoD and other national payloads. That's the way it was always intended. It's a national resource. But certainly no one could have anticipated that the balance of power in the world would shift so dramatically.

The payload complement of the shuttle, of course, has also evolved more toward international space-station development, more toward scientific payloads. The DoD flights have tapered off at this point, but the shuttle still has a military role to play. I think this role will probably be pivotal in extending the first two space radar lab missions into a third one, which will be in partnership with the DoD to map the globe. Once and for all, we will have a digital database of the entire globe, if you can imagine that and the kind of things that will enable in terms of geodesy.

We constantly find that parts of the world are improperly charted. Now, we have a global positioning system [GPS]—a constellation of satellites that has been so useful in just about every walk of life, whether it's out camping in the wilderness or on a sailboat in the middle of the ocean. It's just about beyond imagining how many different applications there can be for GPS. But it's valuable only if you can tie it to terrestrial coordinates.

If those are properly mapped, then the two synchronize nicely. The applications are clear for civil aviation: being able to chart the world so that your on-board navigation system knows not only where it is, but what the altitude of the terrain is. Even without radar, you can avoid the terrain in all types of weather. The safety applications of that alone are just phenomenal.

USNI: So the shuttle is more of a commercial enterprise these days than it once was.

Readdy: I'm not sure I'd use the word "commercial," necessarily. NASA has been trying to develop the commercial launch industry, and you have seen traditionally military booster rockets such as the Delta and the Atlas develop more and more into commercial launch platforms. NASA is not in competition with the commercial world as a vehicle for launching communication satellites. We are in the technology business, in partnership with industry developing new technologies, and the satellites we launch are going to advance the state of the art of scanning the universe.

USNI: Given the new international cooperation in space, namely, between the Russians and Americans, do you foresee a time when some sort of international consortium will design and build the next generation of spacecraft?

Readdy: We are already cooperating on the international space station. It is truly international in that the Russians are one of the partners, and they're making significant contributions in terms of launches, logistics, and modules. The shuttle missions to the *Mir* are just stepping stones, developing the operational techniques, the interfaces, to take the next step. We'll continue that series until we start building the space station.

Commercial joint ventures are currently being negotiated between Russian and American firms, between Rockwell and the Energia works in Moscow, between Lockheed and the Krunachev Rocket Factory in Moscow. They are in their infancy, but the international space station may become a springboard to launch some future effort, perhaps back to the Moon, which would be a likely place to prototype the hardware required to go farther, maybe to Mars.

USNI: Russia does not have a shuttle or anything similar to it.

Readdy: Not today. The Russians developed their own space shuttle, called *Buran*, which means "snowstorm." As a matter of fact, they were thinking of flying it in 1988 to precede STS-26 in our own return to flight after the *Challenger* accident.

Buran was a major development effort for them. It was produced by Energia, and it was similar to [our] space shuttle in many aspects. When we formed this joint partnership, the Russians had always planned to have a shuttle-like vehicle to resupply their space station, and they were planning to launch a next-generation *Mir* station. Of course, we already had an operational space shuttle program, so the marriage was obvious.

USNI: How difficult was it adjusting to flying spacecraft as opposed to aircraft?

Readdy: There are many similarities. The launch phases of the space shuttle are very similar to being catapulted off a pitching carrier flight deck at night. Most of that is in the hands of the catapult officer. My hand is on the stick, but that's only to talk on the radio or to push the engage button if I need to take control. It's eight and a half minutes versus three seconds, but it's still the same kind of ride, the same kind of physical sensation.

Once you get on orbit, it's a spacecraft for a week and a half or two weeks. It's very much like life at sea. Everything has to be shipshape, you stand watches, and it's very much a team environment.

Rendezvous and docking, I'd say, are like any kind of coordinated operation at sea where you have a formation of ships or aircraft. I'd liken the final approach and the physical docking to flying formation and finally doing aerial refueling. The tolerances are similar in that we're talking about inches and very small increments of closure, typically about an inch a second when you finally dock. You're working with a 100-ton orbiter and 120-ton space station, so you want to do everything very carefully, and you want the alignment to be precise.

USNI: What about reentry?

Readdy: For our landing at the Kennedy Space Center, which occurred just after sunrise, we did our deorbit burn over Australia. That was the last powered event of our flight. From Australia, our orbital track took us over the Pacific in darkness. As we started to sink into the atmosphere, we were surrounded by a pink-orange glow so bright we could read our checklists by it. We were into a right-hand turn pretty much the entire time. Our orbital path took us over Vancouver, British Columbia, then Chicago, then down the Appalachians, and over Cecil Field, Florida. We arrived over the Kennedy Space Center at about fifty-five thousand feet at Mach 1 and then started a right-hand turn all the way around, landing on Runway 15, after about four million miles over ten days and 160 orbits.

The actual manual flying of the orbiter was much like flying a dive-bombing pattern. The outer approach is a 20-degree dive at three hundred knots and then at about seventeen hundred feet you shallow to an interglide slope of about a degree to a degree and a half. You put the landing gear down at three hundred feet above the ground and then continue to decelerate to land at a speed of approximately two hundred knots.

That entire evolution, I think, is similar to coming on board a ship. The tolerances are very exacting. Even though the runway is long, no engines are running at this point, so you're intent on flying the proper glide slopes. As soon as you touch down, you deploy the drag chute and then lower the nose to the runway. The drag chute is so powerful that you need only the absolute minimum amount of braking. We stop with three thousand feet of runway remaining.

USNI: How big a blow was the failure of the hatch to open during STS-80 in November 1996, thus preventing space walks that were to test space-station building techniques?

Readdy: It was a big surprise, quite frankly. I'm sure we could have opened the hatch if we had really wanted to, but a space walk was low on the list of priorities for that particular flight. It was one of those nice-to-do activities. So the decision was made not to risk opening the hatch and have it jam in an intermediate position while trying to get it closed.

No black magic is involved. If it's an engineering problem, we'll figure it out and fix it. I can guarantee you that as long as we continue flying in space there will be other surprises. Our job is to minimize them. I'm sure we'll run this one to ground and we won't have this problem again. It was certainly disappointing for the crew members who had trained to evaluate tools and techniques for a space station, but those same objectives will just wind up on another flight downstream. One primary objective for the flight was to deploy the wake shield facility and to grow ultrapure materials in space for microelectronics. The other was to deploy an ultraviolet telescope and retrieve it at the end of the flight. Each of those was accomplished.

USNI: You say surprises happen all the time. Did anything surprise you on your latest mission?

Readdy: Shortly after we got into orbit, after main engine cutoff, our Number Two auxiliary power unit [APU] shut down inexplicably. Nothing on board indicated any malfunction, and the ground team pulled all their data and looked at it for days. We were concerned—because there was no obvious explanation, from where we were sitting—that the mission might be shortened. We had contingency plans for expedited transfer and rendezvous, so we were thinking seriously about it.

The ground team was confident that we would not have a recurrence on any of the other APUs. As it turns out, detailed troubleshooting revealed that, in the most recent design change of the APUs, the polarity of two wires in the drawings was changed. So all APUs on all the orbiters were rewired before they were cleared to fly again.

USNI: What about the next stage of the shuttle? Some of these orbiters seem to be getting a bit old.

Readdy: It seems to some people that we've been flying these things for a long time. The shuttles have been around since 1981, so they've been flying for fifteen years. But each individual orbiter, the airplane portion of it, was intended to fly a hundred missions. And we're nearing about twenty missions on each orbiter. So they still have an incredible amount of life left in them from their original design. I flew A-6s off the *Coral Sea.* That was flying a thirty-five-year-old airplane off a forty-five-year-old aircraft carrier, neither of which got the kind of tender loving care that the orbiters do.

These things are young pups—teenagers. They're at 20 percent of their intended lifetime, and there isn't any reason to think that they wouldn't be flying for the next fifteen or twenty years. There are several second-, third-, and fourth-generation spinoffs that I'm sure NASA would like to take advantage of in terms of increased payload, reliability, reduced maintenance time per mission—all the things you would typically do with a fleet airplane over its lifetime. It has happened to every airplane that I've flown in the Navy. I think it's going to be at least fifteen years before we have a new launch system to replace the space shuttle.

USNI: Do you think we will live to see a Man-to-Mars mission?

Readdy: Without question. If we really wanted to throw money at the problem, I think we could have gone to Mars ten years ago. It's no longer a question of technology.

At this point, I think we need to focus on advances in propulsion technology rather than spending tens of billions of dollars on a mission that will take the better part of a year to get there and almost the same amount of time to come back. Just as the jet engine eclipsed the propeller in World War II and the rocket engine was the enabling technology for our initial exploration of space, there is going to be another advance in propulsion technology. The science fiction writers, I'm sure, already know what it is. Whatever it is, it will open exploration beyond the Moon.

USNI: Will the Mars spacecraft be more Apollo-like or shuttle-like?

Readdy: The initial Apollo spacecraft was going to look like a kind of rocket ship that landed on its tail rather than a lander that left the base of a larger craft. During Apollo, we ended up doing lunar rendezvous, in which the landing craft detached from the service module, went down to the surface, did a lunar orbit rendezvous back up to the command and service module, and then eventually jettisoned what was left into the surface of the Moon.

Mars has a different atmosphere and a different gravity, factors that will dictate whatever kind of lander you choose. I doubt if it's going to be any kind of winged aircraft, because the atmosphere is corrosive with dust and wind.

With budgets shrinking, the possibility of mobilizing an Apollo-sized effort is slim—even with the results we have from recently discovered Martian asteroid fragments, the micrometeorites that landed in the Antarctic. I'm not sure that's a compelling enough argument to demand a human mission to Mars within the decade. Of course, that's what President [John F.] Kennedy directed for a Moon landing in the early 1960s.

USNI: What recommendations do you have for young people contemplating a career in the space program?

Readdy: Currently, the different career fields that would compel one to get into the astronaut business are virtually unlimited. The space program favors any kind of hard science—biomedicine, chemistry, physics, astronomy, astrophysics. The number of possibilities is almost endless.

My advice would be to do whatever you're truly interested in, and do it with the most professionalism that you can, so that you can be competitive. It's a very competitive process. There may be four thousand applicants for a dozen jobs when NASA comes looking for volunteers. You need to do something that you enjoy, because the odds are so staggering against being selected. It has to be worth doing in and of itself—not just a means to an end.

I am sure the number of people who fly in space will increase over the years. I'm sure, for instance, that we'll have people living in space, on the Moon, and elsewhere. But for the moment, the number of possibilities in terms of being a crew member are limited.

To a young naval officer, I would say the same thing. Warfare specialty makes no difference. I know during the last go-round that we were looking at submariners, Civil Engineering Corps officers, surface warfare officers, and certainly aviators and flight officers. All the career fields in the Navy now have become so technical and specialized that it's almost a logical extension into the technical, specialized world of the astronaut business. One last thing: When NASA comes looking for volunteers, be sure to raise your hand. If you don't raise your hand, they can't pick you. Don't ever count yourself out.

USNI: Do you perceive a public relations problem with the space program? It seems that something could be done to stimulate more interest with the general public.

Readdy: First of all, the space program is not only fascinating, it's necessary. It is one of the few investments we actually make in our future. Most people don't understand what a trivial amount is spent. Less than a penny out of every federal tax dollar has built everything we have done in space, including not only the space hardware but all the NASA field centers and all the contracts across the country. We're also talking about educational programs. All the money is spent on this planet, in this country, developing technologies that have been the enabling link for things such as electron microscopes, ultrasound imagery, portable pacemakers—things that make life better on Earth.

I think it's a very compelling story and one that most people in the media know. But it's not always popular, because it's perceived as a choice on Capitol Hill—housing or space, welfare or space, people programs or space. In fact, what we do in space is a people program.

It is still exploring, it is still adventure, it is still the future. And that kind of sells itself. I think the trouble lies with people who tend to get a little bit jaded as they grow older. They grew up with the space program. It's like having grown up with color TV and not remembering that it wasn't always there.

I think the space program is a fantastic national treasure. It's something that continues to keep the United States at the forefront. If you want to see what would happen to this country if we stopped leading the world in communications and aerospace technology, just look at the U.S. automobile and steel industries in the last twenty to thirty years. I don't think we want that to happen to our country in the aerospace world, where we continue to have an edge.

USNI: What is your forecast for the future of the space program?

Readdy: We're building the future right now. We're already doing the test and evaluation on the international space station hardware, and not only building and testing it on the ground. In fact, STS-79 flew some space-station hardware to give it a shakedown cruise.

The first launch of the space station is going to occur in November 1997. That's what we'll be building for the next five to six years. At that point, the space station will be on orbit for decades as a research platform. Its crews not only will be doing planetary science, meteorology, and characterizing the world's environments, they also will track the functions of the human body in space.

When you're able to subtract gravity from the equation, you're better able to understand human physiological effects—on the vestibular system, for example. It turns out that osteoporosis has quite a parallel to what we experience in long-duration space flight—porosity and loss of bone mass over a long period of time. So we will be able to tackle many scientific issues.

USNI: How much did we learn from Shannon Lucid's unintentional longevity in space?

Readdy: We had already learned a tremendous amount from our Skylab astronauts twenty years ago. We had our own space station in Skylab, and the final crew on board flew for three months. We've also learned a tremendous amount from our Russian colleagues, and we've had two long-duration crew members of our own, Dr. Norman Thagard and Dr. Shannon Lucid. I think folks have forgotten that Norm got to spend an extra month in space waiting for the *Specter* module to arrive and then for the *Atlantis* to get up there for the first docking mission.

Shannon got to spend an extra six weeks waiting for the *Atlantis* again, but I think that shows you the tremendous versatility of the space shuttle. In a little bit over a year we have flown the *Atlantis* with four different cargo bay configurations to four different *Mir* station configurations. It's amazing what a versatile workhorse we have in the space shuttle, and I think it is definitely going to be the mainstay for building an international space station.

Thomas E. Ricks

GREG E. MATHIESON / MAI

Mr. Ricks is the Pentagon correspondent for *The Washington Post.* He delivered the following remarks at the U.S. Naval Institute's 124th Annual Meeting and 8th Annapolis Seminar in April 1998.

■

I want to address what I fear may be a decline in American military professionalism. But I want to begin by talking about a dog I saw when I was writing my book about the Marine Corps.

I was in Hartsville, South Carolina, visiting a former Marine. The guy had been an artillery officer for a few years during the Vietnam War, but had been out for twenty years. I walked into his house, and he said, "Mr. Ricks, meet my dog, Brittany."

I said, "Hi, Brittany."

He said, "Brittany, tell Mr. Ricks, would you rather be in the Army or be dead?" And the dog rolls over and puts his four paws in the air. I thought to myself, "Now that's one powerful culture that the Marine Corps has. Not only is the guy thinking like a Marine after twenty years out, his *dog* is thinking like a Marine."

I want to focus today on how to preserve the warrior culture, and on the threats to it. Specifically, I want to focus on what I consider to be an internal threat to the warrior culture. By that, I mean the decline of American military professionalism, to borrow a phrase I first heard from Richard Kohn, a military historian at the University of North Carolina.

The argument I want to make is that, partly as a result of the attacks on military culture in recent years, the officer corps has become less professional in its outlook and behavior. In reaction to those attacks we have seen a creeping politicization of the officer corps. This rightward movement is, I believe, an inappropriate response. A much more powerful and appropriate response would be to return to the longstanding U.S. military tradition of nonpartisanship.

Let me tell you up front here that I have no military experience. I speak as a largely admiring outsider who spends a lot of time around the U.S. military. I hope you will listen to me, but I hope you will also listen to the views of people with far more experience than I, such as Adm. Stan Arthur, who argues that there is an increasingly large and worrisome gap between the military and American society.

What do I see changing in American military professionalism?

First, I see a sense of separation between this military and this society. This is not a thought original with me. I think Admiral Arthur put it best in his essay, published by the Army War College, in which he worried that the U.S. military thinks it has become better than the society that it protects. In the same vein, I see a tendency in some military commentary these days to dwell on the weaknesses of American society without seeing the strengths of our society. This is a bit ironic, because today, for the first time in twenty-five years, we have an economy that is the envy of the world.

There was a small story deep in the foreign pages of *The Wall Street Journal* this week that said the United States has replaced Japan as the most competitive nation in the world economy. We now enjoy the lowest peacetime unemployment rate since Eisenhower was president—and it is occurring even as we enact a free trade agreement that some predicted would suck jobs out of this country. Over the last twenty-five years, since the oil shock of 1973, this society has made a dynamic transition from having an industrial-based economy to having an information-based economy. The rest of the world is struggling to keep up with that change.

I think that many in the U.S. military fail to appreciate the immensity of that transformation. I sometimes wonder if we actually have moved to a maneuver warfare society, yet still have an attrition-oriented military. The writer Ralph Peters commented recently that we have a military that all too often talks Sherman but acts McClellan. I agree. Who do you think knows more about maneuver warfare, the information warriors at Microsoft, or the Army officers who talk expeditionary, but want to upgrade a seventy-ton tank?

Anybody who has read my book knows that I am an admirer of Marine Corps culture. It is healthy culture, one that works. It is flexible and adaptive. It is more intellectually supple than the other services. Even so, every other Marine captain I meet seems to believe that American society is troubled, even collapsing. Yes, this society does face major problems. We need especially to do a better job of educating our youth intellectually and morally. But I do not think, as some have argued in the *Marine Corps Gazette* in recent years, that the next war that the U.S. military fights will be on American soil.

The second trend I see is the politicization of the officer corps. Until recently, this was purely anecdotal—the cracks we've all heard, when we are in official or semi-official settings, about President Bill Clinton. But lately statistical evidence has emerged to support this anecdotal evidence. Duke University professor Ole R. Holsti last summer released data that confirm that not only has the American military grown more conservative over the last twenty years, but also more partisan.

It turns out that every four years since 1976, Professor Holsti, who is a specialist in foreign policy and public opinion, had polled four thousand Americans listed in *Who's Who* on their views on foreign policy and politics. He also had polled people attending the National War College and senior officers at the Pentagon. But, not being a specialist in military affairs, he never had separated out his data on the views of military officers. When he did, the results were startling.

In 1976 one-third of senior military officers interviewed said that they were Republicans. In 1996, that share had doubled to two-thirds. The ratio of conservatives to liberals in the military went from about four to one in 1976, which is about where I would expect a culturally conservative, hierarchical institution like the U.S. military to be, to twenty-three to one in 1996. This came even as you have more women and minorities in the senior officer corps—which indicates to me that a big chunk of the white male officer corps is marching toward Rush Limbaugh territory. For the purposes of comparison, this rightward swing came as there was a much smaller shift toward conservatism in civilians polled by Professor Holsti. They were 25 percent Republican in 1976 and 34 percent in 1996.

But the most worrisome trend that Professor Holsti detected was a sharp decline in nonpartisanship. This used to be the single largest category in the U.S. officer corps: independent, nonpolitical, or no identification. In 1976, more than half of officers polled said that they were independent or nonpartisan. Now, only a quarter say they are.

Evidence from the field suggests that these numbers are accurate. When I was in California in December, for example, a Marine told me that his commander routinely played the commentaries of Rush Limbaugh over the loudspeakers, so, the commander explained, everyone can enjoy it while they work. Whether or not you like Rush Limbaugh, to play that sort of commentary for your unit during duty hours strikes me as unprofessional.

What all this indicates, I think, is a major change, largely unreviewed, in the nature of the U.S. military professional. In *The Soldier and the State*, the classic text on U.S. civil-military relations, Professor Samuel Huntington said that nonpartisanship is a pillar of U.S. military tradition. It appears to me that over the last twenty years, that pillar has begun to crumble.

Yes, there are historical reasons for this to occur—it is explainable. The Vietnam War destroyed the hawkish wing of the Democratic Party associated with Henry "Scoop" Jackson. After that war, many people who were pro-defense no longer felt there was a home for them in the Democratic Party. At the same time, white Southerners as a class moved toward open identification with the Republican Party. But explainable is not the same thing as excusable.

Why should this trend be worrisome? For many reasons, most of them obvious, about the relationship between our military and our democracy.

But one important reason may not be so obvious: It can hurt military effectiveness. Historically, politicization of the officer corps has led to military ineffectiveness. When people are promoted for their political views, rather than their combat leadership or management skills, military effectiveness suffers. Take it far enough and you get a banana republic military, one that by definition is better at politics than at fighting.

Combine these two overarching trends—a separation from society and a politicization—and you move toward having what Harvard political scientist Michael Desch has called a "semi-autonomous military." It is, I think, a military that is not always responsive to civilian control, one that in some ways is beginning to act as its own interest group. I worry sometimes that the traditional rivalries among the services are now being extended to other Washington players, so that the way the Army, Navy, and Air Force used to jostle each other is now being applied to their interactions with the White House and the Congress. This can lead to trouble.

When you start acting like an interest group, when you start playing in politics, you're going up against the heavy hitters in their game, not yours. I think we got a whiff of this with Senate Majority Leader Trent Lott's demands to the Navy last year over shipbuilding contracts for his home state. One of his aides sent a note to the Navy with the title, "How To Make an Unhappy Man Happy." It read like a multi-billion-dollar ransom note: Nice Navy you got there, terrible if something were to happen to it. This is the same Trent Lott, who in the middle of the Kelly Flinn mess, told the Air Force to "get real."

What is happening here? This is, I think, the U.S. military being treated like an interest group by people who say, "Okay, you want to play politics, let's play politics." I think we got another whiff of this from 1992 to 1995 on Bosnia policy, with a chairman of the Joint Chiefs and a U.S. military in Europe determined not to go into Bosnia and doing their best to undercut explicit national policy on Bosnia. This begins with Gen. Colin Powell running an op-ed piece in the middle of the 1992 presidential campaign opposing candidate Bill Clinton's view on Bosnia, which was the single largest foreign policy issue in that campaign. We subsequently saw a variety of actions by the U.S. military in Europe as it split with the Clinton administration's policy that the Bosnians were the victims of Serb aggression. I wonder if that opposition interfered with the Army's planning for Bosnia.

I remember standing in December 1995 on the Bosnia end of that blown-up bridge over the Sava River that leads from Croatia down into

Tuzla and talking to an engineer from the First Armored Division. I said, "Didn't you guys realize you'd have to do this?" He said, "Sir, until five weeks ago, we never thought we were coming here." This was a guy who, it seems to me, had been misled by his superiors about the likelihood of a U.S. intervention in Bosnia.

I'm not saying that there should not be military dissent. In fact, I think the great tradition of loyal dissent in the military needs to be revived. It is clearly the obligation of the military professional to give his or her best opinion, most especially when the superiors are perceived to be moving in the wrong direction. But I think thought needs to be given to the proper mode of dissent.

As Eliot Cohen has observed, think of how difficult it would have been for President [Franklin D.] Roosevelt back in World War II, when he overruled the advice of his senior military leaders and decided to invade North Africa. Think of how much more difficult his job would have been if he had to consider what that dispute would look like two days later when it was pasted all over the front pages of *The Washington Post*, *The New York Times*, and *The Wall Street Journal.* There is a lot to be said for arguing the policy until the point of decision, and then moving out smartly and executing that decision with all your might.

I want to leave you with two broad questions and a few thoughts about remedies.

My first question has to do with the kind of puritanical swing I see going on in parts of the U.S. military these days. In the Marines especially, I frequently encounter an open religiosity, wearing one's religion on one's sleeve, that I think has unintended side effects. It can encourage hypocrisy, for example: A Marine officer told me recently that he thought his colonel was becoming more openly religious the closer the promotion board got. It's not just the Marines, though. An officer at the Air Force Academy told me that if you don't attend the Monday morning Bible meeting in his department, you were out of the loop for the week. Is it appropriate to begin a lunch meeting at the Pentagon with an open prayer to Jesus Christ? Is it appropriate on the Army's new Officer Efficiency Report to ask for the judgment on the morality of the officer in question? What happens if the person making that judgment believes that abortion is immoral, and the officer being rated recently had a perfectly legal abortion, perhaps to ensure that she could deploy to the Gulf to fly her attack helicopter? Could the great and colorful leaders of the past, the Chesty Pullers, the George Pattons, pass the sort of tests we see nowadays?

The other question may prove the most significant. This is one first posed by Andrew Bacevich, a retired Army colonel who now teaches at Boston University. What, he asked, will happen to a politicized and conservative U.S. military when it finds out that congressional conservatives are not necessarily pro-military? We got a hint of this with Senator Lott's comments about Lieutenant [Kelly] Flinn a year ago.

I doubt it will be the Democrats who take the defense budget down $20 billion dollars to $50 billion dollars annually. They are too vulnerable in that area—they resemble the schoolboy nervously whistling past the school bully, saying to the Pentagon, "Look, we'll give you $250 billion dollars a year as long as you promise not to beat us up." A Republican in the White House will not have that problem. If a deficit hawk such as John Kasich lives in the White House in a few years, he might look at the Social Security problem and decide to solve it by trimming the defense budget—the domestic equivalent of Nixon going to China. What then happens to a politicized military? Would the toothpaste crawl back in the tube? Or would it become more alienated, more distrustful of the political system? I think anyone who points to problems is obliged also try to offer solutions. What can be done?

First, I think we need to reflect on what it means to be a professional military officer nowadays. There are a lot of assumptions out there, not all of them correct. Today's junior officer seems to assume that to be an officer is to be a Republican. You see this in surveys out of the Naval Academy and out of West Point. Also, Lieutenant Flinn, a junior officer, seemed to assume that it is okay to disobey orders if you really, really dislike them. I think that the conservative "Lieutenant Limbaugh" and the insubordinate Lieutenant Flinn are both wrong, and in the same way: Both have fallen away from military traditionalism.

As part of that reflection, we need to think about reviving the tradition of loyal dissent, to think about the proper channels for military dissent.

Second, we need to think about ways to narrow the gap between the American military and society. I would love to see the draft reinstated, but I don't think that is going to happen. There are other things that can be done short of that. Expand ROTC at elite institutions, such as the Ivy League. Expand Navy and Marine ROTC at historically black colleges. If the Navy says it can't find the engineers it needs, the Marines can go it alone—they need an awful lot of grunts who don't need to know anything about engineering. The Army has ten thousand black officers. Why? Because for decades it has had a very strong presence in historically black colleges. There were, the last time I looked, about a thousand black officers in the Marine Corps. You need to go ask.

Related to this gap, you might also shorten the service requirement attached to attending Annapolis and other academies, so that you get more people cycling back out into society. There is a declining number of veterans in Congress. If you're not going to have people who understand the military in Congress, you're going to have trouble. For the same reason, send officers needing graduate work, whenever possible, to civilian institutions.

Use the reserves more creatively. From my perspective, the reserves have been abused in recent years, almost cavalierly. In 1995 I hitched a ride to central Haiti to spend some time with a Special Forces A Team. The guy who drove me up was a reservist who was the manager of a Federal Express office in Atlanta, yet they assigned him to six months of driving a HumVee. Who do you think knew more about "just-in-time" logistics, the guy driving the HumVee, or the colonel in charge of logistics? Another example: Everybody these days loves to talk about information warfare, but is there a reserve unit of information warriors in Silicon Valley? The reserves could be a real bridge to American society.

Finally, on the enlisted side, Admiral Arthur has suggested that we need to think about prep schools for the enlisted, just as you have for the academies. Expensive, yes, but if you want to build a bridge to American society, it's a good thing to think about.

In conclusion, I think that the answer to attacks on the warrior culture is not to become politically conservative. That sort of reaction, I think, is part of the problem, not part of the solution. It compounds the problem by further warping military culture. I think the answer is to re-assert military traditionalism. Of course, saying that is the easy part. The hard part is how you do it in the environment of the 1990s. How does military traditionalism fit into a gender-integrated military? Answering that question is difficult. I think you begin by enforcing standards, which aren't political. How you answer the question may be one of the most significant acts the younger people here perform in their military careers.

Robert Timberg

LINDA MCCABE / U.S. NAVAL INSTITUTE

Mr. Timberg is chief of *The Baltimore Sun's* Washington bureau. He is a 1964 graduate of the U.S. Naval Academy and a combat veteran, U.S. Marine Corps, of the Vietnam War. He is the author of the highly acclaimed story of five Naval Academy graduates with ties to the Reagan administration, *The Nightingale's Song.*

■

I cannot help being struck by an amazing contrast—between a conflict that was a defining event in my life and a new reality. Things have changed. My son Craig, who is twenty-five, vacationed recently in Vietnam. He and his fiancée biked through the Mekong Delta, into the Central Highlands, then up Route 1 over the Hai Van Pass to Hué, where they caught a bus to Hanoi. I spoke to Craig there by telephone. The small hotel where he was staying plays the theme from the movie, *The Sting*, when it puts you on hold. They were headed for Haiphong the next day. On their journey they stopped and paid their respects at some familiar places—Quang Ngai, Chu Lai, Da Nang, An Hoa, The Arizona Valley, Hué, Khe Sanh, The Rock-pile.

So things have changed. But let me take you back to a time many of you remember well—a time when a lot of men died.

In 1995 we noted a milestone of some importance: the thirtieth anniversary of the first U.S. ground units landing in what was then South Vietnam. It was an unopposed landing. Signs reading WELCOME TO THE GALLANT MARINES greeted the troops. Bud McFarlane, one of the principal figures in *The Nightingale's Song*, commanded the artillery battery that went ashore on 8 March 1965.

That was thirty-one years ago. On 30 April 1975, twenty-one years ago, the U.S. ambassador to South Vietnam climbed aboard a helicopter clutching a folded American flag and lifted off the roof of the U.S. Embassy in Saigon. With that, the nation of South Vietnam ceased to exist, and the curtain was drawn on this nation's longest war.

Now, the United States has established full diplomatic relations with its old enemy, Vietnam.

We lost the Vietnam War, with all that meant in terms of U.S. prestige abroad and in terms of this nation's ability to carry out its international commitments, at least for a time—an extended time.

But the Vietnam War did something else. It fractured a generation of young Americans, creating a divide that may never be bridged. This generational fault line is what I've tried to examine in my book. On the surface, I've chronicled and woven together the lives of five men, three of whom—Oliver North, Robert McFarlane, John Poindexter—were caught up in the Iran-Contra Scandal. James Webb, one of the most decorated Marines of the Vietnam War, is a best-selling novelist and served as secretary of the Navy. John McCain, a Navy pilot who survived more than five and a half years as a prisoner of war, is a U.S. senator from Arizona. All five men are Naval Academy graduates, as I am. All were touched in varying ways by the Vietnam War and its aftermath. And all became well known—for better or worse—during the presidency of Ronald Reagan.

In *The Nightingale's Song*, I recount their lives, which have intersected over the years in fascinating ways, in order to explore the generational fault line that first appeared in American society during the Vietnam War and which, I believe, continues to haunt the nation three decades later. That fault line cuts between those who served in the armed forces during the Vietnam War—and I am talking about liberals, conservatives, and everyone in between—and those who used money, wit, and connections to avoid serving.

The Nightingale's Song is by no means a defense of the Vietnam War. Basically, I do not take a position on the war. Like you, I do not think any war is a good war. But let's face it; some are better than others. World War II was a good war. The enemy was well defined, and so was the threat. For me, though, the crucial issue during Vietnam was how one answered the summons, how one responded to the call to arms.

If you believed the war made sense, you had an obligation, I think, to serve. That means you did not play the deferment game, get married, have a baby, or, I must add, join the National Guard. Not in those days.

If you felt the war was a mistake, I think you had to keep faith with your generation by opposing the war in a manner by which you put yourself in peril, a kind of peril that in some way mirrored the danger that other members of your generation were experiencing in the jungles or in the rice paddies, in the air or on the sea in Southeast Asia. That meant standing up to the draft—walking into your draft board saying, "I am John Smith, I am 1-A, and I am not going to go." That also meant you faced jail. Frankly, if a lot more young men had done that, I believe the machinery of the Selective Service System would have ground to a halt, the war would have ended, and lot of blood would never have been spilled. As it was, most men used a vast smorgasbord of deferments—often relying on a large network of draft counselors—to beat the system and avoid or evade the draft.

What is this generational fault line I am talking about? I define one part as those who served as enlisted men and junior officers during the Vietnam War. The other part is made up of their contemporaries, men of roughly the same age who did not serve. In simple terms, I am talking about those who went and those who didn't.

What does that mean? The war was not the problem. Vietnam was hell, but so were all wars: World War I, World War II, Korea, no doubt the

Peloponnesian War. The problem with Vietnam was the homecoming. Many had seen friends and comrades die. Many others came home maimed themselves. And yet, when they got back to the States, they were condemned by many as baby killers; some were spat upon. It was as if they had barely dragged themselves out of the primordial sludge. There was no recognition that what they had done was something that they and many others, including their government, viewed as an important mission.

Across this generational divide, meanwhile, they saw their unbloodied contemporaries flourishing. Not only was no stigma attached to what used to be called draft-dodging, the other half of this generation—as Jim Webb has said—wore their antiwar credentials like combat decorations. Or it had not affected their lives at all. They were unbloodied and prospering.

That was what turned Vietnam into what has been called an indigestible lump. It was as if a social contract had been broken, as if we had gone to bed one night and awakened to find the whole world changed. Bob Bedingfield, a chaplain who served with Ollie North's regiment in Vietnam, probably put it best. "What that does," he said, "is dislocate loyalty. It says I can never trust the system again. That is now the filter through which I interpret the world."

A friend of Jim Webb, another Vietnam veteran, put it more strongly. He said, "There's a wall ten miles high and fifty miles thick between those of us who went and those who did not. And that wall is never going to come down."

I think that is too strong. But I also believe that this generational fault line is more crucial than most people suspect. Look back at the history of this nation since the onset of the Great Depression. The election of Franklin D. Roosevelt in 1932 ushered in a period in which most Americans looked on the government as an institution that could be trusted to have the best interests of the people at heart. FDR led us through the Depression and World War II. Right up through the Kennedy years, this nation, despite its faults—most notably the racism that has stained it from the beginning—seemed driven by an unquenchable idealism and a willingness to sacrifice to help others.

The Vietnam War, reinforced by the Watergate scandal, changed all that. How many people trust their government today to do the right thing? The answer, I am afraid, is "Not many." And as I see it, this is why. You cannot march millions of men and thousands of women off to war, then, when they come home, tell them it was all a big mistake, without sooner or later paying a price—especially when the other half of their generation paid no price to speak of.

I had been to Vietnam, been wounded, had moved on, and become a newspaperman. I did not read books about Vietnam. I did not join veterans' organizations. By choice, I never covered the military. Sometime during the dark couple of years after I was wounded, I realized I needed to move on, build a new life, and if not forget about Vietnam, put it off to the side. And so I did, quite successfully.

By the 1980s, I was the White House correspondent for *The Baltimore Sun*. Then, in 1986, the Iran-Contra scandal blew all over Washington. And right at the heart of it were three Naval Academy men—Oliver North, Bud McFarlane, and John Poindexter. I did not know any of them well, but I thought of them as men imbued with the highest ideals of public service. And so I started asking myself a question: What the hell is going on here?

I covered the Iran-Contra affair for the *Sun* for the next year. I knew a constitutional crisis when I saw one, and this was most assuredly a constitutional crisis. But almost from the beginning I began to smell the Vietnam War in it. And that is what finally became compelling for me—to see what Iran-Contra said about my generation and, for that matter, the past three decades of American history. And that quest gave rise to another question: Was Iran-Contra, at least in part, the bill for Vietnam finally coming due? I concluded that it was. I also believe that if I am right, the country got off cheaply.

But I wanted to know more about this generation of well-meaning if ill-starred warriors, and Iran-Contra took me only so far. Jim Webb's novels, and Jim Webb himself, took me further, showed me how a Vietnam veteran could take the anger and bitterness that afflicted his generation and give it a voice, make it real.

John McCain added the final piece to the puzzle. He had the worst war of any of the five principals in the book—five and a half years in North Vietnamese prisons, thirty-one months in solitary, brutally tortured. He left prison crippled. And yet, almost immediately after descending from the plane at Clark Air Force Base in the Philippines, he began putting Vietnam behind him. He told himself that whatever destiny had in store for him, good or bad—and it had both—he was going to fulfill it, prison or no prison. And somehow he did. At least that is what he says, and if he is covering up, he sure puts on a good show.

Within months of his release, when people asked John McCain how he felt about the men and women who had demonstrated against the war, whose actions may well have extended the time he and his comrades spent in prison, he had an unvarying answer: "That doesn't bother me," he said. "The right of the American people to loudly disagree with the actions of their government is one of the things we were fighting for."

And so, when President Bill Clinton extended diplomatic recognition to Vietnam, standing on the podium with him was John McCain, the senior senator from Arizona. When Senator McCain is asked how he feels about President Clinton's actions as a young man, most notably his efforts to avoid the draft, his response may surprise you. He says, "Look, that's not an issue. The American people elected Bill Clinton their president." All of which tells me there are still a few people in Washington who truly believe in America.

A reviewer from *The Boston Globe* took great pains to say *The Nightingale's Song* had vividly illuminated this generational divide to which I refer but had done little to close it, to bring about healing. He assumed that was my purpose. It was not. Everyone is always talking about reconciliation. Jim Webb, whom I describe as the kick-ass troubadour for a generation of combat veterans, spoke for many of us when he said, "I don't want to be reconciled."

In *The Nightingale's Song*, I was talking to a number of different audiences. To my comrades, I was saying that I share their pride in having served. To others, those too young or too old to have served in Vietnam, I was saying that the fabled Vietnam generation was not made up solely of antiwar protesters. It was not just Janis Joplin and Woodstock and Jimi Hendrix and phony gurus like Timothy Leary and the Weathermen and Abby Hoffman and the rest of the Chicago Seven. It also included millions of men and thousands of women who actually set foot in Vietnam. To the other half of our generation, I was saying, "I know you think you were smarter than us, and more sensitive, and lived on a higher moral plane, and you probably thought you had more reason to live. But that is not what you looked like to us."

Don Walsh

DAVID HOFELING / U.S. NAVAL INSTITUTE

In January 1960, Capt. Don Walsh, U.S. Navy (Retired), and Swiss copilot Jacques Piccard navigated the U.S. Navy's bathyscaphe *Trieste* into the Challenger Deep, the deepest spot in the World Ocean. The record still stands. Walsh also was a member of Operation Deep Freeze in 1971, spending more than a month on the ice in Antarctica and earning recognition for his contributions there by having an Antarctic mountain ridge named for him.

Today, Walsh is president of International Maritime, Inc., an Oregon-based consulting company that has completed projects in twenty nations. He is one of twenty living honorary members of the Explorers Club, an honorary life member of the Adventurers Club, and a fellow of England's Royal Geographic Society. He was technical advisor for such films as *Gray Lady Down, Raise the Titanic, The Hunt for Red October,* and *The Abyss.* The interview appeared in the April 2000 issue of *Naval History.*

■

USNI: In a *Naval History* interview a few years ago, Jean-Michel Cousteau referred to you as the Buzz Aldrin of the ocean. What do you think he meant by that?

Walsh: I've known the Cousteau family for many years. I know Jean-Michel well. I've been a guest in the Cousteau home. We go way back, so I believe that was a compliment and not a complaint.

USNI: We thought he might have meant that Jacques Piccard received more of the credit for your expedition to the Challenger Deep, comparing you to Aldrin and Piccard to Neil Armstrong.

Walsh: Well, it's a tad nationalistic. Europeans tend to favor the European, and Americans tend to favor the American. I think that's just human nature. The Piccards, of course, are a dynasty. I don't think any family in the history of exploration has had three generations who, essentially, all established world records. Auguste, of course, was a great balloonist. He was basically a physicist, but he set the world altitude record in the early 1930s in a balloon. And of course, his son Jacques was with me in the *Trieste.* And now Jacques's son Bertrand is the first man to fly a balloon around the world. So they're a dynasty of explorers and scientists in Europe, and, understandably, the press treatment would probably favor them. I don't think it's any kind of a deliberate spin; it's just the way people see the news and report it. It doesn't trouble me.

USNI: What was it like competing against the space program at the time?

Walsh: It was pretty tough, because the advent of the space program came at just about the time we brought the *Trieste* to the United States. We and this inner spaceship we had didn't even enjoy a year of primacy. NASA already was off and running. The Navy's entire undersea program has lived in the shadow of the space program. Of course, our project seemed to be under wraps from the beginning.

I remember presenting the program to Adm. Arleigh Burke. Of course, the Navy doesn't require lieutenants to go the chief of naval operations to get approval for programs, but nobody wanted to make the decision. I kept getting handed up the chain until one day I ended up in front of Admiral Burke.

So I briefed him on the program. And he said, "How many of you are in this thing?"

And I replied, "It's just myself and Piccard."

Then he said, "Are there any other Navy people associated?"

And I said, "There's Lt. Larry Shumaker, who's the assistant officer in charge. He'll be in charge of the topside aspects."

The admiral then said, "Well, if this thing doesn't come back up, you tell Shumaker that you're the lucky one, because I'm going to have his lower appendages."

Arleigh Burke said what he meant and meant what he said. So I got the approval from him, but he put a condition on it. He said, "There'll be no publicity, none at all." I looked at him in surprise, because if we were successful, this was going to be quite a coup for the U.S. Navy.

"The science guys and the research and development engineers in the Navy," he said, "have been promising me spectacular things. We were going to put up the first earth-orbiting satellite." They had lit off a rocket at Cape Canaveral, and it shot into the ocean rather than into space. So Admiral Burke said that he didn't want any more of these promised science spectaculars that turn out to fizzle.

"If you do it successfully," he said, "then we'll have the publicity. But until then, just keep your mouth shut and go do it."

So we didn't really have a ramp-up to this great event. There was no general knowledge of what we were doing. Although *Life*, *National Geographic*, and improbably, *The London Daily Mail* got a whiff of it, the Navy's chief of information bought their silence by saying they could go on the trip but they couldn't tell anybody. And they didn't. Does Macy's tell Gimbel's? They were inside, and the door was shut. They essentially had scoops. And so, off we went to Guam. That was good coverage.

The London Daily Mail had a wonderful foreign correspondent, Noel Barber. He was out of the trench coat–Lowell Thomas school. When the Dalai Lama came out, Barber hired horses and rode a hundred miles into Tibet to greet him and get the scoop. He was a wonderful raconteur. During the evenings in Guam, when we'd all go out for dinner, we didn't talk about the *Trieste*, we sat around and listened to the reporters tell stories about their adventures. It was great fun.

USNI: Were you at all trepidatious before your dive to the Challenger Deep?

Walsh: No. People say, "Well, you're just being modest." And my wife says I've got a lot to be modest about. But the fact is, the whole strategy of the testing of the bathyscaphe, over nearly a year, was to make increasingly deeper test dives. When we got it, it was configured for only twenty-thousand-feet diving depths. We had to reengineer it, enlarge it, and buy a new cabin for it, to be able to go to thirty-six thousand feet. And so we did a few test dives in San Diego, then shipped the whole thing to Guam.

At Guam, we started out at four hundred feet in the harbor and worked our way offshore, in increasingly deeper water. And we actually brought the world's depth record home to the United States in November of 1959, when we made a dive to eighteen thousand feet. The previous record, of course, was held by the French Navy, at 12,500 feet, which actually is the average depth of the ocean. That was set in 1954. So we captured the record again in '58, and by early January 1960 we dove to twenty-four thousand feet. Then twelve days later we made the deep dive. It was all incremental.

So I say it was just a longer day at the office, and people think I'm trying to be clever. But that's the truth. All the manipulations we did to make it dive were the same whether we were diving a thousand feet or thirty-six thousand feet. And we got to know it intimately. I'd put on a boiler suit, scrape rust inside that tank, and help paint it. Everybody turned to. We were a small team—only fourteen people. And we worked seven days a week, dawn to dusk, at Guam. You build a certain confidence in your equipment.

USNI: Why do you think no one's done it since? Is it a cost/benefit matter?

Walsh: Yes, it is. If you can dive to twenty thousand feet, you can cover 98 percent of the sea floor. For engineers and bean-counters—even the users—98 percent is pretty good.

Having said that—the last 2 percent is about the size of North America, in terms of unexplored ocean floor. Today, four manned submersibles can dive to twenty thousand feet. We did have five, but the U.S. Navy has resigned from the game. We had the *Sea Cliff*, which replaced the bathyscaphe *Trieste*. In 1982, that was converted to a twenty-thousand-foot submersible by adding a titanium hull, among other features. So the *Trieste* left service, and the *Sea Cliff* went into service.

That was soon followed by the *Nautile*, the French six-thousand meter, or twenty-thousand-foot submersible, in the mid-1980s. The Russians bought the two *Mir*s—actually made in Finland—in the late 1980s. And then the fourth country to get into the game was Japan, which built a *Shinkai*, at sixty-five hundred meters. The extra five hundred meters means that the Japanese now have the deepest-diving manned submersible in the world.

USNI: Why is the U.S. Navy out of the game?

Walsh: Beats the hell out of me. I wish I knew. We pioneered manned submersibles. Sure, the Piccards invented and developed the bathyscaphe, but it was perfected in our Navy. And this led us on to other submersibles. Most that exist in the world today are based largely on work that began in the U.S. Navy R&D establishment. And all of the Remotely Operated Vehicle (ROV) technology came out of the Navy, principally the U.S. Navy lab in San Diego. The same goes for the Autonomous Untethered Vehicles (AUVs). So much of this early work was started by the Navy in the sixties and the seventies, which was sort of the golden age of undersea vehicles. But over the years, the Navy has just pulled clear of all of it. I guess it doesn't see any operational need.

Having said that, I think that the state of technology in the civil sector, for ROVs and AUVs today, is such that the Navy is probably better off just buying what it needs, or contracting to have built what it needs, rather than being involved in the R&D.

The genesis of civil involvement in deep submersibles rested in the navy lab system, with submarine force involvement. And it's all kind of gone away. The Navy doesn't do that kind of R&D anymore, and it really doesn't contract for much of it. It's not even a sponsor of new developments, which are all being done in the civil sector.

We've just resigned from the game. That's an all-embracing statement, but essentially it's correct. It just seems to me today—as it did a long time ago—that being able to go deep in the oceans, to maintain a presence anywhere in the oceans, and to be able to work anywhere on the floor of the oceans, is pretty important. But after we made the deep dive, the Navy restricted the *Trieste* to twenty thousand feet. From then on, the U.S. Navy did not have an ultimate-depth capability.

USNI: Why was that restriction made?

Walsh: The Navy felt the new cabin that was built for it was not safe and didn't want us to use it anymore.

There is an apocryphal story—well, maybe it's true. When we were on board the *Trieste*, getting ready to make the deep dive, my leading chief petty officer was on board a destroyer escort called the *Lewis*, some distance from our support vessel.

A radioman came around with his clipboard, looking for Lieutenant Walsh. He said he had a message from Washington. The chief said that Lieutenant Walsh was on the *Trieste*, but that he'd certainly give this message to him at the earliest possible opportunity. The message said: "Don't make the dive." The chief gave me that message about five years ago. That shows how much confidence we had in each other and in the device, a confidence that probably wasn't shared in Washington.

USNI: You brought up the ROVs and the AUVs. That brings me to a question about Robert Ballard. What do you think of his adventures and his ability to have them funded by public means?

Walsh: Well, I think it's wonderful. I don't know what hold he has over these people. Normally, that kind of deal stems from a personal relationship with somebody like the secretary of the Navy or somebody who controls resources; both policy resources as well as physical resources.

Bob has been able to do it across several changes of top-level personnel in Washington, and that's a remarkable thing that he's done; to gain access to navy assets and resources for these jobs. I'm sure he's not paying market rate, if he's paying at all. It's not only remarkable, it's unique.

In the old days of exploration, people like Richard Byrd had hybrid expeditions with Navy assets. How many of his flights were done with Navy air, and how did he get the time off, as a serving naval officer, to do these things? There was a lot more flexibility in those days that isn't present today.

So what Bob is doing is truly remarkable in the sense that he's been able to plow straight ahead, get access to these assets, and do some interesting things. He's a great communicator. He gave a talk once to some educators in a meeting I attended in England. He said that when he did dives on the deep-sea vents, the black smokers, with the *Alvin*, he'd get a few letters a week from students who were interested in what he was doing. When he found the *Titanic*, he said it went to hundreds of letters a week.

Here was something that was recapturing young people's imaginations. From a scientific point of view, finding the *Titanic* was probably far less valuable to society than working with the deep-sea vents and trying to explain them. He has developed a formula that allows him to connect with a large body of the public, with the underlying message that not only are strange and wonderful things happening in the sea, but there's almost nothing that has been lost or dropped into the sea, in man's history, that we can't find and study.

USNI: What do you think he might find in his next expedition?

Walsh: The next expedition, I understand, is the Black Sea, which is an anaerobic basin, where the water is oxygenated down to a certain depth; it's a very shallow layer on top. And that's because the sill depth at the

Sea of Marmora is high enough that only the top layer moves in and out and gets oxygenated. Of course, biological and chemical processes use the oxygen quickly.

After the oxygen is depleted and not being recharged, the result is an anaerobic body of water. The notion is that ancient wrecks will not, perhaps, deteriorate as rapidly as they do in an oxygenated area, which can support chemical breakdown of substances or support bacteria that facilitate that breakdown.

My question is: If we've got two life systems on our planet—beyond the traditional photosynthetic sun-based system—that exist in the absence of oxygen, couldn't bacteria microbes that live in the Black Sea have adapted to a virtually no-oxygen environment and still be able to carry on the deterioration of organic materials?

Chemosynthetic organisms live around the hydrothermal vents on the sea floor. Microbes known as archae live under very high temperature and pressure within the rocks. This gives us a clue about whether there might be life on other planets. These microbes are able to live in extraordinarily tough environments. And so we need to go back and start looking and sampling from other planets in our solar system, to see whether or not there might not be life at this level there. If something can live in conditions as brutal as that, why couldn't they adapt in the Black Sea?

Very few archeological expeditions have gone into it, so it's virgin territory. Trade and shipping were very active in early civilizations around the edge of the Black Sea. One of our best-known oceanographers, Willard Bascom, judges that about 15 percent of all ships that sailed in ancient times never got to their destination. And so Bob's going in an area that is like a big bank.

USNI: You were talking about technology transfer. Has deep-sea exploration brought us anything similar to what the space program has brought us? Or is it all intangible?

Walsh: That's a good question. In the case of sea exploration, we're really talking about technology that has migrated to other segments of the science. A lot of that know-how, those technological building blocks, might be borrowed by another project, without having to pay for the technology again. That's technology transfer, but that's intramural. When they say technology transfer, most people talk about it as extramural.

Undersea technology probably has not had that much extramural transfer, but has produced a lot of intramural benefits. Things that we developed for the *Trieste* have shown up in other programs over the years. We had the first underwater manipulators—the artificial hands—and the first high-resolution sonar. The first ROVs were a technology transfer from the U.S. Navy lab to profit-making companies. But that is intramural. So it depends on how you ask the question, when you're talking about technology transfer.

A little bit has gone the other direction. For example, take Europa, the water-covered moon of Jupiter. Its outer skin is ice, with some icebergs sticking out of the crust. It appears that surface disturbances were caused by thermal venting from inside. The ocean on Europa has been determined to be about a hundred kilometers deep—thirty-three miles. That's a pretty deep ocean. So the biggest ocean in our planetary system may be on the Europa moon, or satellite, of Jupiter.

So what is being discussed now is the development of a Europa lander with the capability of boring through this ice crust to put an ROV or an AUV into the ocean. This would be able to determine whether or not things are living in the water and to analyze water-dissolved gases, salinity, and other characteristics. So U.S. companies that build ROVs have been approached. Antarctic Lake Vostok, an ice-covered lake, would be a good prototype experimental area, but the dilemma now is whether we want to contaminate Lake Vostok with our atmosphere.

Right now, we're studying the ice layers on Greenland. I think we've been able to core down to about three hundred feet, which represents something like 250,000 years of earth's climate. It's just like tree rings. Here we actually have a sample of the atmosphere, earth's atmosphere, a quarter of a million years ago. But have we contaminated it? That's the dilemma on Lake Vostok—that we will open it up and contaminate it. Or will we?

USNI: Do treasure hunters have a role in the understanding of history?

Walsh: I'm glad you asked that question, because it's something I've been working on recently. Underwater archaeologists and salvors need each other. Even in a big country like ours, or a European country like France or Great Britain, underwater archaeology ranks below ballet in terms of government support. I won't say it doesn't get any respect; of course it does, because it's an academic discipline. But it doesn't get a lot of public funding for the conduct of research.

Working in the deep ocean is terribly expensive. A good first-class oceanographic research ship with a manned submersible or an ROV system on board might cost forty-five thousand to sixty thousand dollars a day. And finding things on the sea floor isn't easy. Ocean water magnifies, so a square mile on the floor of the ocean is huge, in terms of being able to sweep through it and find small objects. That's a slow, time-consuming business. Virtually nothing that has been lost on the floor of the ocean cannot be found, if you can pay the price.

So a marine archaeologist had better know very well where something is before he goes out, because you can burn up your budget quickly and come home empty-handed. This is not good for an academic or a program manager. I think there's a place for people—I would prefer to call them "shipwreck diving companies" rather than the pejorative-sounding "treasure hunters"—who have a different motive to search for, locate, and classify things. These companies work with the additional incentive of being able to recover artifacts, market them, and sell them.

Now, that may sound bad. But these two communities—the shipwreck diving companies with a profit incentive and access to the technologies and the search methodologies, and the archaeologists who have the research and historical information to identify, classify, and to conserve artifacts properly—need to get together. The archaeologists will never be able to afford deep-water work. It's just too expensive. Very few in fact will ever have a chance to do it. And so, if the archaeologists just say, "off with their heads" to the deep-shipwreck people, they're never going to get out there to do their work. The shipwreck people are not going to take them. And they certainly won't cooperate if they are ruled out by governments and laws and regulations. If they can't work, that's the end of it. Nobody will go in the deep sea. So it's a Pyrrhic victory if you get rid of the shipwreck companies.

I visited one of those companies recently, so it's on top of my mind. They're very careful. They are working with governments, and they don't take anything without permission. They welcome archaeologists and government officials to go with them on these trips. Every find is documented, and the disposition of each item is auditable.

The deal they usually work out is: 75 percent of cultural items goes to the government, to museums and archaeologists, and 25 percent is retained by the company. In the case of trade goods and gold—the freight, if you will, of the times—75 percent stays with the shipwreck exploration company and 25 percent goes to the government. They can swap shares back and forth, but that's the basic opening deal.

The shipwreck exploration company takes all the risk and does all the research to find the wreck. Once they have a target, they send down the

ROVs and classify it. They have their own archaeologists on staff, and when they start recovering artifacts, they conserve them in a way generally accepted by all marine archaeologists, as far as methodology goes. So they're doing all the work, taking all the risk, and then they share with the local government.

USNI: The trouble with that is, all of them don't have equal integrity.

Walsh: Deep shipwreck work is not a subtle thing. It takes a big ship, a big staff, and a very sophisticated ROV system or a manned submersible, all of which costs a lot of money. So they have to find investors. It's all very high-visibility. Governments can track these activities and insist that the appropriate things be done, in terms of employing archaeologists and having some control over the artifacts being removed.

Now you might say, "Look, when you get beyond territorial waters, who's going to track you?" The Mediterranean, which is the richest trove, and the Black Sea are all government waters. I think it's easier than you think to put some controls and constraints on the shipwreck-locating and diving operations being conducted by these private companies.

And so I think that, instead of being adversaries, the direction for archaeologists to take is to work out a set of rules and regulations and protocols to get everything they want. But they need to recognize the only way that these expeditions are going to get funded. And museums can't house all the artifacts, anyway. The world does not have ten thousand maritime museums. A lot of museums say, "No. Don't send us any more stuff. We've got plenty."

I saw a videotape when I was in France late last year of a Roman ship that was carrying roof tiles that looked just like the tiles you see today. How many of those can a museum handle? I think there's enough to go around.

The archaeologists and the governments get first pick, and the rest of it is handed off to the shipwreck diving company to market and thus finance future expeditions. I think you can control it in a way that satisfies everybody.

USNI: What have you enjoyed most about your career?

Walsh: You know, the great thing about doing this kind of work is not only the work itself, but also the people you meet. I was once loaned to the State Department for a couple of months to lecture in the Indian Ocean region and the Middle East as a sort of advance man just before the third UN Law of the Sea Conference. My role was to give talks to people of consequence in these countries, to demonstrate what was possible at the time in uses of the sea. The notion behind it was to communicate the State Department position that, "If you affiliate with the American position on the sea, then these things can be yours."

It was great for me, because I was able to go to India, Iran, Pakistan, and Ceylon. I was gone for about two months. One of the people I had the pleasure to meet was sitting in the front row when I was lecturing in Ceylon. He certainly looked familiar. It was Arthur C. Clarke, who lives in Ceylon. And so we became friends. We went skin-diving in Trincomalee, and I was a guest in his home. That's what I mean about meeting people.

I remember we stayed at the old officers' barracks in Trincomalee, which was a huge naval base from World War II. The Sinhalese Navy had two forty-foot Vosper patrol boats. When they left at night, the whole base turned off its lights. Arthur had brought along his Celestron telescope and gave me a personal tour of the heavens as we sat outside in wicker chairs. You know, I can't think of a better guide for space. He's an example—one of my best—of the people I've had the chance to meet while touring around.

James Webb

DAVID HOFELING / U.S. NAVAL INSTITUTE

Mr. Webb is the creator, executive producer, and co-writer of the Paramount Pictures movie, *Rules of Engagement.* He received the Navy Cross, the Silver Star, two Bronze Stars, and two Purple Hearts during his service in the Marine Corps in Vietnam. He won an Emmy Award for his reporting on the Beirut bombing in 1983, served as assistant secretary of defense and secretary of the Navy in the Reagan administration, and is the author of several best-selling books. The interview appeared in the April 2000 issue of the Naval Institute's *Proceedings.*

■

USNI: Obviously, the subject of rules of engagement plays heavily on the readers of this magazine. How did the film, *Rules of Engagement*, come about?

Webb: I conceived the idea in 1989, when Scott Rudin began producing after having been president of production at 20th-Century Fox. He had read Bob Timberg's article in *Esquire*, which was the seminal article for his book, *The Nightingale's Song*. We had a discussion that boiled down to the notion of military loyalty. Timberg's article had struck him, when it mentioned that, although I did not particularly like Oliver North, if I'd been working in the White House at the time of the Iran-Contra activities, I would not have let him do what he did. This led to a discussion of Marine Corps loyalty, as opposed to what you see in the civilian world. I made a comment that basically was: "In the Marine Corps, loyalty means you will die for somebody even if you don't like them." He said, "You know, there's a movie in that."

The whole issue of the rules of engagement weighed heavily on my mind: first, from having fought in Vietnam; second, from having represented a so-called "war criminal" for six years, which was written about some time ago for the Naval Institute Press [Gary Solis, *Son Thang*, 1997]; third, from having been a journalist in Beirut when the Marines were there, with unbelievably ridiculous rules of engagement; and fourth, from having been secretary of the Navy during the Persian Gulf incidents of 1987 and 1988.

The theme has run deep over the past forty years, and I thought we should show the American people what the modern military has to deal with on a daily basis, when it is placed in politically complex environments. So I came up with an idea, using a Marine Expeditionary Unit (MEU) having to rescue an embassy under siege, because the government of that country, as a protest against something the Americans had done, pulls away its police protection. The MEU commander must make a decision to fire into a crowd after some of his Marines are killed. He then becomes, on one hand, something of a hero. But on the other hand, he is court-martialed for murder. The loyalty then plays in when he sees he's in trouble, and a lot of people are trying to take advantage of him for political reasons. He sees that the one person he really trusts to defend him is a Marine whose life he saved in Vietnam and who was shot up badly and became a Marine Corps lawyer.

USNI: Does the movie resolve anything about rules of engagement?

Webb: As originally written, this film would have been harder on the viewer. You'll still be debating, when you walk out of the theater, whether what the MEU commander did was right. The thing I'm proudest of, in terms of what has survived through the filmmaking process, is the kind of rhetoric that you're going to hear. I refer especially to one speech, delivered by Samuel L. Jackson: "No matter what happens here, do you realize I will never command anything again? And do you know what that means?" The average civilian in this country has no comprehension of what command is. Halfway through this film, the viewer knows that, whichever way it goes for this guy, he has lost the most precious thing to him, professionally—the right to command troops. That, to me, is emotionally satisfying. World War II is easy in Hollywood. There has never before been a film that expressly addresses the modern American military and the issues it faces.

USNI: Why do you think the public is so ignorant about what a combat commander has to go through?

Webb: The level of ignorance is extremely high. A big part of that is because Hollywood has become, in many ways, the articulator of our culture—to ourselves and to the world. Right now, 60 percent of the money Hollywood makes is in international sales. If you look at the films that have been done about the U.S. military—anything after World War II—they are simplistic on these issues, and they are not positive. You see a repetitive theme, either about the corruption of U.S. military leaders or the depiction that Americans just shoot things up, without restrictions.

The conversations I've had with the people in Los Angeles responsible for marketing this film have been quite informative. They had no comprehension that we had any restrictions on us, even in a place like Vietnam. Where does the average American get his information? From the movies.

Many people have asked me over the past ten years what the hell I'm doing, working with Hollywood. I don't think I'm going to do this solely or forever, because most of the things you hear about Hollywood are true. It's a very difficult place on philosophical issues and also because of the competitive nature of the beast. The Writers' Guild typically registers about thirty-four thousand screenplays a year, and they make 260 feature films. The process of getting your product through that system in some ways depends on quality, but in a lot of ways it depends on relationships and political content. So people who have more traditional views have a very tough time there. What has survived in this film, I think, is going to be good for the country and will be satisfying for people who care about the military.

USNI: Take us through your on-and-off relationship with this project.

Webb: For nine years, I was the sole writer and co-producer with Scott Rudin, who did *Angela's Ashes*, *Sister Act*, *The Firm*, and *Sleepy Hollow*. He's one of the dominant producers in Hollywood, and he's very content-oriented. When Billy Friedkin became the director, Scott was doing *Angela's Ashes* and *Sleepy Hollow* in England. So Friedkin brought on Dick Zanuck, the son of Darryl Zanuck, to produce. At that point, with Scott off in England, they formed their own ideas. They brought in another writer and, without my direct involvement, came up with some changes to the story. Some of them were things that I may not have done myself, but that's Hollywood.

I found two scenes deeply objectionable, and I communicated that to them. Without going into detail, one scene involved the Marine Corps in Vietnam, the other involved the Vietnamese community in the United States. Those two constituencies, for lack of a better term, are more important to me than making a movie. I could just see people saying, "Webb went to Hollywood and sold out. He's turning his back on the people he says he cares about."

So it was sort of like "SecNav, round two." [Webb resigned as secretary of the Navy in the Reagan administration.] I took my name off my own film. Luckily, over the course of the next year, as they shot the film and edited it, either they had second thoughts about what I had said, or they decided on their own. It doesn't matter; they realized that those two scenes would have been extremely bad for the film. So they edited both of them down to the point that they were acceptable. I went to a screening, and I agreed to come back on as executive producer, with a "story by" credit. In the process, I lost my screenwriting credit.

USNI: Based on what we've heard, that is extraordinary in the movie business. Maybe they did realize that they were going to alienate the Marine Corps, a major portion of the potential audience.

Webb: Probably the most unfortunate occurrence in the shooting of the film was that Dale Dye was technical adviser. In my view, he should have been more loyal to the Marine Corps and backed me on what I said. This was my movie, and he never even called me to talk about the fact he was on the project. It was very clear to me where his loyalties were. If there's anybody I'm really disappointed in, it's not the Billy Friedkins and the Dick Zanucks of the world. What do they know about the military? It's people like Dale Dye, who should have known that he did not have the experience to make the judgment that he made, which cost us an entire year of wrangling. Most people in Hollywood think that Dale Dye was an infantry Marine. He was not.

USNI: How serious is the apparent gap between the civilian and military cultures?

Webb: To start, it depends on how you comprehend or perceive the problem. Tom Ricks's book, *Making the Corps,* is representative, I think, of many people who have not served in the military, who have gone to elite schools, and who are part of the ruling veneer in this country. Their worry is that the military is becoming more dangerous as a separate entity. And the military is beginning to view itself, through its leadership, as a separate entity.

In my view, the danger is the other way around. And it's been that way for thirty years. But it's become more markedly so during this particular administration. The elites of this country have been separating themselves from the obligations of serving and have less and less comprehension of the military. As a result, they have more of a cavalier view of how the military should be used. They have very little personal or emotional connection to military service.

I started seeing this twenty years ago, when I was a committee counsel in the Congress. Typically, members of Congress had some military service; the staffers typically did not. When things really got bad, and we started Indian Ocean commitments around 1979, it may as well have been the Mexican Navy out there when it came to explaining what was going on to the staffers. By the way, the same is true in the media. The typical reporter twenty years ago didn't have military service, but his or her editor did. Now, most members of Congress and most editors lack military service. Where do they go to get that understanding? That's part of the problem.

The other part of the problem is that senior military leaders have been unable to perceive this change as it relates to their responsibility for articulating how the military operates. They're still ten years behind, with most of them believing that it is somehow a political act to confront the political process when the political process needs to be confronted. As little as ten or fifteen years ago, the uniformed people could back off a bit, because the room in a typical congressional hearing was inundated with people who understood the basics. The military leaders didn't need to state them. They need to state them now. And when these statements come from people outside the process, they do not have the same impact as they do when they come from people in uniform. The Marine Corps has done very well. The other services have not.

The danger, to me, is real, and it comes from a veneer that's been defined by academic background and class. We have moved from issues of race to issues of class in this country, very subtly. And people are only now beginning to comprehend it.

With studies like the Triangle Study of the so-called military elites, people had better be paying close attention to the exact words being used and how the military is being defined from the outside. To coin the phrase "military elites" is a pretty dangerous thing, a contradiction in terms. You're not born to be an admiral, even though some believe they were. More than any other institution in this country, the military is basically a socialist meritocracy. You work your way up; you are evaluated on intangibles; and you're rewarded not with pay but with things like command. And when they start characterizing a military elite, and then carefully carve it away, the next step is going to be to carve the leaders away from their own troops. Just watch.

Watch out for these civilian-designed attitudinal surveys that go straight to the troops. The intellectual elites in this country want to say that the military elites don't understand their own troops; their troops have evolved as society has evolved, and these intellectuals know what's best for the military. That's what's going to happen.

USNI: Might that be a root problem in regard to recruiting and retention?

Webb: I would argue that the problem—from the evidence of the Marine Corps and from being out and talking to the people who really care, who want to lead—is not that the leadership is too traditional. It has become too obedient to the political process to the point that it will not define the military culture to the political leadership.

[Commandant of the Marine Corps, Gen.] Bob Barrow saved the Marine Corps. He was the guy, back in 1979, during the Carter administration, who really drove the stake into the ground and said, "This is what the Marine Corps is. If you don't like it, fire me. If you don't like what I'm saying, fire me." Barrow wasn't the first guy to say it, but this was a defining moment for the Marine Corps. And the Marines have said, basically, "We know who we are; we know what our traditions are; we know how to lead; we know how to fight; and we're going to take care of our people."

When members of the other services see the leadership at the top cut into the political process, that's when you get the sort of confusion that I see. Maybe there are people who write for *Proceedings* who have different views, but to me that seems to be the difference between the Marine Corps and the other services. And it does affect recruiting and retention.

USNI: You've been a vocal critic of military leadership, and you were especially tough in your 1996 speech at the Naval Institute's Annual Meeting. I'm sure you remember that. Has anything changed since then?

Webb: Yes, I remember. Let's back up to that speech. The biggest problem at the time was the cascading effect of the Navy leadership's failure to defend its culture after the Tailhook incident. In 1992, I wrote a piece for *The New York Times*, basically saying that the problem wasn't the Navy's culture. The problem was the admirals who were standing there saying we have a flaw in the culture, or who were allowing the civilian process to say that we had a corrupt culture.

If that were true, if the Navy's culture was permanently flawed and that was what caused Tailhook, then every one of those guys should have resigned. And if the culture wasn't structurally flawed, if this was an isolated incident that happened on one part of a hotel, where some people got out of hand, then they should have spoken up, and the whole thing might have taken a different turn. You tell me that what happened in a mosh pit at a Woodstock celebration last summer was less notorious than what happened at Tailhook? That was much more notorious. There were actual rapes in the mosh pit at Woodstock '99. But where were the media?

Obviously, there was something else going on at Tailhook. Some agenda leftists were seizing the event to break the Navy culture. And the admirals stood silent, when the civilian leaders were saying that the culture was broken. The admirals created that culture. They were a part of it. If they didn't agree with what the civilians were saying, they should have spoken up.

This wasn't something that I got up every day and made a speech about. When we reached the point where promotions—that already had been approved through the sacrosanct promotion process—were then required to have a second look by a group of Senate staffers, then something was inalienably wrong with the Navy's leadership.

I brought my fourteen-year-old son with me to that Naval Institute conference. When I got there, I told him, "I do not want to make this speech; I don't know how people are going to react to it. But it has to be said." And this became quite an education for him over the next several months.

When you ask whether things have changed since that speech, I think that the tragedy of Adm. [Jeremy M.] Boorda's suicide, the visibility of what happened to [Commander in Chief, Pacific, Adm.] Stan Arthur, and the things that were written about them caused a sort of second look at what was being done to the Navy. I think that gave the Navy some breathing room for a number of reasons. But I think—or would have hoped—that with that breathing room, there would have been a lot more aggressive argument from the top leadership of the Navy regarding force structure and other important issues.

I don't see how you can have a United States Navy with three hundred ships—no matter how efficient each one of those ships might be—and still perform what needs to be done on behalf of the nation's security, especially if we are going to be the nation that we say we are. Again, it's a question of having the uniformed leadership at the top understanding that it's different now; it's different than it was ten years ago, and they need to be saying it. Some of them are, but most of them aren't.

USNI: What would you say your biggest accomplishment was in your public service?

Webb: It's hard to say. I was a committee counsel for four years in the Congress, and that was a time when veterans' issues were extremely visible. I think probably the most important thing that I did was to create the legislation that countered the Carter discharge program.

After President [Jimmy] Carter had given amnesty to all the draft evaders, he turned around and created a program that would have upgraded hundreds of thousands of discharges of people who were deserters, attitude cases, et cetera. I worked day and night for six months on that. And we eventually brought what we called "historical standards" to many of those discharges. We could not stop the Carter administration from upgrading the discharges, but we could stop people from getting veterans' benefits, unless they met historical standards. That was very important to preserving the dignity of the people who had served. It was unbelievably emotional and contentious. We were right, in my view. It's hard to look at a guy who lost his arm, telling you, "I went to Vietnam. My cousin deserted. And now they're going to give my cousin veterans' benefits." He said, "I never felt any bitterness toward my cousin, except that they're going to treat him the same way they treat me." Those were the distinctions that we were having to deal with. I could write a book on how a bill becomes a law just based on that piece of legislation.

I think the most important thing I was involved with in the Pentagon, when I was ASD [assistant secretary of defense] for three years, was the creation of the Reserve Affairs Staff. We had all seven guard-reserve components, all four active services, plus political and career civilians all on one staff. And making that work—where we became central to resourcing mobilization, manpower flow, and medical care—was a tremendous leadership experience.

My goal as secretary of the Navy was to reinvigorate the admiralty and give it more responsibility. I think we did that in a number of different ways. And toward the end, even though I fell on my sword, I made some speeches that still resonate about the United States as a Pacific nation and why we are a maritime nation; not in the sense of having to ram four aircraft carriers up through the Kola Peninsula, but why we need this force structure in the day-to-day operational environment in which we exist. By having fought that issue, and refusing to back down on it, I can still talk about it with some veracity.

USNI: Did you know you were "falling on your sword" at the time?

Webb: No. We almost had it done. I've been criticized for being intransigent, because I resigned. But you don't survive four years in Congress, putting twenty bills a year through the House floor, by being intransigent. When I was ASD, over three years on the Defense Resources Board, we lost only one issue.

We argued the issue over which I resigned for three months. I had written a paper in 1984, laying out exactly how I believed the force structure of all the services should change, moving into the twenty-first century. And I was the first guy in the [President Ronald] Reagan administration to argue that we should reduce our ground and tactical-air presence in NATO. So this wasn't just more bucks for everybody; it was a plan for how to reconfigure the U.S. military. As I said, for three months we negotiated how to meet this $11 billion decrement that we had been given, without dropping force structure.

[Secretary of Defense Frank] Carlucci basically came in and said, "I want everybody to give up force structure." To him, it was, "when times are good, everybody gets more; when times are bad, everybody gives something up." My view was that if we could survive the decrement and keep force structure intact for one year, people would understand that the Navy, in the current environment, is different from the other services. That was the gamble. And we were so close.

USNI: What was your biggest regret during your public service?

Webb: Having resigned as secretary of the Navy. That's it.

USNI: Why did you decide to leave public service and go into literature and filmmaking?

Webb: From the time I left the Marine Corps, I've done both. I have an unwitting career. Actually, I wrote my first book after my first year in law school. It was a small book on Micronesia and American strategic interests in the Pacific.

So I just became fascinated with writing and started *Fields of Fire*. From that point forward, I'd write for a while and then do something in government for a while. When I resigned as secretary of the Navy in 1988, I was asked by the Republican National Committee to run against [Senator] Chuck Robb [D-VA]. They offered me $400,000 start-up money. Part of me was saying, "If I run for the Senate, people are going to forget what I just did. They're going to think I resigned just so I could make more noise and run for the Senate."

Then I also sat down and thought that if I were to go into government at any level beyond where I'd been, I should be financially secure. I also thought that I should have all of my curiosities basically taken care of. You're a prisoner when you're in government at that level. Even when I was SecNav, I was locked up in some of the best hotels in the world. You could travel all the way to the Philippines, but you couldn't go see anything. I'm lucky enough now that I can get people to pay me to go places I want to go and see things I want to see.

And then there's the side of me that loves to make stories. As I said, particularly on the film side, if you really care about the cultural issues, the place where our culture is being articulated is Los Angeles. I've been in and out of there for ten years. I'm not saying I'm going to do it for the rest of my life. And at some point, I might go back into government. I haven't decided.

USNI: Do you have the same type of relationship with the filming of *Fields of Fire* as you had with *Rules of Engagement*?

Webb: Having learned how Hollywood operates and feeling how important the Vietnam story is, especially because it's never been done right, I decided to do *Fields of Fire* outside the studio system. It's harder. But if you sell a story or a novel into the studio system, into what they call "development," they own it; they own it creatively, they own every one of those characters, and they can do anything they want. All they have to do is pay you out.

With *Fields of Fire*, the only reason to go through this drill was to try to get it right. It's a much harder way, but it's going to be much more satisfying in the end. It took me an entire year to get the rights to shoot this in Vietnam, right in the An Hoa Basin, where I was. We got the NVA [North Vietnamese Army] to play themselves. And the Marine Corps is going to help us. The problem is that there are very few people in Hollywood, on the development or on the money side, who connect emotionally with a positive view of Vietnam service. It's taken me a lot longer than I ever thought it would, but we're very close. I think we're going to get it done this year.

USNI: What advice would you give to young people who are contemplating a military career?

Webb: First of all, I think you've got to make that decision for yourself. My son just turned eighteen and is very interested in going into the Marine Corps. I'm really proud of him for that. But, at the same time, if he were doing it purely because somebody else wanted him to, then he would be in the wrong place.

That aside, I really wish we had more of a citizen soldiery. I wish we had more people in the country going through the military, because it's the greatest experience in the world in terms of helping you understand the cultural makeup of the country and how you can work together. Whether you're in for three years or for thirty, you take that back to your community, and you have a totally different understanding of this country by having served. There's no greater thing a young person can do than to be responsible for other people in the military environment. It helps you learn who you are, how to make decisions, and how to lead.

Whether someone going in should remain for a career is a big leadership question. I wouldn't even put that on a young person. I'd put that on the admirals and the generals. We get so many good people in the U.S. military, and we always have, with a few small blips here and there. Even in bad times there are some really great people coming in the military. And the question always has been whether they are inspired, whether the leadership and the nation will convince them that what they're doing is important. Napoleon said that there are no bad regiments; there are only bad colonels.

Caspar Weinberger

DEPARTMENT OF DEFENSE

Mr. Weinberger was secretary of defense in the Reagan administration and is currently the publisher of *Forbes* magazine. The interview with Secretary Weinberger appeared in the May 1990 issue of the Naval Institute's *Proceedings.*

■

USNI: How could you, during your tenure as secretary of defense, have forecast the seemingly inevitable austerity measures the defense budget is now facing?

Weinberger: I don't think we were interested in forecasting austerity measures; we were interested in trying to rebuild the defenses of all three of the services, and the Navy certainly needed rebuilding fully as much as the other two. We were concentrating on that, and we knew it was a long-term job. We knew that carriers took, for example, seven to eight years. We cut the time and cost as much as we could. But our interest was in trying to regain the necessary deterrent strength as quickly as possible in all of the services. So we were not thinking about austerity measures, because we didn't think they were warranted, safe, or justified.

USNI: If you were secretary of defense today and were in charge of allocating the funds, how would you do so?

Weinberger: First of all, I'd try to get more funds, because I don't think anything yet warrants the assumption that we no longer fully need the strong defenses that we regained and built during the 1980s. I would try to meet the principal needs as we did during the time I was secretary. We would rely on recommendations from the services, but they would obviously not be final. We would make our own decisions, but we would try to maintain both conventional and strategic strength, and we would do it on the basis of what we felt were the capabilities of potential enemies, such as the Soviet Union, which has an enormous capability militarily, which has not been reduced at all.

I noticed recently in *The New York Times* that it was just assumed that the Soviets are about to move six divisions out of Europe. That's a comforting assumption for anybody who wants to cut the defense budget, but it is, at this point, based entirely on rhetoric—nothing that could not be changed or reversed, even if they should go beyond the rhetoric.

USNI: Speaking of rhetoric, and borrowing some from Ronald Reagan and his presidential campaigns, would you say that the U.S. armed forces are better off today than they were five years ago?

Weinberger: Because we invested the amount necessary to make them better off. We regained a great deal of readiness, we had substantial modernization, we increased stocks of ammunition, and we added a lot more training time, steaming time, and maneuver time. All of those things have sharpened and strengthened the armed forces very much. I measure it from 1981, when we took over.

The real worry is that in the last four years some reductions have begun, which, when the items already in the pipeline are delivered and no more are forthcoming, could weaken the armed forces. And I'm sorry to see those reductions coming. But I think right now our Panama activities are excellent proof of the readiness and strength of the military forces, just as were the Grenada operation and our attacks on Libya.

USNI: Do you think five years from now you would say the same thing?

Weinberger: I would worry very much about that, because you can't maintain the kind of strength that we have, or that we need, if cuts of the magnitude being talked about very casually now are actually made. You cannot maintain or reacquire military strength without spending money. While a lot of the public and a lot of people in Congress would like to do that, it simply can't be done. So I think inevitably there will be a serious weakening of the military strength if these cuts are put into effect. A lot of people say we won't need this much military strength. That, too, I think, is a very dangerous assumption to make on the basis of what we've seen so far.

USNI: How do you feel your six tests for use of military force have stood the test of the past five years?

Weinberger: I think they're good guides and that they've stood the test quite well. Fortunately, we've not had to make those decisions very often. We made them, for example, in the Persian Gulf, where I was a strong advocate of our going in to help Kuwait keep the oil flowing through the Gulf. That was actually not a combat situation in many ways, but it was a situation in which we committed the armed forces to activities in which the risk of combat was there.

We went to Panama in response to what appeared to be, and what were, attacks, and perhaps continuing attacks, on the authorized American military presence in the Canal area. That was fully warranted within the six tests rule.

USNI: Do you think these tests will hold up five years from now?

Weinberger: I think so, yes. I think they're a proper set of guidelines to have. You have to bear in mind there are a lot of people in the United States, some in the government, who want to use U.S. forces very quickly and without any careful, mature consideration of either the risks or the propriety of such use. Many people feel that you can make some kind of a diplomatic showing if you send a battalion or two into a tense situation.

My feeling has always been this: Vietnam demonstrated that you should not commit U.S. forces to combat unless the situation is serious enough to require it from our overall national interest and security viewpoint, and unless you're willing to commit enough military power to win. The idea of simply committing U.S. forces because you hope their presence will frighten somebody into doing what you'd like them to do is, I think, a very wrong approach. I would never want to be secretary of defense and have any kind of situation in which I asked American servicemen and women to commit their lives to combat unless we planned to support them and to win.

USNI: I believe one of the tests concerns popularity among the American people.

Weinberger: No, one of the tests is whether or not there is some reasonable anticipation of public support for the action. The point that I made was that you can't fight a war against an enemy and against Congress at the same time. As a matter of fact, it's true of all the actions of our type of government. You have to have public support. You should have it. If you don't have it, you shouldn't continue. Those points were made at the time when some people were talking very casually about our possibly beginning attacks on Cuba or things of that nature.

My point is that you can't expect the American people to support a military action when, for example, they open their newspapers some morning and find that we've invaded Cuba. The American people must have some kind of understanding of how important any decision to commit American forces is; and that it must be a decision required by our national interests, as, for example, the Persian Gulf activities were; and that we're going to commit enough resources and have enough staying power to win. We are not going to do what we did in Vietnam, which was to add more and more incrementally but never with any intention of winning.

USNI: Of all the services, which do you think should get the franchise for low-intensity conflict?

Weinberger: I don't think that it's a question of giving anybody the franchise. First of all, it's a question of availability of trained forces for specific missions. The Marines are clearly in that category and would receive some assignments.

The next question would be: How close are the forces? Can they be inserted into the area, if required, as quickly as possible? I don't think it's bad that Marine Corps and Army infantry capabilities overlap—in the sense that both are trained and able to do amphibious landings, and both are trained to be inserted behind lines or in low-intensity conflicts, or to deal with terrorist incidents. To my mind, whoever gets the call would depend a great deal on the availability, combat readiness, and preparedness of the troops in that particular situation.

Many stories going around are total myths, such as the one that Grenada was fought under a plan that required the use of all armed services to satisfy all of the Joint Chiefs. This is total, complete nonsense. We used Marines and we used paratroopers because both were available. Marines were available because they were under way, combat-loaded to replace a Marine unit in Lebanon, and they were turned south toward Grenada. The Army units, the paratroop units, were there, were ready, and were needed to get into the airfields.

It depends on a great many factors. I never thought of the services as being that separate; I think of them all as being committed to serve the national interests of the United States.

USNI: How would you adjust service shares of a future budget, if you were in that position now?

Weinberger: According to needs measured by the nature of the threat. We need a capability to do a number of things, some of them simultaneously, perhaps. People used to talk, years ago, even in my confirmation hearings, about whether we should be prepared to fight one and a half wars or two and a half wars. I always thought that was total nonsense. We have to be prepared to do whatever the situation requires. The Soviets are perfectly capable militarily—were then and are now—of mounting two wars at once and perhaps a few other small subsidiary actions. We have to be prepared to be strong enough so that they will never be able to succeed in those. That's the essence of deterrence.

So I would think we need a counterterrorism capability, for which we have very well-trained people; we need some swift reconnaissance capabilities for situations of great risk, such as the SEALs [sea-air-land teams] are able to do; and we need carrier battle groups because we may not always have airfields in areas where we need them. We must be prepared for many different kinds of situations, and we try to anticipate those by measuring the capabilities inherent in potential enemies' military forces. What we acquired in the 1980s were the things necessary to deter anyone—not specifically the Soviet Union—from feeling they could make a successful attack against our interests anywhere. That's what we must have.

USNI: We'd like to ask you to anticipate a little bit, to look into the future. Somebody's got to sit down and say, "The Navy gets this percentage, the Army gets this percentage. . . ."

Weinberger: Well, it varies from year to year. It varies on the basis of readiness, how much deferred maintenance there is that needs to be made up, whether or not this is a year in which carriers are coming to completion, whether or not you have a new Navy plane that is going to require heavier expenditures than the year before. You can't do it by any kind of a percentage allocation; you have to do it by need.

The principal problem we had in 1981 was that we needed everything. People used to ask me about our highest priority. Our highest priority was to regain overall military strength to deter attack. That required the allocation of very large sums for virtually everything. It was truly unfortunate that we got ourselves into a situation of that kind, because when you cut back, as we did in the 1970s—more than 20 percent, measured in real terms—then you get yourself in a situation where, in order to make up and regain your strength, it's a lot more expensive than if you'd kept pace a little bit better all along. We would never have needed 7 percent, 9 percent, and 10 percent increases in the defense budget if we'd maintained, on a regular basis, a 3 percent increase over inflation all through the 1970s. Instead of that, we had a 20 percent decline.

USNI: So what you're saying is, if all the pieces of the pie are spoken for, you make the pie bigger?

Weinberger: It isn't a question of being spoken for. Nobody has any right to any particular portion of the total or any percentage. I never went on the basis that all the services could have everything they wanted, although, again, that's one of the myths that you read about. What we did was give a little more discretion in carrying out policies made by the Defense Department to the services—but we didn't abdicate responsibility to them and let them pick their own budgets, or say, "Everybody get a third and you can do what you wish with it."

What you have to do is recognize that, in some years, one service will need more than the others. For example, the Air Force was assigned the ground-based missiles. So the Air Force needed enough money for a modernization program to get the MX. That created an increase in the Air Force budget, not because it was the Air Force, but because that mission of the Air Force needed a great deal of money that year.

For the Navy, we had one year in which we had authorized two carriers, which saved us close to two billion dollars by getting them both authorized the same year. That required a fair amount of money in year one, and an increasing amount of money in years three, four, and five. And increased the Navy budget. The same was the case with the six-hundred-ship Navy.

The Army needed a great deal of modernization on the conventional side, and the Army has some nuclear responsibilities, as well.

So all of these things are going to make the service shares different from year to year, and what you have to look at are overall needs. Those needs are measured best by looking at the overall threat, not just the threat based on comforting rhetoric such as we're getting now from the Soviet Union, but the threat based on military capabilities that the Soviet Union still has.

USNI: Speaking of comforting rhetoric from the Soviets, overcaution is sometimes worse than recklessness. How can we apply that analogy to U.S.-Soviet relations?

Weinberger: Well, by always having enough. That's one of the things I always insisted on in the actions that we took in Grenada and Libya, and in the Persian Gulf. The Joint Chiefs would come in with some recommended force levels and force strengths, and I would invariably double it. I never wanted to have a situation, such as the attempted rescue of the hostages from Iran, with not enough military strength on hand to do the job.

As far as the overall totals are concerned, we have to be sure that we have enough to deter attack, and we deter attack because the other side recognizes that they do not have enough to win, if they should attack. You must try to get inside the minds of the Soviet Union or any other potential enemy. And that, in turn, means that you are going to have a very difficult time computing the equations of deterrence. How much is enough?

But the other problem is that you will never know that you haven't got enough until it's too late to do anything about it. So yes, you err on the side of caution. You err on the side of having perhaps more than some people sitting down in some academic atmosphere will say you really require. I never felt sufficiently confident in my own ability, or anybody else's ability, to say what was precisely enough. So I always felt that we should have at least enough so that the Soviets, by any kind of calculation, would never feel that they could make a successful attack. This is not an offensive force; it's a strong enough defense so that they would be, in effect, deterred from launching an attack.

USNI: Many recognize the political climate in the Soviet Union now as undergoing a real change from past years. How far must the Soviets go for you to trust them?

Weinberger: What we're seeing now, first of all, is confirmation of the fact that the Warsaw Pact nations were never a very reliable set of allies for the Soviet Union. Of course, it's very gratifying to know that people who have had to live under the thumb of communism for forty years, who have never known anything else, hate it so much that they're willing to take major risks and ultimately win their own freedom. But as far as my thinking was concerned, I never regarded the Warsaw Pact nations as terribly reliable allies for the Soviets, except in the sense that they had been sufficiently intimidated by the Soviets and had sufficient Soviet troops in their own countries, so it would be very difficult for them to be in open revolt against the Soviet Union. I just didn't think they would ever be very strong allies. But the Soviets have nearly four hundred thousand troops in East Germany. They have two divisions or more in Poland, and have had them there since the end of World War II. That gave them—and still gives them—a very strong base from which to launch an offensive.

As far as the Soviet Union itself is concerned, we have not seen any major reductions in the Soviet military strength. The only thing we've seen is that in compliance with the INF [Intermediate Nuclear Forces] treaty, they are bringing home some of the SS-20s, as required. They're supposed to bring them all home. They may very well be going to do that. But some of these missiles may still be available to them in the future. The Soviet Union has a system of government under which they could take out the five hundred thousand people they've talked about from their military and turn them back into farmers. But they could turn them into an army the next day without any kind of a vote or any kind of discussion or any kind of a roll call or any debates or editorials or anything else. We don't have that kind of system. We don't want it. But it gives the Soviets a degree of military leverage that we have to recognize.

So it's more than just the rhetoric that would be required. I would want to see a very substantial dismantling of Soviet military strength and a real change in the kind of military capability that they retain, a truly defensive military strength. They talk about that. They say they're doing it now. But from the Soviet point of view, the idea of defense means moving out from their homeland, farther and farther, in rings that pretty soon cut all the way out to the Pacific areas, including the Fijis, for gosh sakes, as a means of defending their homeland. That is a much broader concept of defense than we have.

I'd like to see a lot of changes of that kind. But so far all we've heard is some totally different kinds of rhetoric than we heard in the 1980s. That's encouraging, but it's nothing that warrants dismantling our commitments to NATO or our own military strength. It is, in fact, a much more sophisticated, clever Soviet tactic for doing the same kind of thing they wanted to do since the end of World War II, and that is to decouple the United States from Europe, and weaken and ultimately dismantle NATO. They were unable to do it by threats, because NATO and the United States quite properly responded by developing a strength that made the Soviet threat impossible to carry out. But now they are achieving their objective by demonstrating, through rhetoric, that there is no threat, so you don't need this activity that is so popular in democracies, of keeping military strength in peacetime.

USNI: In a tighter budget situation, which programs do you think are marginal and, thus, possibly expendable?

Weinberger: I think the second Midget [small intercontinental ballistic] missile is totally marginal and basically undesirable. It costs a huge amount of money and it isn't going to give you nearly the kind of strengths that continuing with the MX program would.

I haven't gone through any of the current plans for two years, but a number of bases are finally being closed now. I would not dismantle overseas strength, and I would not dismantle modernization, because the Soviets have not only a very large advantage in numbers, but have very much greater advantage in modernization. I don't think you can, or should, make significant cuts in our defensive strength or defense budget. I think that when everybody accepts the fact that that is going to happen, then you make it a foregone conclusion and you remove the whole issue from debate. I don't think it should be. I think this idea of "peace breaking out" is all very nice, but it's really a license to some congressmen, who always oppose defensive strength, anyway, simply to spend more money on more politically popular domestic programs.

But there are a few things that you could cut. There are many things we recommended to be cut. The Congress regularly adds a great many things that we don't want and don't need. They require you to continue production of an aircraft, for example, for a long time beyond what you need, because they are made in somebody's district. That means you have a lot of things in the defense budget that the Defense Department and the services don't want. Those are things that could go.

USNI: If you could have done anything differently during your term as secretary of defense, what would it have been?

Weinberger: I suppose to have been more persuasive with the Congress to continue the defensive strength that we needed. They started to cut back in 1986 and we still had a lot to do at that time. There are probably some other things, but you can't take actions every day for seven years without having something that perhaps could have been done differently. And that's one that comes to mind.

Herman Wouk

COURTESY OF HERMAN WOUK

After graduating from Columbia University in 1934, Mr. Wouk worked in radio and wrote for the *Fred Allen Show* from 1936 to 1941. He joined the Navy after Pearl Harbor and reported on board the destroyer-minesweeper USS *Zane* (DMS-14) in February 1943 at New Caledonia. Later, he transferred to a sister ship, the USS *Southard* (DMS-10) and was her executive officer at war's end. He took part in eight Pacific invasions, earning several battle stars while serving on the two vessels.

He began writing *The Caine Mutiny,* for which he was awarded the 1952 Pulitzer Prize for fiction, in June 1949 while on a reserve training cruise on board the USS *Saipan* (CVL-48). He is one of America's most widely read authors. In a rare public appearance, he delivered the following at the Naval Institute's 121st Annual Meeting and 5th Annapolis Seminar in April 1995.

■

I was signing books today at the Naval Institute's book store, something I haven't done in thirty or forty years, but the Navy is different. I must have signed about a hundred copies of the Naval Institute's special edition of *The Caine Mutiny*, and I was thinking to myself, well, after all, here is sure immortality for a work of fiction. But then I remembered the other side of the picture.

Not very long ago a gentleman named Alan Dershowitz, the wild-haired legal light who is a member of the squadron of lawyers escorting O. J. Simpson through his ordeal, told me a story. Alan teaches at Harvard Law School, and when I met him recently—he's an old friend of mine—he said to me, "Herman, I don't know what's becoming of the students who go to law school these days. For years I've taught first-year law, and, of course, I've used the court writings in Dostoevski's great novels *Crime and Punishment* and *The Brothers Karamazov* and I've also used *The Caine Mutiny*. And do you know, in this year's class, nobody had heard of *The Caine Mutiny*?" He must have seen how my face fell, because he said, "Don't worry, they haven't heard of Dostoevski either."

The overwhelming tribute to this early work of mine is most gratifying, but I have to tell you that *The Caine Mutiny* did not, at its outset, have this kind of reception in the United States Navy.

Grave reservations were vocally expressed at this model of imperfection—Captain Queeg—who was presented realistically as a regular naval officer. Now, the turn came when Adm. [William M.] Fechteler, who was then chief of naval operations [1951–53], was speaking at a banquet like this one. During the question-and-answer period, one courageous soul raised his hand and asked: "Admiral, have you read this new novel, *The Caine Mutiny*, about the Navy?"

The admiral said, "Yes, I have." The brave officer persisted, "What did you think of it, Admiral?" And the admiral growled, "Well, in a long naval service, I've met every one of those sons of bitches but never all on one ship." The boss man had spoken and *The Caine Mutiny* was in.

But there was still another barrier that the old *Caine* had to cross, and that was Hollywood. My wife Sarah and I were then a very young couple with a baby, and I was anxious for a movie sale. The major studios wouldn't touch it because there seemed to be no chance of getting naval cooperation for a film about Captain Queeg. But an enterprising young producer, Stanley Kramer, offered us a very modest deal with a still more modest option. In other words, we were paid a small amount for a six-month option; then, if he decided he wanted the book, I would get a sum—which at that time meant a lot to us—for the rights.

However, there was a catch. I had to get naval cooperation for the filming of *The Caine Mutiny*! Well, my baby was hungry, and so were we. I went to the Navy, to the public relations department, and spoke with the admiral there. He was not all that anxious to lay his head on the chopping block for saying, "Okay, let's film *The Caine Mutiny*." So we had an unsuccessful discussion, some talk of making Queeg a reserve, notions like that.

I went home and, discouraged, told Sarah, "no deal." And I wrote Kramer a letter saying, "I'm very sorry, I believe navy cooperation is quite impossible; I think our deal is off, and I'm perfectly willing to return your advance." The next day, Kramer exercised the option and grabbed the rights, obviously assuming I'd gotten a better deal from someone else. That was the origin of the film.

And, of course, ever since then—thanks, I think, in part to the magnificent performance of Humphrey Bogart as Captain Queeg—I can say that, even though he's my own creation, he's passed into legend. I've heard from all over the world, from people who say, "I personally served under that guy."

I've heard it here in the United States from the Air Force, from the Army, from the Coast Guard. I heard from an airman in England who wrote, "How the hell did you find out about Wing Commander [So-and-So]?"

I want to talk tonight about another commanding officer whom I created. Again, people often say to me, "I know that guy, I served with him," or "Victor Henry, Pug Henry—he's a friend of mine." But nobody knows who he was except me, and now you're going to hear the story and how I thought of him.

When *The Caine Mutiny* first came out and Admiral Fechteler had yet to give it his imprimatur, I got a letter from a gent who is gone now, may he rest in peace—Rear Adm. Dan Gallery. Some of you may have known him—an original, very brilliant officer, the one who captured the U-boat, U-505, and brought it back to our shores; it's the submarine that is now at Chicago's Science and Industry Museum. Dan wrote me, "I don't care what they're saying, this is a great book and I'd like to meet you," and we became very good friends. When I told him years later that I was working on a major panoramic book about World War II in which Leyte Gulf would be a prominent part, he said, "Well, if you're going to write about Leyte Gulf, you should talk to [Adm. Robert B.] Mick Carney [CNO 1953–55] because he was Halsey's chief of staff."

So I went and visited Mick Carney in his home in Georgetown. About the Battle of Leyte Gulf, Mick spoke the straight Halsey line: "Given the information at the time, he couldn't have made any other decisions." If we have a question-and-answer period, we can discuss that. But then he said, "So you're writing about World War II and about the Navy's part in it. I want to tell you a story. When I arrived at Pearl Harbor for a new tour of duty shortly before the war, I went to see Adm. James Richardson, who had just been recalled as commander in chief of the U.S. Fleet after recommending that the Pacific Fleet be pulled back to the West Coast because of the way it was exposed in Pearl Harbor."

Of course, at the time Mr. Churchill wanted the fleet advanced to Singapore so as to overawe the Japanese. Neither Admiral Richardson's advice nor Churchill's was acceptable to FDR, Singapore being impossible and the West Coast being politically impossible as well, and so Admiral Richardson was recalled. He said to Carney, "I want you to know something: there's a war coming, it's absolutely inevitable, and you guys are going to fight it. We're too old; we'll be out to grass. You had better understand what the situation is here in the fleet. We don't have the torpedo depots far forward. We don't have the logistical infrastructure. I have grave doubts about the torpedoes that we have." And he proceeded to tell Carney, then a commander, everything that was wrong with the situation in the Pacific and the danger to which the Navy and, therefore, the United States, was exposed.

Carney said to me, "This was a turning point in all my days, this conversation with Admiral Richardson. I suddenly realized where I was and where I was heading with my life. I was a go-go career officer, I was regarded as a comer, and that had been my life until then. With this conversation, I all at once realized that I was also responsible for the safety of the United States of America. That changed my whole way of thinking about myself, my career, and my aspirations."

And that was when I got the flash of the character who became Victor Henry. Victor Henry is not a great leader. He is no Mick Carney, destined for CNO. He goes through the entire war, he has various posts, he has many disappointments, he misses one blue-water assignment after another because he's diverted into diplomatic jobs, which he does well. The characteristic of Victor Henry, this comer who never quite makes it, is that he does things so well that he's given things that do not necessarily lead straight to flag rank. He reaches flag rank, but he is not a naval officer whom anybody would ever have heard of, had I not created him and made him a hero of *The Winds of War* and *War and Remembrance*.

He's not a brilliant strategist like Raymond Spruance. He's not a celebrated, flamboyant leader like William Halsey. What he is, is a backbone naval officer, and it is the Victor Henrys who create the victories for the Spruances and the Halseys.

I don't have to tell anybody in this room of the troubles that the Navy has been through in recent years, and these are endemic troubles of armed services. But because of the Victor Henrys, the Navy sails on and will—and with another word or two concerning the larger situation which the Victor Henrys may think about when they're off-duty, I will close these remarks.

On the United Nations at the entrance are carved the words, "Nation shall not lift up sword against nation, neither shall they learn war anymore."

You and I look at the television day by day and read the headlines about the events in Rwanda, in Bosnia, in the Middle East, in the Far East, and we hear of terrible events that don't even surface in the headlines, and this carving seems like a cruel mockery of reality.

There are really two views of war that come down to us in our Western cultural heritage. There is the view of Thucydides, the first and I think still the greatest of true historians. It stems from the Greek rational view of human nature, of mankind, and of society. He traces the Peloponnesian Wars to completely realistic facts, the confrontation of Athens and Sparta, the unstable balance between them, which led to the kicking off of a war with all the things that happen in war: reversal of alliances, bullying of the weak by the strong, shifts and counter-shifts of events, great invasions, invasions that succeed, invasions that fail. The book of the Peloponnesian Wars is not finished, but what comes out of this unfinished masterpiece is a sense of deep pessimism about the possibility of war ever ceasing. It seems to be built into human nature and human society.

But we inherit another view of war. It is those words carved at the entrance to the United Nations: "Nation shall not lift up sword against nation, neither shall they learn war any more," or in the Hebrew:

Lo yi•sa goi el goi che•rev,
lo yil•me•du od mil•cha•ma

This same view of war is expressed in Psalms, "The meek shall inherit the earth." It is spoken again in the Sermon on the Mount, "Blessed are the meek, for they shall inherit the earth."

We look around us and we wonder, where lies the tilt in the balance between these two diametrically opposed views, which seem equally powerful insights into human nature and human aspiration? A son of mine lives in Israel and has fought in the Israeli Navy. My grandson, Barak—four and a half years old—flew here last week with his parents to celebrate the Passover with us. When he grows up, by a supreme paradox he will probably serve in an armed service that speaks Hebrew, the language of Isaiah, who said, "Nation shall not lift up sword against nation, neither shall they learn war anymore."

And if you ask me where I come down on this clash of views, I say to you that, as a historian and a realist, Thucydides is my great teacher, but as a simple man of faith, my prophet is Isaiah.

■

Note: Admiral Carney's recollections of his meeting with Admiral Richardson can be found in *Air Raid: Pearl Harbor!* edited by Paul Stillwell and published by the Naval Institute Press in 1981, page forty-nine.

Anthony Zinni

L. BRACKENBURY / DEPARTMENT OF DEFENSE

Gen. Anthony Zinni, U.S. Marine Corps, served as the commander in chief, U.S. Central Command, leader of Operation Desert Fox (December 1998) and operations against Iraq. The interview appeared in the May 1999 issue of the Naval Institute's *Proceedings.*

■

USNI: As liaison between military operations in the Persian Gulf region and the civilian leadership, what do you see as the most difficult part of your job?

Zinni: Our region is a seriously volatile one. The Middle East peace process, the situations in Iraq and Iran, and the price of oil obviously affect us and tend to overlap in their military, political, and humanitarian dimensions. Keeping these in sync is difficult because of their complexity and number.

Obviously, CinCs [commanders in chief] are involved in engagement planning and operations with the civilian side of our government—the non-uniformed side. In the United States, we rely on an interface among the Joint Staff, OSD [the Office of the Secretary of Defense], the State Department, the NSC [National Security Council], and the other agencies. And when the particular CinC is not directly involved, sometimes it's difficult to sort through all the policy issues.

Another problem is the way we're organized. The State Department is organized to face the world differently from the way the Unified Command Plan operates; the geography is different. In fact, our geography is even different from OSD's and the Joint Staff's. So you have four different outlooks, and that can be significant.

For instance, in our AOR [area of responsibility], we have Pakistan, but we don't have India. We have most of the Arab world, the Middle East, but we don't have Israel. The State Department does it differently. Its Near East Department, for example, includes Israel with the rest of the Middle East, and India and Pakistan are together. That can change your perspective. So keeping everything in sync, given these organizational differences, becomes a challenge. Fortunately, in Central Command we have a good relationship with the State Department. We don't always see things eye-to-eye, but we work hard to create a strong relationship with our ambassadors on the ground and the forward desk officers who influence our part of the world—Central Asia, Southwest Asia, Africa, and the Middle East. But it requires constant attention and constant interaction because of all the complexities and the differences in organization and approach.

USNI: Would it help if all the agencies were in sync, territorially?

Zinni: It could help in some ways. But we're talking about political-military interface. It's all a matter of perspective. By looking at it from a purely military dimension, you might end up with a lot of problem areas—having more than one major theater of war in one CinC-dom and none in another.

Command-and-control and balance of forces could be at odds with an organization that tries to align itself along national-interest or ethnic/religious-affinity lines. Military points of view may not match political ones. And political ones may not match the way things lay out logically—ethnically and culturally—on the ground. So it is difficult to get it all aligned just right.

USNI: The cat-and-mouse game that Iraq has been playing in the no-fly zones seems to be feeding a volatile situation. You have said that you would need a deliberate campaign and more assets to rectify the situation. Why don't we ask for more assets and mount a deliberate campaign to get the job done?

Zinni: First of all, we have to put in context the threat that these aircraft present to us. Obviously, anybody who can shoot at you, and has demonstrated the intent to shoot at you, is dangerous.

But in reality, Iraqi aircraft have never fired a missile at us. In reality, they've never shown any indication to do more than assert sovereignty by crossing the line and running back. In reality, when they have been used in some sort of air-defense posture against us, it has been as the bait, not as the trap or the shooter. In reality, when we look at the Iraqi Air Force and its levels of pilot training and aircraft capability, it is not a major threat to our aircraft. Now, does that mean that it isn't possible for them to shoot down our aircraft? Of course it's possible. Is it probable? No.

They've shown no determination or will to engage. In fact, they've shown just the opposite. If anything, they don't want to come out when we're over Iraqi skies. They usually show up when we're on our way out, and they turn and run if we give any indication of turning around to meet them. They won't ever put themselves in a position to engage within missile range. There's no doubt in my mind that the Iraqi pilots understand the differences between their skills and the skills of our Navy, Marine Corps, and Air Force pilots.

So why should we go after their airfields? We can do damage to airfields, we can blow up a lot of concrete, and we can damage a lot of buildings. But the probability of eliminating airplanes by doing that is very slim, because Saddam Hussein disperses them to other airfields, and he moves them a lot. So it would be difficult.

Why don't we get them with TacAir [tactical aircraft]? The airfields are located in areas that have what we call Super MEZ [missile engagement zones]. Do we want to mount a campaign to get those airplanes? The additional assets we would need would have to be Desert Fox–like. We would have to go against very heavy air defenses to get those airplanes. And we would put pilots at greater risk than they are now. So what would be the benefit? Is that really what we want to do? In addition, what would be the political impact of launching another strike? Is that the right thing to do?

What do threaten us are surface-to-air missiles, not airplanes. Their airplanes try to lure us within missile range. He [Saddam] understands that. We can take measures to minimize the threat to our airplanes by flying at different altitudes, by not flying in known missile engagement zones, and by placing heavy emphasis on our own intelligence. If he [Saddam] shows any indication of threatening us, we take action—not necessarily toward the specific system that threatens us. It's not just the missiles themselves; it's also the radars, the early-warning systems, and everything that ties them together. We reserve the right to strike any part of the Iraqi air defense system if we're threatened by any other part of it.

That's what we've been doing, systematically, deliberately, and methodically. We have seen a steady attrition of his air-defense assets. We see him now pulling back into the center, after he had flooded the north and south. Obviously, this has been a loser strategy for him.

So to make the simplistic case that going after his airfields will eliminate the threat doesn't make sense to me. Anyone can question the strategy. The only way you can guarantee that Saddam leaves the scene or that the threat goes away is to be willing to put boots on the ground and troops into Baghdad. When you're willing to make that commitment, you can make some assurances, but doing anything short of that makes assurances very difficult.

USNI: Since Saddam Hussein seems sometimes to have used the no-fly zones to his advantage, how effective are they?

Zinni: The purpose of the no-fly zones is to prevent him from using fixed-wing aircraft and attack helicopters against his own people—the marsh Arabs, the Shiah in the south, and Kurds in the north. They were set up in conjunction with the security zone in the north and the no-drive zone in the south, which prevented him from enhancing ground forces to do the same thing.

If the purpose of the no-fly zones was to prevent him from oppressing these people, then they've been successful. We have enforced these no-fly zones for eight years, and we have denied him the use of that space. I guess if you look at it from the perspective of an eight-year commitment of force, you might reach a different conclusion. But if you look at it from the perspective of a poor Kurd or a Shiah on the ground, you might say that they've been saved a lot of pain and agony. So how you measure it determines how you answer that question.

USNI: The people of the United States supported Desert Storm and its aftermath overwhelmingly. Now, it seems that many have become jaded and wonder whether recent operations are worth risking American lives and the substantial financial investment. How do you address the skeptics?

Zinni: I would address them in two ways. First, I would define our national interest there. This is the repository for most of the energy source that drives the global economy—65 percent of the known oil reserves and 40 to 45 percent of the known natural gas reserves. More is to be tapped just to the north, in the Caucasus and Central Asia. Pipelines may flow from there.

Energy drives our economy, and for the foreseeable future, no alternate sources of fuel are going to drive that economy for at least the next half-century or more. We import 18 percent of our oil from this region, and it appears that this number will go up. Over the course of the next few years, it could increase to as much as 23 to 25 percent. So, one-quarter of our direct oil supply could be at risk.

In addition, Japan, the Far East, and Western Europe have a greater reliance on this oil. Recently, when we had fluctuations in the economies of Asia and other parts of the world, we saw what happened to our economy. Imagine Japan with no oil—75 to 80 percent of its oil comes from the Middle East. The same goes for Western Europe. What does that do to our economy?

And what happens to the oil we get from regions like Latin America or Africa—which makes up the other 75 percent—when the demand goes up? Who says they'll sell it to us at the current price? So it isn't just the 18 to 25 percent you might lose from the Middle East; you might lose more of what we get now, in greater portions, to competition.

Aside from oil, we all know that instability in this region tends to spread like wildfire. Extremism, fundamentalism, and terrorism do not stay confined to this region. And if you don't contain it, if there is no force of stability, it tends to branch out.

What happens in the Balkans is influenced by what happens in this part of the world. The Middle East can shoot problems through Africa, which can shoot up into Eastern Europe, up into Central Asia, and out toward Southwest Asia. These problems tend not to stay confined. They can even become global and transnational, in terms of drug trade, drug production, and the exporting of terrorism. This region is the confluence of three continents. What transits through the Suez Canal, Bab el Mandeb, and the Strait of Hormuz? It's the old Silk Route. Can we afford to lose access to this region?

As for the financial investment, Central Command owns no assigned forces—not one division, not one carrier battle group. Everything comes to me from somebody else. In other words, I borrow the forces to police this area. So we're not doing this with any extra force structure. I do it with minimal infrastructure in the AOR, usually from bases provided to us by the countries there. We do it with pre-positioning supplies and equipment. Nothing requires constant manning, or permanent bases, or a lot of military construction money.

We do it with burden sharing, which I think is unmatched anywhere in the world. The Saudis, the Kuwaitis, and others put up hundreds of millions of dollars a year to support our troops with assistance in kind—food, water, fuel, basing rights, overflight rights. They build facilities for us, as the Saudis have done now, after [the explosion at] Khobar Towers, when we moved to the desert. They've just put two hundred million dollars in building facilities for our troops. So the burden-sharing is significant.

Their military forces have slowly but surely increased in quality. They don't have the demographics to match the threats of Iran and Iraq; they just don't have the numbers of people. But they have high-quality forces. They have F-15s, and they have other things that we allow within limits, in terms of technology release.

Who do you think benefits from these billions of dollars of investment in their own defense? How much of those billions of dollars goes to the U.S. defense industry, so that they can stand with us as partners and provide for their own defense?

Look at what our interests are, what it costs us, and the benefits we get from what our friends in the area do. We always tap the Saudis and others to provide money for other causes around the world, and they're always there to do it.

So, is this worth it? Day-to-day, in noncrisis situations, we have sixteen thousand to twenty-three thousand troops out in the Gulf, depending on whether a carrier battle group or MEU/ARG [Marine Expeditionary Unit/Amphibious Ready Group] is in or out. At the height of a crisis, it's at about twenty-eight thousand. So essentially, a division reinforced is taking care of this region of the world. And not one soldier, sailor, airman, or Marine would go away if Central Command went away today.

USNI: The global stake in all this leads to another question. How well can the United States rely on its European allies?

Zinni: Obviously, the British fly with us and are committed to us. And the French fly Southern Watch with us, although right now they're not—post–Desert Fox. That may resume. We have Dutch, Italian, British, and others who send ships to participate in maritime intercept operations with us in the region. It's obvious what they did during Desert Storm and the commitment they made. When we were building up for Desert Thunder [ultimately aborted in 1998], we had commitments from a number of countries. Some we never called on, because it was halted. Saddam capitulated. Some we did deploy—the Australians, New Zealanders, Eastern Europeans, and some Latin Americans.

I think each individual situation has different levels of commitment. In the region, the support from the GCC [Gulf Council Countries] gets little attention or credit. The Arab League foreign ministers have condemned Saddam, and his foreign minister burst out red-faced and upset that he couldn't turn them. They've taken a stand. They have allowed us to use their bases and strike from them.

We never have had a situation where we couldn't do what we had to do because somebody denied us access. Sometimes, we confuse the actual support they give on the ground with what they feel they have to say publicly. They may say they don't agree with use of force in this situation, or that they are concerned about the plight of the Iraqi people. At the same time, they're letting us use their bases.

USNI: What about the French?

Zinni: First of all, when we went into northern Iraq, the French provided a brigade, and that brigade was chopped to our operational control. They provided air support. It was a full-up joint force with its own air and logistics ground forces. It was very significant and very, very capable. It was an effective mobile force.

The French stayed with us until 1996, when for political reasons—because they disagreed with our approach to the Kurds—they pulled out. But from 1991 to 1996, the French and the Brits were the ones who stuck with us.

When we went into Somalia, they provided a brigade—again, French Marines, Legionnaires, the best troops they had, with their own air support and logistics. And once again, they chopped that whole organization to our operational control. They took one of the toughest and most remote sectors, and they were with us, side by side, in Somalia.

They're with us in the Balkans today. They were with us in Desert Storm. We have conducted noncombatant evacuation operations together out of Africa. They have evacuated American citizens. We don't always see eye to eye politically. But militarily, on the ground, they've been fantastic. They're one of our most valuable allies, when we can get them.

We sometimes focus on the political difficulties and miss the positive things. I'm always fond of saying that the main street in the little Pennsylvania town where I grew up was named Lafayette Street. We ought to think back to what the French did for us during the Revolution, as well as what they did for us in the War of 1812. And we should remember what we did for them in World Wars I and II. My father was in World War I and deployed with the American Expeditionary Forces to France. It's a long relationship, one that gets strained by politics—but what doesn't?

USNI: Getting back to the current situation in Iraq, in Senate testimony you said, "We don't go into pursuit unless there's a good reason to do that." What constitutes a "good reason"?

Zinni: A good reason would be if they made a deliberate attempt to engage us and we knew we had the assets in theater to pursue. Another would be if they were truly to violate the no-fly zone and bomb Shiah or marsh Arabs. And another would be if they were to attack Kuwait or Saudi Arabia. But nothing like that has happened.

USNI: How much more difficult is it to execute a mission like Desert Fox without the larger coalition of Desert Storm?

Zinni: First of all, we have to keep the Iraqi military capability in perspective. It's roughly half of what it was in Desert Storm. We know a lot more now than we did leading up to Desert Storm. Obviously, we didn't know that Iraq was going to invade Kuwait and we were going to be at war. But now we have nine years of intensive intelligence on this country. Ever since Desert Storm, because of sanctions, the Iraqi military has atrophied and not modernized at all. It relies on black-market and self-manufactured parts to keep things going. They're pretty innovative, and they do a remarkable job. But how much of that can keep their forces going?

We also look at the training they receive, the quality of their personnel, and their morale. We've seen executions of officers, mass arrests and releases of officers, and rotations of units to ensure that no loyalty buildup would threaten Saddam. That takes its toll on a military. At the same time, the technological capability of our forces has increased since Desert Storm. The increases on our side and the decreases on their side have allowed us to shape the kind of force we need immediately. When you add it up, we're able to do a lot more now with less force than we would have been able to do ten years ago.

USNI: I heard at least one senior leader from Desert Storm say that the coalition was more trouble than what it was worth, at least when it came to accommodating and coordinating. How do you feel about that?

Zinni: I think what might be considered the coalition, if it really means the regional coalition, has come a long way. Obviously, Desert Storm has taught us a lot about interoperability and communications. Coalition operations are always harder than solely U.S. operations. Joint U.S. operations are hard enough. Combat identification and interoperability of systems make it tough enough to put a joint force on the ground. Adding coalition forces for combined operations makes it even more complex, brought on by differences in culture and language, incompatibility of equipment, doctrinal incompatibility, and procedural incompatibility. All those things have to be worked through.

It points up the value of our exercise program. We do a lot more exercising now with coalition forces in the region than we did before Desert Storm, and these exercises teach us a lot. We've also set up the mechanisms to connect them.

USNI: Does U.S. involvement in Bosnia and now Kosovo have any effect on the way you do your job?

Zinni: It could. Let me tell you why. As I told you, we draw forces from other commands. We own no assigned forces. If you look at recent events in our AOR, we had only one carrier battle group present. We've had to increase the percentage of time we've had MEU or ARG cover. And we pulled those out of the Mediterranean. When we shoot TLAMs [Tomahawk land-attack missiles], the easiest way to keep our minimum numbers up is to pull shooters from the Mediterranean. So if Kosovo or Bosnia flares up and those forces can't be spared, then we have a problem. We are forced to do things that further upset the stability of our force. We may need to pull forces that are in the process of working up, or pull them out earlier, or extend forces in place. And that becomes more disruptive of our rotation and readiness and our operational tempo.

So what happens elsewhere in the world, whether it's in the Pacific, or in the Mediterranean—or anywhere else for that matter—can affect us because we have a force that tends to be globally oriented now, as opposed to regionally oriented, especially in our case.

USNI: Are the troops in the Gulf being given awards and combat pay?

Zinni: Yes. We do have awards in the region. Three areas come into play. One is overall recognition, like the Armed Forces Expeditionary Medal for units involved in the operations—and in some cases, in ongoing operations, like Southern Watch and Northern Watch.

Combat-zone tax-exclusion pay is received for areas where there is a terrorist threat or a threat in the immediate proximity of units like those in Kuwait and Saudi Arabia. There is also individual imminent-danger pay, which is received by our forces who fly.

When we do specific operations like Desert Thunder or Desert Fox, we recognize units with unit awards, too. We feel the awards program is pretty healthy in the area and we do our best to try to recognize everybody and also to make sure that those who face imminent danger receive the benefits and the pay.

USNI: How do you rate the morale of the troops?

Zinni: Overall, morale has been good. As a matter of fact, I'm amazed at how high it is. The things that affect morale most, when you get down to individual units or components, seem to me to be the quality of training and the sophistication of the operation.

For example, an Army battalion task force in Kuwait undergoes unbelievable training. They prepare elaborate plans. They can shoot all their weapons; they can maneuver; they have all the assets, even full-time close air support. Those units really gear up for it. And they come back much better trained.

Flying missions in Southern Watch tends to get fairly routine. The pilots are not going through the kinds of more complicated and sophisticated proficiency training that they might at home. We worry about atrophy of skills. So we've adjusted the tours to accommodate any loss in proficiency or training. Sometimes the breakdown might seem unfair. Those who have longer deployments may deploy fewer times. But in the end, it tends to balance itself out, or pretty close to it.

It has been a long commitment. I run into troops who have been to the desert ten and eleven times in their careers. It gets hard. We have done a lot of work to improve quality of life out there. The Saudis have built a friendly-forces housing complex to the tune of several hundreds of millions of dollars. So it is a little more tolerable, and that tends to pick up morale.

At Christmas time, when I went with the secretary of defense and a USO show, I was amazed at the spirit of the troops. And I'm not saying that just because you would expect me to say it. I've been there when they've had major complaints. But I've seen a commitment on the part of our commanders to make life better. The services have begun to adjust. The Navy and Marine Corps have contended with long deployments for decades and are more used to it. The Air Force was taking it out of hide. Now, [Air Force Chief of Staff] Gen. [Michael E.] Ryan has reorganized the Air Force. He's looked, by his own account, at how the Navy and Marine Corps have done this. So he's creating expeditionary groupings—a workup phase, a ready-for-deployment phase, a deployment phase, a recovery phase. It will be much more like a MEU or a carrier battle group. We are beginning to see the other services setting up family support structures for continuous deployments.

But the number of deployments takes its toll and I'm aware of that. But I don't think this is going to change for a while. I just think the demands of the post–Cold War world are going to make this the routine, and I think it's important to make adjustments.

I have been surprised when I hear talk about retirement and pay. I was not aware of how focused even very junior members of the military have become on these issues. I'm amazed at the young sergeants and the young petty officers, who really think about these things, who have looked at the long term. Part of this is because they're much smarter, they're much more aware of where they're going in their lives, and they think beyond tomorrow. Part of this is because the economy is so good and offers and opportunities are out there. Another part of this is that we have a much more family-oriented force than we ever had before.

I remember a time in 1989: I was a regimental commander in Okinawa, and Gen. [Al] Gray was the commandant at the time. He came out and visited us. We were on the beach waiting for things to happen during a night amphibious landing. He said to me, "You know, we crossed a major milestone in the Marine Corps recently. We now have more dependents than we have Marines." And it struck me as something that probably nobody had focused on except somebody like General Gray. It was a tremendous watershed.

I don't think that trend has changed. It has probably continued upward. When I stood in front of my platoon as Second Lieutenant Zinni in 1965 at Camp Lejeune, North Carolina, two men were married out of forty. When I was the commanding general of the 1st Marine Expeditionary Force, something like 43 percent of the force was married. You're talking about a force where the average rank is lance corporal.

And when my son stands in front of a platoon, which he may well do when he graduates this summer, he's going to be looking at a platoon where eighteen or nineteen Marines are married.

So when you start looking at platoons that are 50 percent married, you have young people thinking differently than they did thirty years ago about life, family pressures, the ability to make ends meet, and the continuous deployments. They think more, I believe, about where they're headed.

My hat is off to the service chiefs, the chairman, and the secretary of defense for changing retirement, increasing pay, and making us more competitive. Those who want to stay can see where they're going to be twenty or thirty years from now. We can make it easier for them to stay. I think also that all of this will help in terms of readiness.

About the Author

Fred Schultz began his magazine editing career in 1980 with Historical Times, Inc. (now Primedia), in Harrisburg, Pennsylvania. There he served in various editorial capacities with *American History Illustrated*, *British Heritage*, *Civil War Times Illustrated*, and *Country Journal*. He also served as contributing editor to *The Historical Times Illustrated Encyclopedia of the Civil War* (New York: Harper & Row, 1986). Mr. Schultz joined the staff of the U.S. Naval Institute in 1989 as associate editor of *Naval History* and *Proceedings* magazines and became editor-in-chief of *Naval History* in 1993. His work, totaling some eighty articles and interviews, has appeared in various publications, including *The Chicago Tribune*, *Maryland* magazine, *Chevron USA*, *Bluegrass Unlimited*, and those mentioned above. He has also written forewords for two books: *Civil War Front Pages* (New York: Random House, 1989) and *Raiders and Blockaders* (Washington, D.C.: Brassey's, 1999). A native of Gettysburg, Pennsylvania, Mr. Schultz currently resides in Annapolis, Maryland, with his wife, Susan, and two dogs, Timber and Foster.

The Naval Institute Press is the book-publishing arm of the U.S. Naval Institute, a private, nonprofit, membership society for sea service professionals and others who share an interest in naval and maritime affairs. Established in 1873 at the U.S. Naval Academy in Annapolis, Maryland, where its offices remain today, the Naval Institute has members worldwide.

Members of the Naval Institute support the education programs of the society and receive the influential monthly magazine *Proceedings* and discounts on fine nautical prints and on ship and aircraft photos. They also have access to the transcripts of the Institute's Oral History Program and get discounted admission to any of the Institute-sponsored seminars offered around the country.

The Naval Institute also publishes *Naval History* magazine. This colorful bimonthly is filled with entertaining and thought-provoking articles, first-person reminiscences, and dramatic art and photography. Members receive a discount on *Naval History* subscriptions.

The Naval Institute's book-publishing program, begun in 1898 with basic guides to naval practices, has broadened its scope in recent years to include books of more general interest. Now the Naval Institute Press publishes about one hundred titles each year, ranging from how-to books on boating and navigation to battle histories, biographies, ship and aircraft guides, and novels. Institute members receive discounts of 20 to 50 percent on the Press's more than eight hundred books in print.

Full-time students are eligible for special half-price membership rates. Life memberships are also available.

For a free catalog describing Naval Institute Press books currently available, and for further information about subscribing to *Naval History* magazine or about joining the U.S. Naval Institute, please write to:

Membership Department
U.S. Naval Institute
291 Wood Road
Annapolis, MD 21402-5034
Telephone: (800) 233-8764
Fax: (410) 269-7940
Web address: www.usni.org